21世纪高等学校电子信息工程规划教材

电子信息工程专业英语导论

瞿少成　吴军其　编著

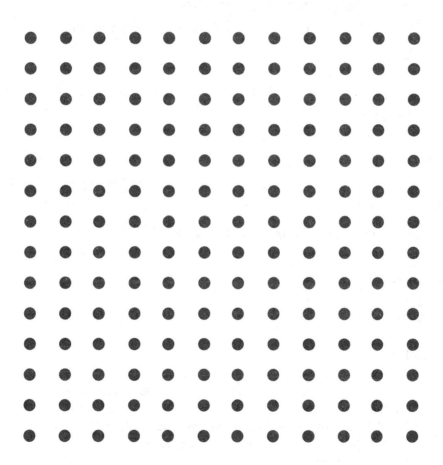

清华大学出版社
北京

内 容 简 介

本书旨在培养学生在专业英语方面的阅读、翻译、表达与写作能力，提高科技英语素养与国际学术交流能力。全书包括专业英语基础篇与提高篇两部分。4个基础篇精选国外教材中的经典文献，涵盖电工与电子基础、电子与通信器件、信号与系统、通信技术等领域；课后附有生词表、难点注释和练习题；每个单元补充了科技英语的特点、翻译要领、科技术语与常用数学公式的表达，并对查阅科技文献的方法与技巧做了简单介绍。提高篇系统地介绍了科技论文的结构、写作与投稿等问题，归纳了中国学生撰写英文科技论文中常见的错误，最后总结了常用应用文写作的要求与规范，并给出了一些实际的范例。

本书可以作为电子信息工程与通信工程专业的专业英语教材，同时适用于相关专业的本科生、研究生和工程技术人员。

本书封面贴有清华大学出版社防伪标签，无标签者不得销售。
版权所有，侵权必究。举报: 010-62782989, beiqinquan@tup.tsinghua.edu.cn

图书在版编目（CIP）数据

电子信息工程专业英语导论 / 瞿少成, 吴军其编著. —北京: 清华大学出版社, 2008.5（2022.9重印）
（21世纪高等学校电子信息工程规划教材）
ISBN 978-7-302-17065-5

Ⅰ. 电… Ⅱ. ①瞿… ②吴… Ⅲ. ①电子技术–英语–高等学校–教材 ②信息技术–英语–高等学校–教材 Ⅳ. H31

中国版本图书馆 CIP 数据核字（2008）第 021386 号

责任编辑: 魏江江　赵晓宁
责任校对: 李建庄
责任印制: 杨　艳

出版发行: 清华大学出版社
　　网　　址: http://www.tup.com.cn, http://www.wqbook.com
　　地　　址: 北京清华大学学研大厦A座　　邮　编: 100084
　　社 总 机: 010-83470000　　邮　购: 010-62786544
　　投稿与读者服务: 010-62776969, c-service@tup.tsinghua.edu.cn
　　质量反馈: 010-62772015, zhiliang@tup.tsinghua.edu.cn
印 装 者: 三河市铭诚印务有限公司
经　　销: 全国新华书店
开　　本: 185mm×260mm　　印 张: 16　　字　数: 382千字
印　　次: 2022年9月第14次印刷
印　　数: 24501~25500
定　　价: 39.00元

产品编号: 022486-03

出 版 说 明

随着我国高等教育规模的扩大和产业结构调整的进一步完善,社会对高层次应用型人才的需求将更加迫切。各地高校紧密结合地方经济建设发展需要,科学运用市场调节机制,合理调整和配置教育资源,在改革和改造传统学科专业的基础上,加强工程型和应用型学科专业建设,积极设置主要面向地方支柱产业、高新技术产业、服务业的工程型和应用型学科专业,积极为地方经济建设输送各类应用型人才。各高校加大了使用信息科学等现代科学技术提升、改造传统学科专业的力度,从而实现传统学科专业向工程型和应用型学科专业的发展与转变。在发挥传统学科专业师资力量强、办学经验丰富、教学资源充裕等优势的同时,不断更新其教学内容、改革课程体系,使工程型和应用型学科专业教育与经济建设相适应。

为了配合高校工程型和应用型学科专业的建设和发展,急需出版一批内容新、体系新、方法新、手段新的高水平电子信息类专业课程教材。目前,工程型和应用型学科专业电子信息类专业课程教材的建设工作仍滞后于教学改革的实践,如现有的电子信息类专业教材中有不少内容陈旧(依然用传统专业电子信息教材代替工程型和应用型学科专业教材),重理论、轻实践,不能满足新的教学计划、课程设置的需要;一些课程的教材可供选择的品种太少;一些基础课的教材虽然品种较多,但低水平重复严重;有些教材内容庞杂,书越编越厚;专业课教材、教学辅助教材及教学参考书短缺,等等,都不利于学生能力的提高和素质的培养。为此,在教育部相关教学指导委员会专家的指导和建议下,清华大学出版社组织出版本系列教材,以满足工程型和应用型电子信息类专业课程教学的需要。本系列教材在规划过程中体现了如下一些基本原则和特点:

(1) 系列教材主要是电子信息学科基础课程教材,面向工程技术应用培养。本系列教材在内容上坚持基本理论适度,反映基本理论和原理的综合应用,强调工程实践和应用环节。电子信息学科历经了一个多世纪的发展,已经形成了一个完整、科学的理论体系,这些理论是这一领域技术发展的强大源泉,基于理论的技术创新、开发与应用显得更为重要。

(2) 系列教材体现了电子信息学科使用新的分析方法和手段解决工程实际问题。利用计算机强大功能和仿真设计软件,使得电子信息领域中大量复杂的理论计算、变换分析等变得快速简单。教材充分体现了利用计算机解决理论分析与解算实际工程电路的途径与方法。

(3) 系列教材体现了新技术、新器件的开发应用实践。电子信息产业中仪器、设备、产品都已使用高集成化的模块,且不仅仅由硬件来实现,而是大量使用软件和硬件相结合方法,使得产品性价比很高,如何使学生掌握这些先进的技术、创造性地开发应用新技术是本系列教材的一个重要特点。

(4) 以学生知识、能力、素质协调发展为宗旨,系列教材编写内容充分注意了学生创新能力和实践能力的培养,加强了实验实践环节,各门课程均配有独立的实验课程和课程设计。

（5）21世纪是信息时代，学生获取知识可以是多种媒体形式和多种渠道的，而不再局限于课堂上，因而传授知识不再以教师为中心，以教材为唯一依托，而应该多为学生提供各类学习资料（如网络教材，CAI课件，学习指导书等）。应创造一种新的学习环境（如讨论，自学，设计制作竞赛等），让学生成为学习主体。该系列教材以计算机、网络和实验室为载体，配有多种辅助学习资料，提高学生学习兴趣。

繁荣教材出版事业，提高教材质量的关键是教师。建立一支高水平的以老带新的教材编写队伍才能保证教材的编写质量和建设力度，希望有志于教材建设的教师能够加入到我们的编写队伍中来。

21世纪高等学校电子信息工程规划教材编委会
联系人：魏江江   weijj@tup.tsinghua.edu.cn

前 言

电子技术与通信技术的飞速发展,促进了新技术、新产品与新设备的不断涌现,要迅速掌握这些新知识与新技能,从业人员就必须不断地提高专业英语水平。为进一步提高电子信息工程与通信工程专业高年级本科生和研究生的专业英语能力,促进人才的高层次培养,我们撰写了这本教材。选材的原则如下。

(1) 语言的规范性与纯正性。本书中的课文选自美国最近出版的电子信息工程与通信工程专业方面的国际权威杂志或经典论文。

(2) 专业知识的广泛性与先进性。选材综合考虑了电工与电子基础、电子与通信器件、信号与系统、通信技术,使读者在学习科技英语的同时也了解最新技术的发展。

(3) 专业知识的全面性。本书不仅重点强调了科技文献的"读",也对"写"与口头表达作了大量的尝试,同时还系统地阐述了科技论文的写作、投稿与应用文写作。

(4) 专业知识的扩展性。作为知识更新极快的专业,必须了解本专业的最权威的期刊,掌握科技文献的查阅方法。

此外,针对同类型教材的不足,结合作者多年来的实际工作经验与学术交流的体会,补充了常用数学名词、数学符号与数学公式的英文表达。

学生学习本书后,能熟悉和掌握大量电子信息工程与通信工程及其相关专业的常用词汇和术语,提高阅读和理解原始专业英语文献的能力,了解本专业一些新的器件与技术,从而增强国际交流能力。

本书由瞿少成、吴军其、罗小巧、姚远和凌毓涛共同编著。其中,姚远博士负责撰写Part 2,罗小巧副教授负责撰写Part 3,凌毓涛博士负责撰写Part 4,吴军其博士负责撰写Part 1与应用文写作部分,瞿少成博士撰写了科技论文的结构与写作初步、投稿指南,以及部分单元中的C部分。

感谢王永骥教授、姚琼荟教授多年的教诲,感谢王继新教授、钱同惠教授多年来对我们工作的支持。此外,应用英语专业的双文庭教授为本书提出了许多宝贵的建议。

由于经验不足,加之作者的水平有限,书中的疏漏之处在所难免,敬请读者批评指正,以便进一步改进和充实我们的工作。

编 者

2008 年 1 月

目 录

基础篇 ··· 1

PART 1　Electrotechnics and Electronics ··· 2
  UNIT 1 ·· 2
    A. Text: Electricity and Electrons ··· 2
    B. Reading: How electricity is generated ··································· 6
    C. 专业英语简介 ··· 9
  UNIT 2 ·· 11
    A. Text: Resistor and Resistance ··· 11
    B. Reading: The measurements of resistor ····························· 15
    C. 专业英语的词汇特征 ··· 17
  UNIT 3 ·· 20
    A. Text: Capacitors and Capacitance ······································· 20
    B. Reading: How does a Capacitor work ································· 24
    C. 专业英语常见的语法现象 ··· 26
  UNIT 4 ·· 28
    A. Text: Transistor ··· 28
    B. Reading: The First Transistor ·· 30
    C. 专业英语翻译的标准 ··· 32

PART 2　Modern Electronics Devices ··· 35
  UNIT 5 ·· 35
    A. Text: The basic components of computer system ············ 35
    B. Reading: Types of Computers and Future Developments ······ 39
    C. 常用的数学名词 ··· 41
  UNIT 6 ·· 43
    A. Text: ARM-The Architecture for the Digital World™ ········ 43
    B. Reading: The Introduce of ARM ··· 46
    C. 数的表示与读法 ··· 48
  UNIT 7 ·· 50
    A. Text: DSP Processor Fundamentals ···································· 50
    B. Reading: Processor Evolution ··· 54
    C. 数学公式的表示与读法 ··· 59
  UNIT 8 ·· 61

  A. Text: Digit-Serial Approach and Reconfigurable VLSI Architectures ················ 61
  B. Reading: High-Performance DSP Design Using FPGAs ···························· 67
  C. 英文摘要简介 ·· 69

PART 3 Signal and System ·· 71
UNIT 9 ·· 71
  A. Text: Mathematical Representation of Signals ··· 71
  B. Reading: Representation of Digital Signals ··· 77
  C. 从句的翻译 ·· 81
UNIT 10 ·· 85
  A. Text: Mathematical Representation of Systems ··· 85
  B. Reading: Comparison of Digital and Analog Techniques ····································· 89
  C. 被动句的翻译 ·· 93
UNIT 11 ·· 96
  A. Text: Fourier Transforms and Frequency-Domain Description ························· 96
  B. Reading: History of Fourier analysis ·· 100
  C. 长句的翻译 ·· 103
UNIT 12 ·· 106
  A. Text: The Sampling Theorem ·· 106
  B. Reading: A/D and D/A Conversions ·· 110
  C. 英汉语序的对比与翻译 ·· 115

PART 4 Communication Technology ·· 117
UNIT 13 ·· 117
  A. Text: Mobile Wireless ·· 117
  B. Reading: Technologies on Fourth-Generation Mobile Communication ············ 124
  C. 文献检索简介 ·· 126
UNIT 14 ·· 127
  A. Text: Fiber Optic ·· 127
  B. Reading: Optical Fiber Communications ·· 135
  C. 文献检索方法简介 ·· 137
UNIT 15 ·· 138
  A. Text: Satellites ··· 138
  B. Reading: Basic Knowledge of Communication ·· 142
  C. SCI 与 EI 简介 ·· 145
UNIT 16 ·· 147
  A. Text: Introduction to Computer Networks ·· 147
  B. Reading: Where Do Security Threats Come from ··· 152
  C. 信息类国内、外重要学术期刊 ·· 155

应用篇 159

- **PART 1　科技论文的结构与写作初步** 160
  - A. Title 162
  - B. Abstract 165
  - C. Body 169
  - D. Others 171
- **PART 2　投稿指南** 174
  - A. 如何选题 174
  - B. 投稿过程与投稿信（COVER LETTER）.. 175
  - C. 审稿过程以及与编辑的沟通 177
  - D. 如何修改论文 179
  - E. How to Give a Technical Talk 179
  - F. 科技论文中常见的错误 181
- **PART 3　应用文写作** 183
  - A. 信函 183
  - B. 简历 188
  - C. 求职信 194
  - D. 合同书 199
  - E. 产品说明书 202

部分参考译文与习题参考答案 211

- UNIT 1 211
- UNIT 2 212
- UNIT 3 214
- UNIT 4 214
- UNIT 5 215
- UNIT 6 217
- UNIT 7 218
- UNIT 8 220
- UNIT 9 223
- UNIT 10 225
- UNIT 11 227
- UNIT 12 229
- UNIT 13 230
- UNIT 14 233
- UNIT 15 236
- UNIT 16 237

参考文献 240

基 础 篇

PART 1

Electrotechnics and Electronics

UNIT 1

A. Text

Electricity and Electrons

You have a strong and wonderful helper. It is always ready to help you. It gives light to your room when you turn on a switch. It shows you TV pictures when you turn a knob. It carries your voice to others when you talk on the telephone. What is it? Yes, the name of this helper is electricity. We are so used to electric lights, radio, televisions, telephones and Internet that it is hard to imagine what life would be like without them[1]. In electricity's absence, people grope about in flickering candlelight, cars hesitate in the streets because there are no traffic lights to guide them, and food spoils in silent refrigerators, to talk over long distance we are left with smoke signals and postcards.

Many years ago, scientists had very vague ideas about electricity[2]. About 2000 years ago, Wang Chong, a Chinese philosopher, discovered that if one rubbed a piece of amber with a piece of fur or wood, he could always produce electricity. Scientists say today that the amber had become charged with electricity. Until the 19th century, no one knew much more about this. As the times went on, many of them thought of it as a sort of "fluid" that flowed through wires as water flows through pipes, but they could not understand what made it flow. Many of them felt that electricity was made up of tiny particles of some kind, but trying to separate electricity into individual particles baffled them.

Then, the great American scientist Millikan, in 1909, astounded the scientific world by actually weighing a single particle of electricity and calculating its electrical charge. This was probably one of the most delicate weighing jobs ever done by man[3], for a single electric particle weighs only about half of a millionth of a millionth of a millionth of a millionth of a pound. The particle is much smaller than you can imagine. To make up a pound it would take more of those particles than there are drops of water in the Pacific Ocean.

They are no strangers to us, these electric particles, for we know them as electrons. Every single thing you have ever seen is made up of thousands of hundreds of atoms, and every atom contains one or more electrons. When large numbers of electrons break away from their atoms and move through a wire, we describe this action by saying that electricity is "flowing" through the wire[4]. Yes, the electrical "fluid" that early scientists talked about is nothing more than electrons flowing along a wire!

But how can individual electrons be made to break away from atoms? The answer lies in the structure of the atoms themselves. In many materials, the electrons are tightly bound to the atoms. Wood, glass, plastic, ceramic, air, cotton ... These are all examples of materials in which electrons stick with their atoms. Because the electrons don't move, these materials cannot conduct electricity very well, if at all. These materials are electrical insulators.

But most metals have electrons that can detach from their atoms and move around[5]. These are called free electrons. Gold, silver, copper, aluminum, iron, etc., all have free electrons. The loose electrons make it easy for electricity to flow through these materials, so they are known as electrical conductors. They conduct electricity. The moving electrons transmit electrical energy from one point to another.

An atom of aluminum, for example, is continually losing an electron, regaining it (or another electron), and losing it again. An aluminum atom normally has 13 electrons, arranged in three different orbits around its nucleus[6]. The inside orbit has 2 electrons. The next larger orbit has 8. The third orbit has only 3 electrons. It is this outside electron that the aluminum atom is continually losing, for it is not very closely tied to the atom. It wanders off, replaced by another free roving electron, and then this second electron also wanders away.

Consequently, in an aluminum wire free electrons are floating around in all directions among the aluminum atoms. Thus, even though the aluminum wire looks quite motionless to your ordinary eye, there is a great deal of activity going on inside it.

If the wire were carrying electricity to an electric light or to some other electrical device, the electrons would not be moving around at random. Instead, many of them would be rushing in the same direction from one end of the wire to the other.

Thus, electricity needs a conductor in order to move. There also has to be something to make the electricity flow from one point to another through the conductor. One way to get electricity flowing is to use a generator. A generator uses a magnet to get electrons moving. Faraday and Henry discovered how magnets could be used to make electricity flow in a wire. Another way is chemical. Volta's voltaic pile, or battery, is a chemical device that makes electricity (or electrons) flow in wires.

New Words and Technical Terms

electricity	[ilekˈtrisiti]	n.	电，电学
electronic	[ilekˈtrɔnik]	n.	电子
switch	[switʃ]	n.	开关
flickering	[ˈflɪkərɪŋ]	adj.	闪烁的，摇曳的，忽隐忽现的
candlelight	[ˈkænd(ə)llaɪt]	n.	烛火，黄昏
refrigerator	[riˈfridʒəreitə]	n.	电冰箱，冷藏库
amber	[ˈæbə]	n.	琥珀
rub	[ˈrʌb]	v.	摩擦
vague	[ˈveig]	adj.	含糊的
particles	[ˈpa:tikəlz]	n.	粒子，微粒
sort	[ˈsɔ:t]	n.	种类，类别
baffle	[ˈbæfl]	v.	困惑，阻碍，为难
astound	[əsˈtaund]	v.	使震惊
delicate	[ˈdelikit]	adj.	精巧的，灵敏的，精密的
atom	[ˈætəm]	n.	原子
bound	[baund]	v.	绑定，限制
detach	[diˈtætʃ]	v.	分开，分离
insulator	[insjuˈleitə]	n.	绝缘体
conductor	[kənˈdʌktə]	n.	导体
wander	[ˈwʌndə]	v.	溜达，闲逛
rove	[ˈrəuv]	v. 漫游；n.	漫游，流浪，粗纱
motionless	[ˈməuʃlis]	adj.	不动的，静止的
random	[ˈrædəm]	adj.	偶然的，随意的
generator	[ˈdʒənəreitə]	n.	发电机
battery	[ˈbætəri]	n.	电池
magnetic	[mægˈnetik]	adj.	磁的，有磁性的，有吸引力的
electrical charge			电荷
electrical energy			电能
electric light			电灯
electrical device			电器设备
electric wire			电线

Notes

[1] We are so used to electric lights, radio, televisions, and telephone that it is hard to imagine what life would be like without them.

我们对电灯、无线电广播、电视和电话是如此的熟悉,所以很难想象离开了它们,我们的生活将会是什么样子。

Be used to sth. 习惯于……；而 used to do sth. 则是表示过去常常做……。

[2] Many years ago, scientists had very vague ideas about electricity.

很多年以前,科学家们对电的概念还是很模糊的。

Have very vague ideas about sth. 对……不是很清楚,知之甚少。

[3] This was probably one of the most delicate weighing jobs ever done by man.

这可能是人类做过的最细致的计量工作之一。

Ever done by man 是过去分词作定语,修饰 weighing jobs。

[4] When large numbers of electrons break away from their atoms and move through a wire, we describe this action by saying that electricity is "flowing" through the wire.

当大量的电子脱离原子的"束缚"并通过导线运动时,这时我们就说电通过导线在"流动"。

We describe this action by saying that 我们就把这种行为描述为……；break away 摆脱,脱离……（的束缚）。

[5] But most metals have electrons that can detach from their atoms and move around.

但是很多金属的电子能够与它们的原子分离,到处漂移。

此处 that can detach from their atoms and move around 是一个定语从句,修饰先行词 electrons。

[6] An aluminum atom normally has 13 electrons, arranged in three different orbits around its nucleus.

一个铝原子通常有 13 个电子,它们排列在原子核周围三个不同的轨道上。此处的 orbit 是指轨道的意思,nucleus 是指核、核子。

Exercises

I. Choose the one that best suits the sentence according to the text.

1. _____ is the wonderful helper to our life according to the passage.
   A. radio   B. television   C. electricity   D. Internet
2. The weight of an atom is _____.
   A. one pound   B. half pound   C. million pounds   D. hard to imagine
3. The tiny particles are _____.
   A. atoms   B. electrons   C. electricity   D. conductors
4. In normal situation, ceramic is _____.
   A. insulator   B. conductor   C. semi-conductor   D. none of the above
5. There are _____ electrons in the second orbit of aluminum atom.
   A. 13   B. 2   C. 8   D. 3
6. In order to make the electricity flow along one direction, we can use _____.
   A. generator   B. battery   C. Volta's voltaic pile   D. All of the above

II. Try to match the following columns.

Electricity	轨道
Electron	原子
Atoms	磁的
Orbit	电，电学
Electrical energy	电能
Magnetic	电子

B. Reading

How electricity is generated

Electricity is the flow of electrical power or charge. It is a secondary energy source which means that we get it from the conversion of other sources of energy, like coal, natural gas, oil, nuclear power and other natural sources, which are called primary sources.

An electric generator is a device for converting mechanical energy into electrical energy. The process is based on the relationship between magnetism and electricity. When a wire or any other electrically conductive material moves across a magnetic field, an electric current occurs in the wire. The large generators used by the electric utility industry have a stationary conductor. A magnet attached to the end of a rotating shaft is positioned inside a stationary conducting ring that is wrapped with a long, continuous piece of wire. When the magnet rotates, it induces a small electric current in each section of wire as it passes. Each section of wire constitutes a small, separate electric conductor. All the small currents of individual sections add up to one current of considerable size. This current is what is used for electric power.

An electric utility power station uses either a turbine, engine, water wheel, or other similar machine to drive an electric generator or a device that converts mechanical or chemical energy to generate electricity. Steam turbines, internal-combustion engines, gas combustion turbines, water turbines, and wind turbines are the most common methods to generate electricity. Most power plants are about 35 percent efficient. That means that for every 100 units of energy that go into a plant, only 35 units are converted to usable electrical energy.

Most of the electricity in the United States is produced in steam turbines. A turbine converts the kinetic energy of a moving fluid (liquid or gas) to mechanical energy. Steam turbines have a series of blades mounted on a shaft against which steam is forced, thus rotating the shaft connected to the generator. In a fossil-fueled steam turbine, the fuel is burned in a furnace to heat water in a boiler to produce steam.

Coal, petroleum (oil), and natural gas are burned in large furnaces to heat water to make steam that in turn pushes on the blades of a turbine. Coal is the largest single primary source of energy used to generate electricity in the United States. In our country, more than half of the country's electricity used coal as its source of energy.

Natural gas, in addition to being burned to heat water for steam, can also be burned to produce hot combustion gases that pass directly through a turbine, spinning the blades of the turbine to generate electricity. Gas turbines are commonly used when electricity utility usage is in high demand. A part of the nation's electricity was fueled by natural gas.

Petroleum can also be used to make steam to turn a turbine. Residual fuel oil, a product refined from crude oil, is often the petroleum product used in electric plants that use petroleum to make steam. Petroleum was used to generate about three to four percent of all electricity generated in our country.

Nuclear power is a method in which steam is produced by heating water through a process called nuclear fission. In a nuclear power plant, a reactor contains a core of nuclear fuel, primarily enriched uranium. When atoms of uranium fuel are hit by neutrons they fission (split), releasing heat and more neutrons. Under controlled conditions, these other neutrons can strike more uranium atoms, splitting more atoms, and so on. Thereby, continuous fission can take place, forming a chain reaction releasing heat. The heat is used to turn water into steam, that, in turn, spins a turbine that generates electricity. Nuclear power was used to generate about 20% of all the country's electricity in 2005.

Hydropower, the source for almost 7% of electricity generation, is a process in which flowing water is used to spin a turbine connected to a generator. There are two basic types of hydroelectric systems that produce electricity. In the first system, flowing water accumulates in reservoirs created by the use of dams. The water falls through a pipe called a penstock and applies pressure against the turbine blades to drive the generator to produce electricity. In the second system, called run-of-river, the force of the river current (rather than falling water) applies pressure to the turbine blades to produce electricity.

Geothermal power comes from heat energy buried beneath the surface of the earth. In some areas of the country, enough heat rises close to the surface of the earth to heat underground water into steam, which can be tapped for use at steam-turbine plants. This energy source generated less than 1% of the electricity in the country in 2005.

Solar power is derived from the energy of the sun. However, the sun's energy is not available full-time and it is widely scattered. The processes used to produce electricity using the sun's energy have historically been more expensive than using conventional fossil fuels. Photovoltaic conversion generates electric power directly from the light of the sun in a photovoltaic (solar) cell. Solar-thermal electric generators use the radiant energy from the sun to produce steam to drive turbines. In 2005, less than 1% of the nation's electricity was based on solar power.

Wind power is derived from the conversion of the energy contained in wind into electricity. Wind power, less than 1% of the nation's electricity in 2005, is a rapidly growing source of electricity.

Biomass includes wood, municipal solid waste (garbage), and agricultural waste, such as corncobs and wheat straw. These are some other energy sources for producing electricity. These sources replace fossil fuels in the boiler. The combustion of wood and waste creates steam that is typically used in conventional steam-electric plants. Biomass accounts for about 2% of the electricity generated in the United States.

New Words and Technical Terms

nuclear	['njuːkliə]	adj. 核子的，原子的，核的，中心的
generator	['dʒenəreitə]	n. 发电机，发生器
magnetism	['mægnitizəm]	n. 磁力，吸引力，磁学
conductive	[kən'dʌktiv]	adj. 传导的
magnet	['mægnit]	n. 磁体，磁铁
shaft	[ʃaːft]	n. 轴
stationary	['steiʃənəri]	adj. 固定的
considerable	[kən'sidərəbl]	adj. 相当大（或多）的，值得考虑的
convert	[kən'vəːt]	v. 使转变，转换
plant	[plaːnt]	n. 植物，庄稼，工厂，车间，设备
furnace	['fəːnis]	n. 炉子，熔炉
blades	[bleid]	n. 刀，刀片
utility	[juː'tiliti]	n. 效用，有用
usage	['juːzidʒi]	n. 使用，用法
refine	[ri'fain]	n. 精炼，精制
fission	['fiʃən]	n. 裂变
reactor	[ri'æktə]	n. 反应堆
split	['split]	v. 分裂，分离
biomass	['baiəumæs]	n. （单位面积或体积内的）生物量
combustion	[kəm'bʌstʃən]	n. 燃烧
uranium	[juə'reiniəm]	n. 铀
neutrons	['njuːtrɔn]	n. 中子
photovoltaic	['fəutəuvɔi'teiik]	adj. 光电的
hydroelectric	['haidrəi'lektrik]	adj. 水力电气的
reservoir	['rezəːvwaː]	n. 水库，蓄水池
penstock	['penstɔk]	n. 水道，水渠，压力水管，水阀门
electric utility industry		电力工业
Steam turbines		蒸汽机
internal-combustion engines		内燃机
gas combustion turbines		燃气机
water turbines, wind turbines, kinetic		水轮，风轮，动能
Residual fuel oil		残余燃料油
crude oil		原油

enriched uranium　　　　　　　　　　浓缩铀
geothermal power　　　　　　　　　　地热能

Exercises

Ⅰ. Which material can electricity get from the conversion of it?

Ⅱ. What's the function of an electric generator?

Ⅲ. How much weight of each kind of material in contribution to the nations' electricity? And why?

C. 专业英语简介

信息技术的飞速发展，给社会带来了重大的变革，各国之间的交流也日趋广泛，各种国际学术会议也不断举行。但是，电子、计算机和控制方面的文献和会议，大部分都是用英文写的。所以，掌握好专业英语的阅读、翻译和书写的方法对我们了解最新的技术动态、吸收先进的科技成果是至关重要的。电子信息专业英语是电子信息专业必修课，同时它也与公共英语密切相关。作为电子信息专业的大学生，他们既有电子信息基础知识，也有不错的公共英语基础，但一看到那些英文文献、英文资料、英文会议时还是会有些不知所措。如何在较短的时间里将专业英语掌握好呢？首先要了解电子信息专业英语的三大特点。

1. 专业性

专业英语的专业性体现在它的特殊专业内容和特殊专业词汇。词汇是构成句子的基本元素，对词汇含义不能确定，就很难理解句子内容，甚至会得出可笑的、相反的结果。很多公共英语在专业领域内被赋予了专业含义，这就要求我们熟悉所学专业。如：Bus（总线）、ATM（异步传输方式）、Port（端口）、Read Only Memory（只读存储器）。

新词汇层出不穷，有的是随着本专业发展应运而生的，有的是借用公共英语中的词汇，有的是借用外来语词汇，有的则是人为构造成的词汇。有些专业词汇是需要对专业知识有相当的了解之后才会明白其意思的。如：

Alternating current　交流电
Parallel circuits　并联电路
Push-pull amplifier　推挽放大器
Sinusoidal oscillator　正弦波振荡器

Tuned circuit　调谐电路
The common base　共集电极法
Secondary winding　二次绕组
Superheterodyne configuration　超外差式结构
Automatic gain control　（GAC）自动增益控制
Matrix circuit　矩阵电路
Quadrate modulation　正交调制

2．灵活性

专业英语一般讲述的是电工电子器件和设备的主要组成部件、工作原理与使用方法，这就决定了专业英语的客观性和灵活性。在学习过程中，尤其是在阅读专业文章时，必须尊重客观内容，不能主观想象。为了表示一种公允性和客观性，往往在句子结构和词性的使用上比较灵活。

如英语动词中有的表示动作，有的表示相对静止的状态。

（1）TV differs from radio in that it sends and receives pictures.

电视与无线电的区别在于电视能够发送和接收图像。（表示状态）

（2）These two RF signals are arranged to differ by a constant frequency by suitable design of the RF amplifier and oscillator tuning circuit constants.

通过合理地设计射频放大器及振荡调谐电路常数，这两个射频信号用于找出一个固定频率。（表示动作）

3．简明性

为求精炼，专业英语中常希望能够用尽可能少的单词来清晰地表达原意。这就导致了非限定动词、名词化单词或词组或其他简化形式的广泛使用。

动名词短语可用来取代时间从句或简化时间陈述句，如

（1）Before it is amplified, the signal should be detected.

（2）Switch off the main supply.

（3）Remove the fuse.

过去分词短语可以取代被动语态关系从句，现在分词可以取代主动语态关系从句，如

In Britain electricity energy generated in power station is fed to the national Grid.

不定式短语用以替换表示目的、功能的从句，如

The function of a fuse is to protect a circuit.

总的说来，与普通英语相比，专业英语很注重客观事实和真理，并且要求逻辑性强，条理规范，表达准确，精练、正式。专业英语有如下显著特点：

- 长句多。
- 被动语态使用频繁。
- 用虚拟语气表达假设或建议。
- 在说明书、手册中广泛使用祈使语句。
- 名词性词组多。

- 非限定动词（尤其是分词）使用频率高。
- 介词短语多。
- 常用 It……句型结构。
- 单个动词比动词词组用得频繁。
- 常使用动词或名词演化成的形容词。
- 希腊词根和拉丁词根比例大。
- 缩略词经常出现。
- 半技术词汇多。
- 缩写使用频繁。
- 插图、插画、表格、公式、数字所占比例大。
- 合成新词多。

UNIT 2

A. Text

Resistor and Resistance

A resistor is an electrical component that limits or regulates the flow of electrical current in an electronic circuit. It is the simplest sort of electrical component. It is used in a circuit for protection and current control. A resistor has two terminals across which electricity must pass, and is designed to drop the voltage of the current as it flows from one terminal to the next.

Resistors can fall into two categories[1]: fixed (Fig. 1-1) or variable. A fixed resistor has a predetermined amount of resistance to current, while a variable resistor can be adjusted to give different levels of resistance. Variable resistors are also called potentiometers and are commonly used as volume controls on audio devices. A rheostat is a variable resistor made specifically for use with high currents. There are also metal-oxide varistors, which change their resistance in response to a rise in voltage; thermistors, which either raise or lower resistance when temperature rises or drops; and light-sensitive resistors.

Fig. 1-1 Fixed Resistor.

Every resistor has resistance. Resistance is a feature of a material that determines the flow of electric charge. The unit of resistance is ohm. In a direct-current (DC) circuit, the current through a resistor is inversely proportional to its resistance, and directly proportional to the voltage across it[2]. This is the well-known Ohm's Law. It can be written in an equation $V=IR$, where V is voltage, I is current, and R is resistance. A high ohm rating indicates a high resistance to current. In alternating-current (AC) circuits, this rule also applies as long as the resistor does not contain inductance or capacitance. Resistance can be written in a number of different ways depending on the ohm rating. For example, 81R represents 81 ohms, while 81K represent 81,000 ohms.

The resistance varies in different materials[3]. For example, gold, silver, and copper have low resistance, which means that current can flow easily through these materials. Glass, plastics, and wood have very high resistance, which means that current can not pass through these materials easily.

Resistors can be fabricated in a variety of ways. The most common type in electronic devices and systems is the carbon-composition resistor. Fine granulated carbon (graphite) is mixed with clay and hardened[4]. The resistance depends on the proportion of carbon to clay; the higher this ratio, the lower the resistance[5].

Another type of resistor is made from winding nichrome or similar wire on an insulating form. This component, called a wirewound resistor, is able to handle higher currents than a carbon-composition resistor of the same physical size. However, because the wire is wound into a coil, the component acts as an inductors as well as exhibiting resistance[6]. This does not affect performance in DC circuits, but can have an adverse effect in AC circuits because inductance renders the device sensitive to changes in frequency[7].

The amount of resistance offered by a resistor is determined by its physical construction[8]. A carbon composition resistor has resistive carbon packed into a ceramic cylinder, while a carbon film resistor consists of a similar ceramic tube, but has conductive carbon film wrapped around the outside. Metal film or metal oxide resistors are made much the same way, but with metal instead of carbon. A wirewound resistor, made with metal wire wrapped around clay, plastic, or fiberglass tubing, offers resistance at higher power levels. For applications that must withstand high temperatures, materials such as cermets, a ceramic-metal composite, or tantalum, a rare metal, are used to build a resistor that can endure heat[9].

A resistor is coated with paint or enamel, or covered in molded plastic to protect it. Because resistors are often too small to be written on, a standardized color-coding system is used to identify them. The first three colors represent ohm value, and a fourth indicates the tolerance, or how close by percentage the resistor is to its ohm value. This is important for two reasons: the nature of resistor construction is imprecise, and if used above its maximum current, the value of the resistor can alter or the unit itself can burn up.

New Words and Technical Terms

represent	[riːprɪə'zənt]	v. 表现，代表
fabricate	['fæbrikeit]	v. 制作
tolerance	['tɔlərəns]	n. 公差，容差
maximum	['mæsiməm]	adj. 最高的，最多的，最大极限的

alter	[ˈɔːltə]	n.	改变
frequency	[ˈfriːkwənsi]	n.	频率
predetermine	[ˈpridiˈtəːmin]	v.	预定，预先确定
resistance	[ˈrizistəns]	n.	阻力，电阻，阻抗
component	[kəmˈpəunənt]	n.	成分、部件
proportion	[prəˈpɔːʃən]	n.	比例
potentiometer	[pəntənʃiˈɔːmitə]	n.	电位计，分压计
rheostat	[ˈriːəstæt]	n.	可变电阻器
varistors	[vəːˈristə]	n.	变阻器
thermistor	[θəːˈmistə]	n.	电热调节器
inductance	[inˈdʌktəns]	n.	感应系数，自感应
capacitance	[kəˈpæsitəns]	n.	电容
graphite	[ˈgræfait]	n.	石墨
nichrome	[ˈnaikrəum]	n.	镍铬合金
cylinder	[ˈsilində]	n.	圆筒，圆柱体
fiberglass	[ˈfaibəglaːs]	n.	玻璃纤维，玻璃丝
cermet	[ˈsəːmet]	n.	金属陶瓷，含陶合金
tantalum	[ˈtæmtələm]	n.	钽（金属元素）
enamel	[ˈinæməl]	n.	瓷釉
direct-current (DC)			直流
alternating-current (AC)			交流
wire wound			线绕的，绕有电阻丝的
metal oxide resistors			金属氧化物电阻器
color-coding			色标

Notes

[1] Resistors can fall into two categories: fixed or variable.

电阻可以分为两类：固定电阻和可变电阻。

fall into 表示"分为"，这个句子也可以说成：Resistors can be classified into two categories: fixed or variable.

[2] The unit of resistance is ohm. In a direct-current (DC) circuit, the current through a resistor is inversely proportional to its resistance, and directly proportional to the voltage across it.

电阻的单位是欧姆。在直流电路中，通过电阻的电流与它的阻抗成反比，与加在其上的电压成正比。

inversely proportional to 与……成反比；directly proportional to 与……成正比。

[3] The resistance varies in different materials.

不同物体的阻抗不同。vary in 依据……而变化。

[4] Fine granulated carbon (graphite) is mixed with clay and hardened.

将精细的颗粒状的碳（石墨）与泥土混合并使其变硬。

be mixed with 与……混合；harden 是 hard 的动词形式，意思是使变硬，使坚固。

[5] The higher this ratio, the lower the resistance.

这个比例越大，阻抗就越低。

这个句型用的是"the+形容词比较级句型"，表示"越……，就越……"。如：The higher the resistance, the lower the current. 电阻越大，电流就越小。

[6] However, because the wire is wound into a coil, the component acts as an inductors as well as exhibiting resistance.

然而，因为导线绕成了圈，这个元件在显示电阻特性的同时，也具有电感的一些特性。

act as 作为……来使用，as well as 也，同时。

[7] This does not affect performance in DC circuits, but can have an adverse effect in AC circuits because inductance renders the device sensitive to changes in frequency.

在直流电路中这并没有影响，但是对交流电路却有反作用，因为电感效应系数使该器件对频率的变化很敏感。

[8] The amount of resistance offered by a resistor is determined by its physical construction.

电阻的阻抗是由它的物理结构决定的。

be determined by 由……决定。

[9] For applications that must withstand high temperatures, materials such as cermets, a ceramic-metal composite, or tantalum, a rare metal, are used to build a resistor that can endure heat.

在必须抵挡高温的场合中，金属陶瓷或者含有金属陶瓷成分，或一种稀有金属钽，就可以用来做成电阻，因为它们可以经受高温的考验。

withstand 抵挡，经受住，endure，忍耐。

Exercises

Ⅰ. Choose the one that best suits the sentence according to the text.

1. When the voltage flows across the resistor, the voltage will _____.
    A. rise   B. drop
    C. no variation   D. all of the above are possible

2. Variable resistors are also called _____.
    A. varistors   B. potentiometer
    C. thermistor   D. metal oxide resistors

3. In a direct-current (DC) circuit, when the voltage is fixed, as the current through a resistor is higher, this shows that its resistance is _____.
    A. lower   B. higher
    C. the same   D. all of the above are possible

4. Compared with copper, the ceramic is _____.
    A. less conductive   B. more conductive
    C. more inductive   D. less inductive

5. When the proportion of clay to carbon is higher, the resistances will be _____.
   A. lower   B. higher
   C. no effect   D. all of the above are possible
6. For applications that must withstand high temperatures, we can use _____.
   A. cermet   B. ceramic-metal composite
   C. tantalum   D. all of the above are possible

II. Try to explain the following terms.

Resistor:

Resistance:

Tolerance:

B. Reading

The measurements of resistor

An ohmmeter measures resistance, and gives you a value of the measured resistance in ohms, kilohms or megohms. Many ohmmeters look like the following diagram (Fig.1-2).

There's an internal source that provides a voltage (Fig.1-3). That source may be a battery or a small power supply. The source drives a voltage divider-two resistors in series. One of those resistors is internal to the meter, and the other resistor is the resistor being measured. An internal meter measures the voltage across the resistance being measured and converts that voltage into a resistance reading. The resistance being measured is connected to the ohmmeter terminals, and the terminals are often colored black and red.

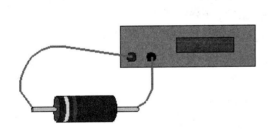
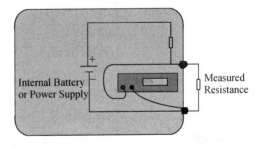

Fig. 1-2 Ohmmeter.   Fig. 1-3 Measure of Resistance using Ohmmeter.

All you have to do to measure a resistance is to connect your resistor to the ohmmeter as shown below, and be sure that the ohmmeter is set to measure resistance. Don't get uptight about which lead goes on which end of the resistor. It doesn't matter. (The resistor is a "bilateral" element and should be the same either way!)

Here's the way you connect the ohmmeter (or digital voltmeter) to the resistor. Here we're using the same resistor as was used above. The ohmmeter shown here includes all of the circuitry shown above including a power supply or battery and an internal resistance. To measure the resistance it applies a small voltage across the resistance.

Besides, the resistance can also be calculated in circuits in series or parallel.

If a circuit contains resistance in series, the total resistance can be calculated by adding all the individual resistance. The formula is straightforward:

$$R_n = R_1 + R_2 + R_3 + \cdots + R_n$$

Here, R is the total resistance, R_1 through R_n are the individual resistance. As an example, suppose two 6 ohm speakers and one 4 ohm speaker were in series.

The total ohm is: 6+6+4=16 ohms

Circuits that contain resistance in parallel are a bit more difficult to calculate net resistance. The formula involves reciprocals. Stated it is that the sum of the reciprocals of the individual resistance equals the reciprocal the total resistance.

The formula appears below:

$$\frac{1}{R} = \frac{1}{R_1} + \frac{1}{R_2} + \frac{1}{R_3} + \cdots + \frac{1}{R_n}$$

If there are exactly two resistances in parallel, there is an easier formula to use:

$$R = \frac{R_1 \times R_2}{R_1 + R_2}$$

New Words and Expressions

diagram	['daigræm]	n. 图表
uptight	[ʌp'tait]	adj. 紧张的
bilateral	[bai'lætərəl]	adj. 有两面的，双边的
individual	[indi'vidjuəl]	adj. 个别的，单独的
straightforward	[streit'fɔ:wəd]	adj. 直接的
circuitry	['sə:kitri]	n. 电路，线路
reciprocal	[ri'siprəkəl]	adj. 互惠的，相应的，倒数的，彼此相反的
		n. 倒数，互相起作用的事物
kilohm	['kiləum]	n. 千欧
megohm	[me'gəum]	n. 兆欧
ohmmeter	['əum,mi:tə]	n. 欧姆计，电阻表
voltmeter	['vəult,mi:tə]	n. 伏特计
power supply		电源

Exercises

1. How to measure the resistance of a resistor by an ohmmeter?

Ⅱ. How to calculate the resistance of a resistor in series circuit?

Ⅲ. How to calculate the resistance of a resistor in parallel circuit?

C. 专业英语的词汇特征

1. 词汇构成

专业英语词汇有其自身的特点，一般来说，可以分为以下几类：
（1）技术词汇

这类词汇的意义狭窄，一般只使用在各自的专业范围内，因而专业性很强。这类词一般较长并且越长词义越狭窄，出现的频率也不高。如：

  bandwidth 带宽   flip-flop 触发器
  super heterodyne 超外差的   superconductivity 超导性
  Amplifier 放大器   quadriphony 四声道立体声

（2）次技术词汇

次技术词汇是指不受上下文限制的各专业出现频率都很高的词。这类词往往在不同的专业中具有不同的含义。如：

  plant   conductor   power

其中，plant 常用含义是植物，但是在专业英语中指工厂、对象、系统，conductor 在日常生活中指售票员和乐队指挥，在电学中表示导体。power 指能量，在电学中指电源等。

（3）特用词

在日常英语中，为使语言生动活泼，常使用一些短小的词或词组。而在专业英语中，表达同样的意义时，为了准确、正式、严谨，不引起歧义，通常选用一些较长的特用词。这些词在非专业英语中极少使用但属于非专业英语。

日常生活中常用下列句子：Then the light is turned on.

在专业英语中，却表示为：The circuit is then completed.

这是由于 complete 词义单一准确，可以避免歧义。而 turned on 不仅可以表示开通，而且还可以表示其他意义，如：

The success of a picnic usually turns on（依赖）the weather.

类似对应的特用词还有：

```
go down——depress        upside down——invert
keep——maintain          enough——sufficient
take away——remove       an once——immediately
push in——insert         a lot of——appreciable
used up——consume        find out——determine
```

（4）功能词

它包括介词、连词、冠词、代词等。功能词为词在句子中的结构关系中提供了十分重要的结构信号，对于理解专业内容十分重要，而且出现频率极高。研究表明，在专业英语中，出现频率很高的 10 个词都是功能词，其顺序为：the, of, in, and, to, is, that, for, are, be。

2．构词法

英语的构词法主要有 4 种：前缀法、后缀法、合成、转化。前缀法和后缀法也叫"派生法"（derivation），专业英语词汇大部分都是用派生法构成的，即通过各种前缀和后缀来构成新词。有专家学者曾经做过统计，以 semi-构成的词有 230 个以上，以 auto-构成的词有 260 个以上，以 micro 构成的词有 300 个以上，以 thermo 构成的词有 130 个以上。仅这 4 个前缀构成的词就达近千个，而常用的前缀和后缀却多达上百个，可见派生法的构词能力非常强。

（1）常用的前缀

inter-   如 intersection interface
counter- 如 counterpart
sub-   如 subway submarine
through- 如 throughput
hyper-   如 hyperons hyper plane
tele-   如 telescope
photo-   如 photosphere
super-   如 superheated
in-   如 inadequate insufficient
im-   如 impossible
re-   如 reuse recharge
over-   如 overwork overload
under-   如 underpay
dis-   如 discharge dissatisfy
ab-   如 abstract
con-   如 confound
ex-   如 exit
trans-   如 transformer

（2）常用的后缀

-ist   如 scientist artist
-logy   如 anthropology

-ism　如 mechanism
-able　如 noticeable stable
-ive　如 reactive effective
-ic　如 electronic metallic
-ous　如 synchronous porous
-proof　如 waterproof acid-proof
-en　如 weaken harden shorten

（3）常用的合成（composition）方法

名词＋名词形式，如 Workshop 工作间，air conditioner 空调

形容词＋名词，如 greenhouse 温室，stainless steel 不锈钢

动词＋名词，如 feedback 反馈，closed-loop 开环，opened-loop 闭环

名词＋动词，如 input 输入，output 输出

介词＋名词，如 forward-bias（正向偏压），outside（在外边）

3．专用词汇和缩略语

专业英语有许多的专业词汇，记住这些专业词汇对于阅读和学习的帮助都很大。

常用的专业词汇和短语组：

air core transformer　空心放大器
air condition　空调
amplitude modulation　调幅
analog multiplier　模拟乘法器
AND gate　与门
Application specific integrated circuit （ASIC）专用集成电路
area code　地区代码
assembler program　汇编程序
audio signal　音频信号
automatic gain control （AGC）　自动增益控制
band pass filter　带通滤波器
bar code　条形码
binary code　二进制码
call control function （CCF）　呼叫控制功能
cathode-ray tube（CRT）　阴极射线管
central processing unit（CPU）　中央处理器
color graphic adapter（CGA）　彩色图形适配器
common emitter amplifier　共发射机放大器
communication channel　通信信道
compact disk　光盘
compact disk read-only memory（CD-ROM）　光盘只读存储器
counter emf　反电动势

coupling capacitor　耦合电容器
differential amplifier　差分放大器
domain name　域名
dry cell　干电池
electromotive force　电动势
electronic engineering　电子工程学
frequency synthesizer　频率合成器
fuzzy logic　模糊逻辑
internet protocol　互联网协议
light-emitting diodes（LED）发光二极管
local call　市内电话
NAND gate　与非门
OR gate　或门
Programming logic controller（PLC）可编程逻辑控制器
Registered trademark　注册商标
RF oscillator　射频振荡器
storage battery　蓄电池
signal generator　信号发生器
silicon controlled rectifier（SCR）可控硅（整流器）
step-attenuator　步进衰减器
square wave　方波
telecommunication satellite　通信卫星
telecommunication system　远程通信系统
the positive-going edge　上升沿
transmission control protocol（TCP）传输控制协议
truth table　真值表
very high frequency　甚高频
very large scale integrated circuit（VLSI）超大规模集成电路
video cassette recorder　录像机
volt-ohm millimeter（VOM）万用表
wideband amplifier　宽带放大器

UNIT 3

A. Text

Capacitors and Capacitance

Electrical energy can be stored in an electric field. The device capable of doing this is called a capacitor or a condenser[1].

A simple capacitor consists of two conducting plates separated by an insulating material called the dielectric [2]. If a capacitor is connected to a battery, the electrons will flow out of the negative terminal of the battery and accumulate on the capacitor plate connected to that side (Fig. 1-4). At the same time, the electrons will leave the plate connected to the positive terminal and flow into the battery to make the potential difference just the same as that of the battery. Thus the capacitor is said to be charged[3]. A battery will transport charge from one plate to the other until the voltage produced by the charge buildup is equal to the battery voltage.

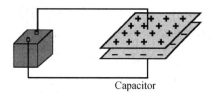

Fig. 1-4 Capacitor.

The ability of a capacitor electrical energy is called capacitance[4]. The standard unit of capacitance is the farad, abbreviated F. However, this is a large unit; more common units are the microfarad, abbreviated μF ($1\mu F = 10^{-6}$ F) and the picofarad, abbreviated pF ($1\ pF = 10^{-12}$ F).

Capacitance is typified by a parallel plate arrangement and is defined in terms of charge storage:

$$C = Q / V$$

Where Q is magnitude of charge stored on each plate, V is voltage applied to the plates[5].

Capacitors can be fabricated onto integrated circuit (IC) chips. They are commonly used in conjunction with transistors in Dynamic Random Access Memory (DRAM). The capacitors help maintain the contents of memory[6].

Large capacitors are used in the power supplies of electronic equipment of all types, including computers and their peripherals. In these systems, the capacitors smooth out the rectified utility AC, providing pure, battery-like DC[7].

New words and Technical Terms

capacitor	[kəˈpæsitə]	n. (= capacitator) 电容器
condenser	[kənˈsist]	n. 冷凝器，电容器
typify	[ˈtipifai]	v. 代表
consist	[kənˈsist]	vi. 由……组成，在于，一致
insulating	[ˈinsjuleitiŋ]	adj. 绝缘的
dielectric	[ˌdaiiˈlektrik]	n. 电介质，绝缘体 adj. 非传导性的
potential	[pəˈtenʃ(ə)l]	adj. 势的，位的 n. 潜能，电压
capacitance	[kəˈpæsitəns]	n. 容量，电容
Farad	[ˈfærəd]	n. 法拉（电容单位）

abbreviated	[əˈbriːvieitid]	v.	缩写，简化，简写成，缩写为
parallel	[ˈpærəlel]	adj.	平行的，并联的
magnitude	[ˈmæɡnitjuːd]	n.	大小，数量，巨大，广大，量级
Voltage	[ˈvəultidʒ]	n.	电压，伏特数
fabricate	[ˈfæbrikeit]	vt.	制作，构成
conjunction	[kəuˈdʒʌŋkʃən]	n.	联合，关联
maintain	[menˈtein]	vt.	维持，继续
peripheral	[pəˈrifərəl]	adj.	外围的 n. 外围设备
rectify	[ˈrektifai]	vt.	矫正，调整
utility	[juːˈtiliti]	n.	效用，有用
electrical energy			电能
electric field			电场
Integrated Circuit（IC）			集成电路
Dynamic Random Access Memory（DRAM）			动态随机存取存储器
Alternating Current（AC）			交流
Direct Current（DC）			直流

Notes

[1] The device capable of doing this is called a capacitor or a condenser.

电能能储存在电场中，具有这种储存能力的器件称为"电容器"。

句中的代词 this 是指示代词，所指代的是上句中的内容，即指在电场的作用下，能存储电能的这种功能。

[2] A simple capacitor consists of two conducting plates separated by an insulating material called the dielectric.

一个简单的电容器是由被称为电介质的绝缘材料隔开的两块金属板组成的。

句子的主语为 A simple capacitor，谓语为 …consist of… 意为 …由…组成，separated by an insulating material called the dielectric 为过去分词作定语，修饰 two conducting plates。

[3] If a capacitor is connected to a battery, the electrons will flow out of the negative terminal of the battery and accumulate on the capacitor plate connected to <u>that</u> side. At the same time, the electrons will leave the plate connected to the positive terminal and flow into the battery to make the potential difference just the same as <u>that</u> of the battery. Thus the capacitor is said to be <u>charged</u>.

如果电容器连接到电池上，电子将从电池的负极流出堆积在与负极相连的极板上。同时与电池正极相接的极板上的电子将离开极板流入电池正极，这样两极板上就产生了与电池上相等的电位差，我们就说电容充上了电。

本段中有两个 that，并且这两个都是指示代词，这两处也正是理解本段大意的关键。下面先来看看第一个 that，这里的 that side 指代的是 the side which is connected to the negative terminal of the battery。第二个 that 指的是前面的 potential difference；to make the potential difference just the same as that of the battery 动词不定式表示目的，这里的 charged 是"充满电的"的意思。

[4] The ability of a capacitor storing electrical energy is called capacitance.

电容器存储电能的能力叫电容。

本句子是一个被动语态，主语部分为 The ability of a capacitor storing electrical energy。

[5] Capacitance is typified by a parallel plate arrangement and is defined in terms of charge storage：$C = Q / V$；Where Q is magnitude of charge stored on each plate, V is voltage applied to the plates.

电容由两块平行金属板组成，其容量根据它存储电荷的多少来定义：$C = Q / V$，其中 Q 是每个极板存储电荷的大小，V 是极板间的电压。

…in terms of…在此意为用……衡量或表示依据……。

[6] Capacitors can be fabricated onto integrated circuit (IC) chips. They are commonly used in conjunction with transistors in dynamic random access memory (DRAM). The capacitors help maintain the contents of memory.

集成电路中就应用了电容器。在动态随机存储器中，通常将电容器与晶体管连接在一起。电容器帮助保存存储内容。

[7] Large capacitors are used in the power supplies of electronic equipment of all types, including computers and their peripherals. In these systems, the capacitors smooth out the rectified utility AC, providing pure, battery-like DC.

所有型号的电子设备，包括计算机及其外围设备的电源储备系统，都使用了大电容器。在这些系统中，电容器能进一步平滑经整流过的公用交流电，使其提供如电池产生的纯直流电一样。

these 指代前句所提到的内容。smooth 在此为其动词形式，意为"消除，使平滑"即"整流"；当作形容词时，为"平滑的，光滑的"。

Exercises

I. Please spell the complete form of the following abbreviation letters.

1. AC_____

2. DC_____

3. IC_____

4. DRAM_____

II. Choose the ONE that best completes the sentence.

1. According the original text, there is a device which can store electrical energy called _____.

A. electric field   B. capacitance   C. battery   D. condenser
2. According the Paragraph Two, which of the following is right? _____
   A. All the capacitors consist of two conducting plates separated by dielectric.
   B. The electrons will not accumulate on the capacitor plate connected to the side which connected to the positive terminal of the battery.
   C. While a capacitor was charged completely, the electricity of the circuit would be not existed.
   D. If a capacitor is connected to a battery, the electrons will flow out of the positive terminal and flow into negative terminal rapidly.
3. Choose the equation which is wrong from the following below _____.
   A. $Q=CV$ B. $10\mu F=10^7 pF$ C. $V=Q/C$ D. $0.1 pF=10^5 \mu F$
4. What can not be inferred from the original text? _____
   A. If a capacitor is charged, the potential difference of the capacitor will be equal to that of the battery.
   B. Capacitors can be fabricated onto IC chips, and it can work without voltage.
   C. The definition of the capacitance is the ability of a capacitor electrical energy.
   D. The capacitors can provide pure DC to the computer and to their peripherals.

B. Reading

How does a Capacitor Work

Let us think that how water flow through a pipe. If we imagine a capacitor as being a storage tank with an inlet and an outlet pipe, so, it is easy to show how an electronic capacitor works.

First, let's consider the case of a "coupling capacitor" where the capacitor is used to connect a signal from one part of a circuit to another, but it don't allow any direct current to flow through it (Fig. 1-5).

If the current flow is alternating between zero and a maximum, our "storage tank" capacitor will allow the current waves to pass through.

However, if there is a steady current, only the initial short burst will flow until the "floating ball valve" closes and stops further flow.

So a coupling capacitor allows "alternating current" to pass through because the ball valve doesn't get a chance to close as the waves go up and down. However, a steady current quickly fills the tank so that all flow stops.

Then, let us consider "decoupling capacitor" (Fig.1-6). Where a capacitor is used to decouple a circuit, the effect is to "smooth out ripples". Any ripples, waves or pulses of current are passed to ground while DC flows smoothly.

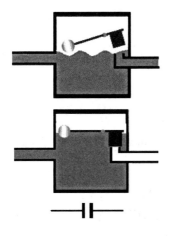

Fig. 1-5 Coupling capacitor.

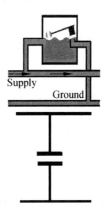

Fig.1-6 Decoupling capacitor.

New words and Technical Terms

capacitor	[kəpæˈsitə]	n.	电容器
ripple	[ˈripl]	n.	波纹；v. 起波纹
pulse	[ˈpʌls]	n.	脉冲
smooth out		v.	消除，使平滑
coupling capacitor		n.	耦合电容器
decoupling capacitor		n.	去耦（合）电容器
ball value		n.	球阀，弹子阀
short burst		n.	短脉冲群

Exercises

Ⅰ. What is the capacitor like?

Ⅱ. What does not a "coupling capacitor" allow to flow through it?

Ⅲ. What does not a "decoupling capacitor" allow to flow through it?

C. 专业英语常见的语法现象

专业英语的语法特点可以归纳为客观、准确和精练，所以在专业英语中经常出现如下的语法现象。

1. 动名词

动名词的作用相当于名词，它在句子中可作主语和宾语。它可以取代时间从句或简化时间从句。例如：

（1）Reading is a good habit. 动名词在句中作主语。

（2）I enjoy working with you. 动名词在句子中作动词宾语。

（3）I am interested in reading. 动名词在句子中作介词宾语。

在专业英语中，动名词的应用相当普遍。它可以令句子精练。例如：通常的表达形式为：

（1）Before it is executed, the program should be loaded into main memory.

（2）When you use the mouse to click a button, you can select an option from a list.

相应的用动名词来表示的精练形式为：

Before being executed, the program should be loaded into main memory.

By using the mouse to click a button, you can select an option from a list.

2. 分词短语

通过使用过去分词可以取代被动语态的关系从句；使用现在分词可以取代主动语态的关系从句。

（1）现在分词短语一般作形容词用，可修饰动作的发出者，有主动的意义。可译成"……××的……"，此时多作定语，在意思上和一个定语从句差不多。如：

Thus the output to the code may be seen as a sequence of 8 pulses relating to channel 1, then channel 2, and so on.

（2）现在分词短语还可以作状语，用来表示方式、目的、条件、结果和背景等；有时可以表示伴随状态。如：

Every evening they sit in sofa watching TV. 现在分词起伴随作用。

（3）过去分词短语一般作形容词用，可修饰动作的对象。如：

A simple capacitor consists of two conducting plates separated by an insulating material called the dielectric.

3．不定式

在专业英语中，不定式短语可以大量地用做状语或定语。当然，它也可以替换表示目的、功能的状态从句。如：

What does a fuse do? It protects a circuit. 可以表示为：The function of a fuse is <u>to protect a circuit</u>. 又如：

Furthermore, we shall prove that a minimum theoretical sampling frequency of order 6.8 kilohertz is required <u>to convey</u> a voice channel occupying the range from 300Hz to 3.4 kHz.

4．被动语态

被动语态在专业英语中用得非常频繁，这主要有两个原因：一是专业文章中在描写行为或状态本身时，注重客观事实或道理，所以由谁或由什么行为或状态作为主体就显得不那么重要了。例如：

All the insulating substances <u>were damaged</u> by sea water. 又如：

The two lamps <u>are held</u> together by the wire.

被动语态使用频繁的另外一个原因是便于向后扩展句子，构成更长的句子，以便于对问题做出更精确的描述，但又不至于把句子弄得头重脚轻。例如：

In the digital computer the numbers to be manipulated are represented by sequences of digits <u>which are first recorded in suitable code, then converted into positive and negative electrical impulses, and stored in electrical or magnetic registers.</u>

在句子中，画线部分用于对 sequences of digits 作更进一步的描述。

5．其他现象

在专业英语中，一些其他的常用短语也经常出现。

（1）在专业英语中，要对概念或术语下定义时，常用以下短语。

be defined as，如 A capacitor <u>is defined as</u> the device where electricity is stored in.

be called，如 This flow of electrons driven through a conductor <u>is called</u> an electric current.

refer to…as…，如 We often <u>referred to</u> these rays <u>as</u> radiant matter.

be regarded as，如 Radio waves <u>are regarded as</u> radiant energy.

be termed，如 The ability of a capacitor to store electrical energy <u>is termed</u> capacitance.

（2）在专业英语中，"主语+be 形容词+to 名词"的结构是很常见的。它用于对某一事物、概念或论点加以定论、叙述。

be necessary to，如 It <u>is necessary to</u> examine the efficiency of the new design.

be adaptable to，如 A living thing <u>is adapted</u> to a special environment.

UNIT 4

A. Text

Transistor

A transistor is a device that is composed of semiconductor material[1]. And it can amplify a signal or opens or closes a circuit, was invented in 1947 at Bell Labs.

There are two types of standard transistors, **NPN** and **PNP**, with different circuit symbols[2]. The letters refer to the layers of semiconductor material used to make the transistor. Most transistors used today are NPN because this is the easiest type to make from silicon. If you are new to electronics it is best to start by learning how to use NPN transistors[3].

Look at Fig. 1-7, the leads are labelled base (B), collector (C) and emitter (E).

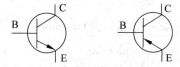

Fig. 1-7　NPN and PNP transistor.

Transistors have three leads which must be connected the correct way round[4]: the common-base, the common-emitter and the common-collector. Please take care with this because a wrongly connected transistor may be damaged instantly when you switch on.

Transistors amplify current, for example they can be used to amplify the small output current from a logic chip so that it can operate a lamp, or other high current device. In many circuits a resistor is used to convert the changing current to a changing voltage, so the transistor is being used to amplify voltage.

Today, transistors have become the key ingredient of all digital circuits, including computers. And, microprocessor contains tens of millions of microscopic transistors.

Prior to the invention of transistors, digital circuits were composed of vacuum tubes, which had many disadvantages[5]. They were much larger, required more energy, dissipated more heat, and were more prone to failures. It's safe to say that without the invention of transistors, computing as we know it today would not be possible[6].

New words and Technical Terms

amplify	['æmplifai]	v.	放大（声音或电子信号）
emitter	[i'mitə]	n.	发射集，发射器
transistor	[træns'zistə]	n.	晶体管

microprocessor	[ˈmaikrəuˈprəusesə]	n.	微处理器
silicon	[ˈsilikən]	n.	硅，硅元素
Prone to			倾向于
Vacuum tubes			真空管

Notes

[1] A transistor is a device that is composed of semiconductor material.

晶体管是一种由半导体材料组成的器件。

本句是一个系表结构的句子，包含有定语从句。that is composed of semiconductor material 用来修饰先行词 device，that 在从句中充当主语。

[2] There are two types of standard transistors, **NPN** and **PNP**, with different circuit symbols.

标准的晶体管有两种类型：NPN 和 PNP，它们的电路标志不一样。

with different circuit symbols 是介词短语作非限定性的定语，故后置且用逗号与中心词分开。

[3] If you are new to electronics it is best to start by learning how to use NPN transistors.

如果你是电子学的初学者，最好现在就开始学习如何使用 NPN 型晶体管。

If you are new to electronics 是一个条件状语从句，在这个从句中，要用一般现在时表示将来时。it is best to 意为 you had better to，最好做……。

[4] Transistors have three leads which must be connected the correct way round.

晶体管的三个极都必须在电路中正确连接。

这里 which must be connected the correct way round…是一个定语从句，修饰 three leads，which 在从句里作主语，从句是一个被动语态。

[5] Prior to the invention of transistors, digital circuits were composed of vacuum tubes, which had many disadvantages.

在晶体管发明之前，数字电路是由真空管组成的，这有很多不足。

Prior to 在……以前，它后面一般接一个名词性的短语，digital circuits were composed of vacuum tubes, which had many disadvantages 这一部分中用到了 be composed of 句型，意为"由……组成"，而 which had many disadvantages 是一个非限制性的定语从句，用来修饰先行词 vacuum tubes。

[6] It's safe to say that without the invention of transistors, computing as we know it today would not be possible.

可以这么说，没有晶体管的发明，今天我们所知的计算是完全不可能的。

It's safe to say that 包含一个主语从句，意为"可以这么说"，其中 it 是形式主语，真正的主语是后面的从句 that without the invention of transistors, computing as we know it today would not be possible, without the invention of transistors 是 that 从句中的条件状语，后面的 computing 是动名词作主语。

Exercises

Ⅰ. Answer the following questions, according the passage.

1. Why most transistors used today are NPN?

2. What is the key ingredient of all digital circuits today?

3. If the transistor not be invented, what about the computing now?

Ⅱ. Write the words according the translation.

TRANSLATION	VOCABULARY
Movement of electrically charged particles	
Electromotive force expressed in volts	
Disposed, liable	
Coming before in time	

Ⅲ. Please translate the English in to Chinese.

The relationship between the electromotive force, the current, and the resistance was discovered by Cerman scientist, George Simon Ohm, at the beginning of the nineteenth century. The unit of resistance was named in his honor.

The relationship, which is called Ohm's law, can be expressed mathematically by means of the following formula:

$$\text{Current} = \frac{\text{electromotive force}}{\text{resistance}} \quad \text{or} \quad I = \frac{E}{R}$$

Where I is measured in amperes; E in volts, and R in ohms. This means that the greater the electromotive force is, the greater will be the current; and the greater the resistance, the smaller the current.

B. Reading

The First Transistor

In 1947, John Bardeen and Walter Brattain, working at Bell Telephone Laboratories, were trying to understand the nature of the electrons at the interface between a metal and a semiconductor. They realized that making two point contacts very close to one another could make a three terminal device—the first "point contact" transistor.

The picture Fig. 1-8 shows the first transistor. It consisted of a plastic triangle lightly suspended above a germanium crystal which itself was sitting on a metal plate attached to a voltage source. A strip of gold was wrapped around the point of the triangle with a tiny gap cut into the gold at the precise point it came in contact with the germanium crystal. The germanium acted as a semiconductor so that a small electric current entering on one side of the gold strip came out the other side as a proportionately amplified current.

Fig. 1-8　The first transistor

　　John Bardeen and Walter Brattain quickly made a few of these transistors and connected them with some other components to make an audio amplifier. This audio amplifier was shown to chief executives at Bell Telephone Company, who were very impressed that it didn't need time to "warm up" (like the heaters in vacuum tube circuits). They immediately realized the power of this new technology.

　　This invention was the spark that ignited a huge research effort in solid state electronics. Bardeen and Brattain received the Nobel Prize in Physics, 1956, together with William Shockley, "for their researches on semiconductors and their discovery of the transistor effect." Shockley had developed a so-called junction transistor, which was built on thin slices of different types of semiconductor material pressed together. The junction transistor was easier to understand theoretically, and could be manufactured more reliably.

New words and Technical Terms

semiconductor	[ˈsemikənˈdʌktə]	n. 半导体
terminal	[ˈtəːminl]	n. 终端
suspend	[səsˈpend]	vt. 吊，悬挂　v. 延缓
ignite	[igˈnait]	v. 点火，点燃
junction	[ˈdʒʌŋkʃən]	n. 连接　接合
triangle	[ˈtraiæŋgl]	n. 三角形，三人一组，三角关系
slice	[slais]	n. 薄片
crystal	[ˈkristl]	n. 晶体，结晶，水晶
germanium	[dʒəːˈmainiəm]	n. 锗

point contact transistor	点接触晶体管
audio amplifier	音频放大器
junction transistor	结式晶体管，结型晶体管

Exercises

Ⅰ. Who invented the first transistor?

Ⅱ. What is the name of the first transistor?

Ⅲ. Why did Bardeen and Brattain receive the Nobel Prize in Physics, 1956, together with William Shockley?

C. 专业英语翻译的标准

翻译是一种语言表达法，是译者根据原作者的思想，用本国语言表达出来。这就要求译者必须确切理解和掌握原著的内容和意思，丝毫不可以离开它而主观地发挥译者个人的想法和推测。在确切理解的基础上，译者必须很好地运用本国语言把原文通顺而流畅地表达出来。随着国际学术交流的日益广泛，专业英语已经受到普遍的重视，掌握一些专业英语的翻译技巧是非常必要的。专业英语作为一种重要的英语文体，与非专业英语文体相比，具有词义多、长句多、被动句多、词性转换多、非谓语动词多、专业性强等特点，这些特点都是由专业文献的内容所决定的。因此，专业英语的翻译也有别于其他英语文体的翻译。

1. 翻译人员必须了解相关专业领域的知识

在专业翻译中，要达到融会贯通，必须了解相关的专业，熟练掌握同一事物的中英文表达方式。单纯靠对语言的把握也能传达双方的语言信息，但运用语言的灵活性特别是选词的准确性会受到很大限制。要解决这个问题，翻译人员就要积极主动地熟悉这个专业领域的相关翻译知识。比如，要翻译 conductor 这个词，仅仅把字面意思翻译出来还远远不够，而且有时用词也不够准确。conductor 在日常生活中的意思是"售票员和乐队指挥"，但在电学中却是"导体"的意思。因此，了解了专业领域，在翻译过程中对语言的理解能力和翻译质量就会大幅度提高。

2. 专业英语翻译标准

关于翻译的标准，历来提法很多。有的主张"信、达、雅"，有的主张"信、顺"，有的主张"等值"等，并曾多次展开过广泛的争论和探讨。但是，从他们的争论中可以看出，有一点是共同的，即一切译文都应包括原文思想内容和译文语言形式这两个方面；简单地说，符合规范的译文语言，确切忠实地表达原著的风格，这就是英语翻译的共同标准。为此，笔者认为，在进行英语翻译时要坚持两条标准。

（1）忠实

译文应忠实于原文，准确地、完整地、科学地表达原文的内容，包括思想、精神与风格。译者不得任意对原文内容加以歪曲、增删、遗漏和篡改。

（2）通顺

译文语言必须通顺，符合规范，用词造句应符合本民族语言的习惯，要用民族的、科学的、大众的语言，以求通顺易懂。不应有文理不通、逐词死译和生硬晦涩等现象。

3. 专业英语翻译过程中要体现语言结果特色

（1）大量使用名词化结构

大量使用名词化结构（nominalization）是专业英语的特点之一。因为专业文体要求行文简洁、表达客观、内容确切、信息量大、强调存在的事实，而非某一行为。如：

A）Archimedes first discovered **the principle that water is displaced** by solid bodies.

B）Archimedes first discovered **the principle of displacement of water** by solid bodies.

译文：阿基米德最先发展固体排水的原理。

前者显然有一个同位语从句。这样的结构出现在一般的英语文章中。但是在专业文章里，你需要将上述结构转换成名词结构。句中 of displacement of water by solid bodies 是名词化结构，一方面简化了同位语从句，另一方面强调了 displacement 这一事实。

（2）广泛使用被动语句

专业英语中的谓语至少有 1/3 是被动语态。这是因为专业文章侧重于叙事推理，强调客观准确。第一、二人称使用过多，会造成主观臆断的印象。因此尽量使用第三人称叙述，采用被动语态，如：

A）**You must pay attention** to the working temperature of the machine.

B）**Attention must be paid** to the working temperature of the machine.

译文：应当注意机器的工作温度。

在一般英文作文中经常使用主动句，但是在专业文章中，以被描述的事物充当主语更为常见。但在翻译成中文时应将其还原成主动句并且句子的主语一般不译出。

（3）非限定动词的应用和大量使用后置定语

专业文章要求行文简练，结构紧凑，往往使用分词短语代替定语从句或状语从句；使用分词独立结构代替状语从句或并列分句；使用不定式短语代替各种从句；介词+动名词短语代替定语从句或状语从句。这样可缩短句子，又比较醒目。如：

The forces **due to** friction are called frictional forces.

译文：由于摩擦而产生的力称之为摩擦力。

这里介词短语 due to 的使用避免了 because 从句的使用，句子变得简洁明了。

（4）大量使用常用句型

科技文章中经常使用若干特定的句型，从而形成科技文体区别于其他文体的标志。例如 It…that…结构句型、被动语态结构句型、分词短语结构句型、省略句结构句型等。如：

It is evident that a well lubricated bearing turns more easily than a dry one.

译文：显然，润滑好的轴承比不润滑的轴承容易转动。

（5）为了描述事物精确，要使用长句

为了表述一个复杂概念，使之逻辑严密，结构紧凑，科技文章中往往出现许多长句。有的长句多达七八个词。如：

The efforts that have been made to explain optical phenomena by means of the hypothesis of a medium having the same physical character as an elastic solid body led in the first instance, to the understanding of a concrete example of a medium which can transmit transverse vibrations, and, at a later stage, to the definite conclusion that there is no aluminiferous medium having the physical character assumed in the hypothesis.

这确实是一个很长的句子，初看上去似乎无从下手。但是在对句子进行分析之后，问题就迎刃而解了。译文：为了解释光学现象，人们曾经试图假定，有一种具有与弹性固体相同的物理性质的介质。这种尝试的结果，最初使人们了解到能传输横向振动的介质的具体实例。但后来却使人们得出了这样一个明确的结论：并不存在任何具有上述假定所认为的那种物理性质的发光介质。

（6）大量使用复合词与缩略词

大量使用复合词与缩略词是科技文章的特点之一，复合词从过去的双词组合发展到多词组合；缩略词趋向于任意构词，例如，某一篇论文的作者可以就仅在该文中使用的术语组成缩略词，这就给翻译工作带来了一定的困难。如：

full-enclosed 全封闭的（双词合成形容词）。

PART 2

Modern Electronics Devices

UNIT 5

A. Text

The basic components of computer system

The basic components that make up a computer system include: the CPU, memory, I/O, and the bus that connects these components together.

John Von Neumann, a pioneer in computer design, gave the architecture of most computers in use today. A typical Von Neumann system has three major parts: the central processing unit (or CPU), memory, and input/output (or I/O). How a system designs these parts impacts the system performance. In VNA machines, like the 80x86 family, the CPU is where all the actions take place[1]. All computations occur inside the CPU. Data and CPU instructions reside in memory until required by the CPU. To the CPU, most I/O devices look like memory because the CPU can store data to an output device and read data from an input device. The major difference between memory and I/O device is that I/O device is generally associated with external device in the outside world.

The system bus connects various components of a VNA machine. The 80x86 family has three major busses: the address bus, the data bus, and the control bus. A bus is a connection of wires on which electrical signals pass through components in the system. For example, the data bus may have a different implementation between the 80386 and the 8086, but both carry data among the processor, I/O, and memory. The 80x86 processor uses the data bus to transfer data among the various components in a computer system. The size of this bus varies widely in the 80x86 family. Indeed, this bus defines the "size" of the processor.

The data bus on an 80x86 family processor transfers information between a particular memory location or I/O device and the CPU. The only question is, "Which memory location or I/O device?" The address bus answers this question.

To differentiate memory location and I/O device, a unique memory address is assigned to each memory element and I/O device. When the software wants to access certain memory location or I/O device, it places the corresponding address on the address bus. Circuitry associated with the memory or I/O recognizes this address and instructs the memory or I/O device to read the data from or place data on the data bus[2].

The control bus is a collection of signals that controls how the processor communicates with the rest of the system [3]. Consider the data bus for a moment. The CPU sends data to memory and receives data from memory on the data bus. This prompts the question. "Is it sending or receiving?" There are two lines on the control bus, read line and write line, which specify the direction of data flow. Other signals include system clocks, interrupt lines, status lines, and so on[4]. The exact structure of control bus varies among processors in the 80x86 family. However, some control lines are common to all processors and are worthy a brief mention.

The read line and write line control the direction of data on the data bus. When both contain logic 1, the CPU and memory—I/O do not communicate with one another. If the read line is low (logic 0), the CPU reads data from memory (that is, the system transfers data from memory to the CPU) [5]. If the write line is low, the system transfers data from the CPU to memory.

The main memory is the central storage unit in a computer system. It is a relatively large and fast memory used to store programs and data during the computer operation. The principal technology used for the main memory is based on semiconductor integrated circuit. Integrated circuit RAM (Read Random Memory) chip is available in two possible operation modes, static and dynamic. The static RAM consists essentially of internal flip-flops that store the binary information. The stored information remains valid as long as power is applied to the unit. The dynamic RAM stores the binary information in the form of electric charge that is applied to the capacitor. The capacitor is provided inside the chip by MOS transistor. The stored charge on the capacitor tends to discharge with time and refreshing the dynamic memory must periodically recharge the capacitor. The dynamic RAM offers reduced power consumption and large storage capacity in a single memory chip. The static RAM is easier to use and has shorter read or write cycles.

New words and Technical Terms

memory	['meməri]	n.	存储，存储器，内存
processor	['prəusesə]	n.	处理器
performance	[pə'fɔːməns]	n.	性能
location	[ləu'keiʃən]	n.	存储单元
signal	['signl]	n.	信号

instruction	[inˈstrʌkʃən]	n. 指令
bus	[bʌs]	n. 数据传送总线，总线
semiconductor	[ˈsemikənˈdʌktə]	n. 半导体
flip-flop	[ˈflipflɔp]	n. 噼啪声，触发器；adv. 连续啪啪声地
chip	[tʃip]	n. 电路，线路
transistor	[trænˈzistə]	n. 晶体管
binary	[ˈbainəri]	n. 二进位的，二元的，二进制的
central processing unit (CPU)		中央处理器
integrated circuit (IC)		集成电路
input/output (I/O)		输入输出
metal-oxide semiconductor (MOS)		金属氧化物半导体
read random memory (RAM)		随机存储器
only read memory (ROM)		只读存储器

Notes

[1] In VNA machines, like the 80x86 family, the CPU is where all the actions take place.

在 VNA 机器体系中，如 8086 系列，CPU 是执行所有事务的地方。

在 the CPU is where all the actions take place 中，主语是 the CPU，where all the actions take place 是关系副词 where 引导的从句充当表语。

[2] Circuitry associated with the memory or I/O recognizes this address and instructs the memory or I/O device to read the data from or place data on the data bus.

与存储器或输入输出相关的电路能够识别地址，并能指使存储器或输入输出设备从数据总线读数据或写数据到数据总线。

本句的主语是 Circuitry，and 前后是并列关系。Associated with the memory or I/O 用于修饰 circuitry。read the data from or place data on the data bus 等于 read the data from the data bus or place data on the data bus。

[3] The control bus is a collection of signals that controls how the processor communicates with the rest of the system.

控制总线是控制处理器与系统其他部分通信的信号枢纽。

that controls how the processor communicates with the rest of the system 是定语从句，修饰主语 the control bus，在这个从句中，又包含了 how 引导的从句作为 controls 的宾语。

[4] Other signals include system clocks, interrupt lines, status lines, and so on.

其他信号包括系统时钟，中断信号，状态信号等。

[5] When both contain logic 1, the CPU and memory—I/O do not communicate with one another. If the read line is low (logic 0), the CPU reads data from memory (that is, the system transfers data from memory to the CPU).

当读写信号都是逻辑 1 时，CPU 和内存—I/O 间不能相互通信，如果读信号是逻辑 0 时，CPU 可以读取内存数据（也就是说系统从内存得到数据）。

Exercises

I. Please answer the following questions according to the text.

1. Please describe the basic parts that make up a VNA computer.

2. What is the difference in memory and I/O device?

3. Please describe how CPU read and write on memory and I/O device.

4. Please describe the major busses in 80x86 family.

5. Introduce the structure of computer as you know.

II. Please explain the meaning of each of the following abbreviations.

CPU

I/O

RAM

MOS

B. Reading

Types of Computers and Future Developments

A computer is an electronic device that can receive a set of instructions, or program, and then carry out this program by performing calculations on numerical data or by compiling and correlating other forms of information.

Microcomputer: A microcomputer is a desktop or notebook size computing device that uses a microprocessor as its Central Processing Unit, or CPU. Microcomputers are also called Personal Computers (PCs), home computers, small business computers, and micros. The smallest, most compact are called laptops. When they first appeared, they were considered single user devices, and they were capable of handling only four, eight, or 16 bits of information at one time. More recently the distinction between microcomputers and large, mainframe computers (as well as the smaller mainframe type systems called minicomputers) has become blurred, as newer microcomputer models have increased the speed and data handling capabilities of their CPUs into the 32 bit, or even 64 bit multi-user range.

Minicomputer: A minicomputer is a mid-level computer built to perform complex computations while dealing efficiently with a high level of input and output from users connected via terminals. Minicomputers also frequently connect to other minicomputers on a network and distribute processing among all the attached machines. Minicomputers are used heavily in transaction processing applications and as interfaces between mainframe computer systems and wide area networks.

Mainframe Computer: A mainframe computer is a high level computer designed for the most intensive computational tasks. Mainframe computers are often shared by multiple users connected to the computer via terminals. The most powerful mainframes, called supercomputers, perform highly complex and time consuming computations and are used heavily in both pure and applied research by scientists, large businesses, and the military.

Supercomputer: In computer science, supercomputers are large, extremely fast, and expensive computers used for complex or sophisticated calculations, typically, machines capable of pipelining instruction execution and providing vector instructions. A supercomputer can, for example, perform the enormous number of calculations required to draw and animate a moving spaceship in a motion picture. Supercomputers are also used for weather forecasting, large scale scientific modeling, and oil exportations.

One on going trend in computer development is microminiaturization, the effort to compress more circuit elements into smaller and smaller chip space. Researchers are also trying to speed up circuitry functions through the use of superconductivity, the phenomenon of decreased electrical resistance observed as objects exposed to very low temperatures become increasingly colder. Computer networks have become increasingly important in the development of computer technology. Networks are groups of computers that are interconnected by communications facilities. The public Internet is an example of a global network of computers. Networks enable connected computers to rapidly exchange information and in some cases, to share a workload, so that many computers may cooperate in performing a task. New software and hardware technology is being developed that will accelerate both of these processes.

The fifth generation computer effort to develop computers that can solve complex problems in what might eventually be called creative ways is another trend in computer development, the ideal goal being true artificial intelligence. One path actively being explored is the parallel processing computer, which uses many chips to perform several different tasks at the same time. Parallel processing may eventually be able to duplicate to some degree the complex feedback, approximation, and assessing functions of human thought. Another form of parallel processing that is being investigated is the use of molecular computers. In these computers, logical symbols are expressed by chemical units of DNA instead of by the flow of electrons in regular problems much faster than current supercomputers and would use much less energy.

New words and Technical Terms

compile	[kəm'pail]	vt.	编译，编辑，汇编
bit	[bit]	n.	位，比特
terminal	['tə:minl]	n.	终端，终端设备
distributed processing	[dis'tribju:tid prəu'sesiŋ]	n.	分布式处理
pipeline	['paip,lainŋs]	v.	流水线操作
vector	['vektə]	n.	向量，矢量
microcomputer	['maikrəukəmpju:tə]	n.	微型计算机
minicomputer	['minikəm'pju:tə]	n.	小型机
mainframe computer	['meinfreim kəm,pju:tə]	n.	大型计算机
supercomputer	[,sju:pəkəm'pju:tə]	n.	超型计算机
microminiaturization	['maikrəu,miniətʃərai'zeiʃən]	n.	微小型化
superconductivity	[su:pəkəndʌk'tiviti]	n.	超导电性
resistance	[ri'zistəns]	n.	电阻
parallel	['pærəlel]	adj.	并行的
approximation	[ə,prɔksi'meiʃən]	n.	近似值

Exercises

Ⅰ. Please answer the following questions according to the text.

1. How many kinds of computers are mentioned in this article?

2. Please describe the characteristics and applied areas of these types of computers.

3. How many kinds of computer are there now? Introduce them simply.

4. What are the development trends of computers as you know?

II. Topic.

1. Talk about the application fields of computer.

2. Discuss the advantages and disadvantages of computer.

3. What do you do with computer?

C. 常用的数学名词

在科技文献中，一般会用到很多数学公式。当阅读国外科技文献时，一旦遇到数学名词与数学公式，大多数人不知不觉会一带而过，如 $f = 1/2\pi\sqrt{LC}$。但在一些很重要的场合，如学术演讲、商务谈判，这些数学名词、数学符号与数学公式的英文表达就显得特别重要。

由于数学学科本身就是一个大的基础学科，包含的内容极为广泛，如数学专业就有数学专业英语，在此仅仅总结最基础的数学词汇供大家参考。

1. 数的分类

复数、虚数	Complex numbers and Pure imaginary numbers
实数	Real numbers
有理数、无理数	Relational numbers and Irrational numbers
分数、小数	Fractions and Decimals
自然数、零	Natural numbers and Zero
整数、负整数	Integers and Negatives of natural numbers
奇数、偶数	Odd numbers and Even
基数、序数	Cardinal and Ordinal numbers

近似数	Approximate numbers
有效数	Significant digits

2. 常见的数学名词

加法	Addition
减法	Subtraction
乘法	Multiplication
除法	Division
比例	Proportion
幂	Powers
对数	Logarithms
根	Roots
根号	Radical sign
符号	Sign
括号	The signs of grouping
小括号（）	The parenthesis
中括号 [ ]	The bracket
大括号	The brace
排列	Permutations
组合	Combinations
微分	Differentials
积分	Integrals
等号	Signs of Equality
不等号	Signs of Inequality
小于	Be less than
大于	Be greater than
方程	Equation
不等式	Inequality
多项式	Polynomial
绝对值	Absolute Value
乘方	Powers
开方	Root-extracting
函数	Function
区间	Intervals
矩阵	Matrix
定义	Definition
定理	Theorem
引理	Lemma
线、角	Line and angle

PART 2 Modern Electronics Devices

相交线、平行线	Intersecting line and parallel line
三角形、四边形与多边形	Triangles, quadrilateral and polygons
矩形、菱形与正方形	Rectangles, lozenges and squares
圆、弧	Circle and Arc
周长	Perimeter
面积	Area
直径	Diameter
体积	Volume

UNIT 6

A. Text

ARM-The Architecture for the Digital World™

ARM Holdings PLC [(LSE: ARM); (Nasdaq: ARMHY)], ranked by Dataquest as the number one semiconductor IP supplier in the world, emerged as a pre-eminent force in the semiconductor revolution[1]. When ARM pioneered the concept of openly-licensable IP for the development of 32-bit RISC microprocessor-based SoCs in the early 1990s, it changed the dynamics of the semiconductor industry forever. By licensing, rather than manufacturing and selling its chip technology, the Company established a new business model that has redefined the way microprocessors are designed, produced and sold[2]. More importantly, ARM has shaped a new era of next-generation electronics: ARM Powered® microprocessors are pervasive in the electronic products we use, driving key functions in a variety of applications in diverse markets, including automotive, consumer entertainment, imaging, industrial control, networking, storage, security and wireless. ARM licenses its IP to a network of Partners, which includes some of the world's leading semiconductor and system companies, including nineteen out of the top-twenty semiconductor vendors worldwide. These Partners utilize ARM's low-cost, power-efficient core designs to create and manufacture microprocessors, peripherals and SoC solutions. As the foundation of the company's global technology network, these Partners have played a pivotal role in the widespread adoption of the ARM architecture and to date; ARM Partners have shipped more than one billion ARM microprocessor cores.

To support and complement the company's RISC microprocessor cores and SoC IP, ARM has developed a strong software capability. Partners have access to an unrivaled range of software-based IP, operating systems (OS) ports and software design services. In this way, ARM provides Partners with a full portfolio of offerings that deliver significant risk reduction and faster time-to-market benefits[3]. In order to support this global technology network, ARM has recently introduced two significant technology advancements that are already in use by key semiconductor companies. The company is now offering its Partners the ARM PrimeXsys™ platform; 'box-ready' IP in the form of platforms targeted at specific applications[4]. The first PrimeXsys platform launched in September 2001 was the PrimeXys Wireless Platform. This is a highly-integrated, extendable platform incorporating all the hardware, software and integration tools necessary to enable ARM Partners to easily develop a wide range of ARM Powered application-focused devices, rapidly and with minimal risk. ARM intends to announce further PrimeXsys platforms in 2002 as the IP market continues to demand more integrated solutions. ARM also introduced the Jazelle™ technology for accelerating Java™ technology that delivers an unparalleled combination of Java performance and the world's leading 32-bit embedded RISC architecture[5]. This technology gives platform developers the freedom to run Java applications alongside established OS, middleware and application code on a single processor. The single-processor solution offers higher performance, lower system cost and lower power than coprocessors and dual-processor solutions.

New words and Technical Terms

peripheral	[pəˈrifərəl]	n. 外围设备
port	[pɔːt]	n. 端口
platform	[ˈplætfɔːm]	n. 平台
middleware	[ˈmɪdlweə]	n. 中间设备，中间件
code	[kəud]	n. 代码，编码
dual-processor	[ˈdju(ː)əl ˈprəusesə]	n. 双处理器
bandwidth	[ˈbændwidθ]	n. 带宽
system-on-chip (SoC)		片上系统
operating system (OS)		操作系统
intellectual property (IP)		知识产权
reduced instruction set computing (RISC)		精简指令集计算机
PLC (abbr. Public Limited Company)		股票上市公司
LSE (abbr. London Stock Exchange)		伦敦证券交易所
Nasdaq (abbr. National Association of Securities Dealers Automated Quotation System)		全国证券交易商自动报价系统协会

Notes

[1] ARM Holdings PLC [(LSE: ARM); (Nasdaq: ARMHY)], ranked by Dataquest as the number one semiconductor IP supplier in the world, emerged as a pre-eminent force in the semiconductor revolution.

被 Dataquest 公司排列为全世界第一的半导体 IP 核提供商的 ARM 上市公司在半导体

革命中显示出了一种卓越的力量。

ranked by Dataquest as the number one semiconductor IP supplier in the world 是主语 ARM Holdings plc 的定语，对主语进行说明和描述。

[2] By licensing, rather than manufacturing and selling its chip technology, the Company established a new business model that has redefined the way microprocessors are designed, produced and sold.

通过许可，而不是制造和出售它的芯片技术，公司重新定义了微处理器设计、生产与销售的方式，从而建立了一种新的商业模型。

By licensing, rather than manufacturing and selling its chip technology 是状语，可译为"通过许可，而不是制造和出售它的芯片技术"。

[3] In this way, ARM provides Partners with a full portfolio of offerings that deliver significant risk reduction and faster time-to-market benefits.

通过这种方式，ARM 提供给合作伙伴一整套旨在降低风险并能快速获取市场利益的投资物。

that deliver significant risk reduction and faster time-to-market benefits 是定语，修饰 a full portfolio of offerings。

[4] The company is now offering its Partners the ARM PrimeXsys™ platform; 'box-ready' IP in the form of platforms targeted at specific applications.

公司现在为合作伙伴提供 ARM PrimeXsys™平台；封装好的 IP 以平台形式解决特殊应用的需要。

[5] ARM also introduced the Jazelle™ technology for accelerating Java™ technology that delivers an unparalleled combination of Java performance and the world's leading 32-bit embedded RISC architecture.

ARM 为加速 Java™技术提出了 Jazelle™ 技术，这样就可以将 JAVA 的优越性能引入世界范围内最重要的 32 位的嵌入式 RISC 结构中。

Exercises

Ⅰ. Please answer the following questions according to the text.

1. Please describe ARM's business model.

2. Please describe the ARM Powered® microprocessors' advantages.

3. What are the differences between ARM and Intel as you know?

Ⅱ. Please answer the following questions.

1. Introduce ARM as you know.

2. Discuss ARM and embedded system in small groups.

B. Reading

The Introduce of ARM

ARM was established in November 1990 as Advanced RISC Machines Ltd., a UK—based joint venture between Apple Computer, Acorn Computer Group and VLSI Technology. Apple and VLSI both provided funding, while Acorn supplied the technology and ARM's 12 founding engineers. Acorn, developer of the world's first commercial single-chip RISC processor, and Apple, intent on advancing the use of RISC technology in its own systems, chartered ARM with creating a new microprocessor standard. ARM immediately differentiated itself in the market by creating the first low-cost RISC architecture. Conversely, competing architectures, which were more commonly focused on maximizing performance, were first used in high-end workstations. With the introduction of its first embedded RISC core, the ARM6™ family of processors, in 1991, ARM signed VLSI as its initial licensee. One year later, Sharp and GEC Plessey entered into licensing agreements, with Texas Instruments and Cirrus Logic following suit in 1993. Over the years, ARM has significantly expanded both its IP portfolio and its licensee base. After the 1993 addition of Nippon Investment and Finance (NIF) as a shareholder, the company began establishing a global presence, opening new offices in Asia, the US and Europe. In April 1998, the company listed on the London Stock Exchange and NASDAQ. ARM is now a global corporation, employing more than 720 people in facilities in eight countries on three continents. With design centre in Blackburn, Cambridge and Sheffield, UK; Sophia Antipolice, France; Walnut Creek, Calif.; and Austin, Texas; the Company also maintains sales, administrative and support offices in France, Germany, Japan, Korea, Taiwan, Israel, the UK and the US. The Company will be opening an office in Shanghai, China during 2002.

This presentation contains forward-looking statements as defined in section 102 of the Private Securities Litigation Reform Act of 1995. These statements are subject to risk factors associated with the semiconductor and intellectual property businesses. When used in this document, the words "anticipates", "may", "can", "believes", "expects", "projects", "intends", "likely", similar expressions and any other statements that are not historical facts, in each case as they relate to ARM, its management or its businesses and financial performance and condition are intended to identify those assertions as forward-looking statements. It is believed that the expectations reflected in these statements are reasonable, but they may be affected by a variety of variables, many of which are beyond our control. These variables could cause actual results or trends to differ materially and include, but are not limited to: failure to realize the benefits of our recent acquisitions, unforeseen liabilities arising from our recent acquisitions, price fluctuations, actual demand, the availability of software and operating systems compatible with our intellectual property, the continued demand for products including ARM's intellectual property, delays in the design process or delays in a customer's project that uses ARM's technology, the success of our semiconductor partners, loss of market and industry competition, exchange and currency fluctuations, any future strategic investments or acquisitions, rapid technological change, regulatory developments, ARM's ability to negotiate, structure, monitor and enforce agreements for the determination and payment of royalties, actual or potential litigation, changes in tax laws, interest rates and access to capital markets, political, economic and financial market conditions in various countries and regions and capital expenditure requirements.

More information about potential factors that could affect ARM's business and financial results is included in ARM's Annual Report on Form 20-F for the fiscal year ended December 31, 2005 including (without limitation) under the captions, "Risk Factors" and "Management's Discussion and Analysis of Financial Condition and Results of Operations," which is on file with the Securities and Exchange Commission (the "SEC") and available at the SEC's website at www.sec.gov。

New words and Technical Terms

shareholder	[ˈʃɛəhəuldə]	n. 股东
workstation	[ˈwɜːksteɪʃ(ə)n]	n. 工作站
royalties	[ˈrɔɪəltis]	n. 版税
litigation	[ˌlitiˈgeiʃən]	n. 诉讼，起诉
forward-looking		adj. 有远见的，向前看的
high-end		高端
single-chip		单片机

Exercises

Ⅰ. Please answer the following questions according to the text.

1. Please tell some variables that could affect ARM's development.

2. Please describe ARM's IP license model.

3. Do you know some applications of ARM's products in China? Please describe simply.

Ⅱ. Please discuss the following the questions.
1. Discuss the applications of ARM's processor.

2. What do you think about the business mode of ARM.

C. 数的表示与读法

1. 数的读法（How to Read Cardinal Numbers）

表示数目多少的数字叫做基数。如 0（zero）、1（one）、19（nineteen）、20（twenty）等。其读法有一些基本规则：

（1）21～99 的基数，先说"几十"，再说"几"，中间加连字号。如 24（twenty-four）。

（2）101～999 的基数，先说"几百"，再加 and，再加末位数。如 156（a/one hundred and fifty-six）；但也有不用 and 的情况，如 850 可以读作 eight hundred fifty。

（3）1,000 以上的数，先从后向前数，每三位数加一","第一个","前为 thousand，第二个","前为 million，第三个","前为 billion（美式）或 thousand million（英式）。如：

1,001　　one thousand and one

284,304　　two hundred and eighty-four thousand three hundred and four

20,654,693　　twenty million six hundred and fifty-four thousand six hundred and ninety-three

850,000,000　　eight hundred and fifty million

（4）幂次的读法，如 10^{18} 读作 one followed by eighteen zeros。

（5）注意：hundred, thousand, million, billion, trillion 等词一般是单数形式。如 two hundred, three million, five trillion 等。

2. 序数的读法（How to Read Ordinal Numbers）

表示顺序的数字称为"序数"，如第一、第二、第三等。序数词一般以与之相应的基数词加词尾 th 构成，如 fourth（第四），但也有特别的地方，主要表现在以下几方面：

（1）one—first；two—second；three—third；five—fifth；eight—eighth；nine—ninth；

twelve—twelfth 等。

（2）以-ty 结尾的词，要先变 y 为 i，再加-eth，如：twenty—twentieth；forty—fortieth 等。

（3）以 one, two, three, five, eight, nine 收尾的序数词，要按照第一条方法变，如

thirty-one—thirty-first　　　eighty-two—eighty-second
fifty-three—fifty-third　　　ninety-five—ninety-fifth
two hundred and fifty-nine　two hundred and fifty-ninth

（4）序数词有时用缩略形式，如

first（1st）；second（2nd）；fourth（4th）；twenty-third（23rd）；
two hundred and thirty-fifth（235th）

（5）序数词表示顺序时，前面常加定冠词，如：The First World War, the third lesson。

3．分数的读法

分数由分子、分母和分数线组成。在英语中，一般用基数词代表分子，序数词代表分母，除了分子是 1 的情况外，序数词都要用复数，具体如下：

$\frac{1}{2}$　　One half

$\frac{1}{3}$　　One third

$\frac{3}{5}$　　Three fifth

$\frac{1}{21}$　　One twenty-ninths

$\frac{3}{178}$　　Three over one hundred seventy-eight

$4\frac{2}{7}$　　Four and two-sevenths

$45\frac{23}{89}$　　Forty-five and eighty-nine over twenty-three

当然，还有一些其他的读法，如 1/2（one by two，或者 one over two）。

4．小数的读法

小数由三部分组成，即整数位区、小数位区和小数点。整数部分按照基数读，小数部分的表达需分别读出每个数，小数点读作 point。

（1）整数位区不为零的小数称为"混合小数"。其读法是整数区按照整数的读法，小数点之后的数字按照小数的读法。如 3.576，读作 three point five seven six。又如 2 050.0357，读作 two thousand and fifty point zero three five seven。

（2）若小数的整数位为零，如 0.45，读作 zero point four five 或 point four five。

（3）若小数是 0.1，0.01，0.001 等，则可读作 one tenth, one hundredth, one thousandth 或 point one, point zero one, point zero zero one。

（4）小数可分为非循环小数和循环小数。如 0.37 读作 zero point thirty-seven；0.3̇7̇ 读

作 zero point three seven recurring；0.2537̇ 读作 zero point two five thirty-seven recurring。

（5）小数有时候需要作四舍五入的近似，如要把数字 483 579 四舍五入到十位，即可得 480 000，英文中读法为：Round off 483 579 to nearest ten thousand。

UNIT 7

A. Text

DSP Processor Fundamentals

In the literature, the definition of a digital signal processor takes many forms. In a strict sense, a DSP is any microprocessor that processes digitally represented signals. A DSP filter for example, takes one or more discrete inputs, $x_i[n]$, and produces one corresponding output, $y[n]$ for $n = \cdots, -1, 0, 1, 2, \cdots$, and $i = 1, \cdots, N$, where n is the nth input or output at time n, i is the ith coefficient and N is the length of the filter. In effect, the DSP implements the discrete-time system. As its name implies, it is assumed that there must be some form of preprocessing if the signals are in the continuous time domain, and this is easily accomplished by an analog to digital converter (ADC)[1].

In general, DSP functions are mathematical operations on real-time signals and are repetitive and numerically intensive. Samples from real-time signals can number in the millions and hence a large memory bandwidth is needed. It is because of this very nature that DSP processors are created with an architecture unlike those of conventional microprocessors[2]. Most DSP algorithms are not complicated and only require multiply and accumulate calculations. Most, if not all, DSP processors have circuitry built and hard wired to execute these calculations as fast as possible.

The signal processing algorithms and functions define a suitable architecture for implementation. We use a simple example of an FIR filter as a basis for the building blocks of the DSP architecture.

One algorithm used to create an FIR filter uses a direct form on tapped delay line structure with $M+1$ taps. The $M+1$ most recent input samples are saved as "filter states". According to Equation (1),

$$y(n) = \sum_{i=0}^{M} c_i x(n-i) \qquad (2\text{-}1)$$

the products of each filter state $x(n-i)$ and its corresponding coefficient c_i are accumulated or added to produce the current output sample $y(n)$. We can also use the signal flow graph as shown in Fig. 2-1 to represent this algorithm[3]. However it is not clear as to the sequence of the computations since it looks like all the operations can be carried out at the same time. Thus, a more accurate picture has to be formed by using *micro-operations* at the register transfer level

(RTL), sequenced temporarily from left to right as seen in Fig. 2-2.

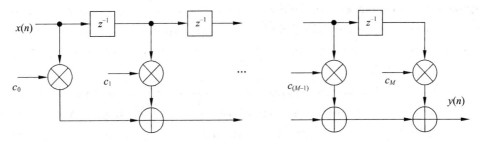

Fig. 2-1 Tapped delay line structure of a FIR filter.

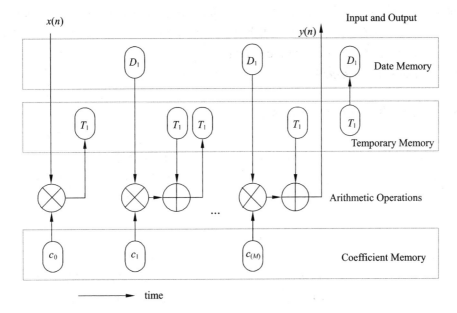

Fig. 2-2 Register transfer level representation of a FIR filter.

The delayed inputs are stored in the data memory D_1 and the coefficients $c_0, c_1, \cdots, c_{(M)}$ are located in the coefficient memory. The contents of both memories are fetched and multiplied together. The result is then added to the temporary memory, T_1 is where the results of the previous taps are stored. This cycle is repeated with a different coefficient until completion, producing the final result as $y(n)$.

We can make certain assumptions for a fundamental general purpose DSP architecture. From our understanding of DSP algorithms, we see that most computations are multiply and add operations. Looking at the example from the previous section, we will require multiple memory units for storage of different data as well as memory for the arithmetic operation sequences. Registers can serve as temporary storage locations and buses will be needed to connect these units together.

At this point, the reader may be tempted to ask how this design is different from a general purpose microprocessor (GPP). If we react the issues central to a DSP function, most DSP calculations are repetitive, require a large memory bandwidth and numeric precision, all executed in real time. One might also argue that modern GPPs have clock speeds and cycles per instruction (CPI) that outperform DSP processors but GPPs have operations and program flexibility that are unnecessary for DSP[4]. DSPs must execute their tasks efficiently while keeping cost, power consumption, memory usage and development time low, especially in the age of mobile computing.

Since many signal processing applications process millions of samples of data for every second of operation, the minimum sample period is usually more important than the computational latency of the processor. We define the sample period as the time between each sequential sample of the input data. The time difference between the input data and the result of its computation is known as the computational latency. Once the initial sample is calculated with certain latency, the subsequent results will however, be produced at the sample period rate. As the number of calculations increases, the relatively larger latency of the processor will be negligible compared to the sample rate.

New words and Technical Terms

outperform	[autpə'fɔːm]	vt. 做得比……好，胜过
flexibility	[ˌfleksə'biliti]	n. 弹性，适应性，机动性，灵活性
latency	['leitənsi]	n. 超低响应时间
delay	[di'lei]	n. 延迟
operand	['ɔpəˌrænd]	n. 操作数
time difference		n. 时差
filter	['filtə]	n. 滤波器，过滤器，滤光器
discrete	[dis'kriːt]	adj. 不连续的，离散的
coefficient	[kəui'fiʃənt]	n. 系数
algorithm	['ælgəriðəm]	n. 运算法则
digital signal processing (DSP)		数字信号处理
development time		程序调试时间
register transfer level (RTL)		寄存器传输级
general purpose microprocessor (GPP)		通用微处理器
cycles per instruction (CPI)		周期/指令
Finite impulse response (IIR)		有限脉冲相应数字滤波器
infinite impulse response (FIR)		无限脉冲相应数字滤波器
analog to digital converter (ADC)		模数转换器
digital to analog converter (DAC)		数模转换器

Notes

[1] As its name implies, it is assumed that there must be some form of preprocessing if the signals are in the continuous time domain, and this is easily accomplished by an analog to digital

converter (ADC).

正如它名字所暗示的，连续时域信号必须要经过某种形式的预处理才能被它所处理，当然这很容易由模数转换器来完成。

句中 its 指代 DSP，as 引导的是状语，it is assumed that there must be some form of preprocessing if the signals are in the continuous time domain 中 that 之后是宾语从句，if 引导的是条件状语从句。

[2] It is because of this very nature that DSP processors are created with an architecture unlike those of conventional microprocessors.

正是由于这一特性，在发明 DSP 处理器时采用了一种与传统的微处理器不同的结构体系。

此句中的 It is…that 是强调句型，这种句型可以强调句子的主语、宾语、状语等，被强调的部分直接放在 be 动词之后，本句是强调状语部分，即 because of this very nature；unlike those of conventional microprocessors 则是用于说明 architecture 的。

[3] We can also use the signal flow graph as shown in Fig. 2-1 to represent this algorithm.

我们也可以用图 2-1 中的信号流程图来描述这个算法。

[4] One might also argue that modern GPPs have clock speeds and cycles per instruction (CPI) that outperform DSP processors but GPPs have operations and program flexibility that are unnecessary for DSP.

也许有人认为现代的通用处理器比 DSP 有更高的处理速度和指令周期，但是通用处理器有许多 DSP 不必要的运算和编程的灵活性。

Exercises

Ⅰ. Please answer the following questions according to the text.

1. Please explain Equation (Fig.2-1).

2. Please describe the meaning of Fig. 2-1.

3. Please describe the meaning of Fig. 2-2.

Ⅱ. Please answer the following questions.

1. What are the differences between Fig. 2-1 and Fig. 2-2?

2. What are the meanings of 'sample period' and 'computational latency'?

B. Reading

Processor Evolution

It is widely known in the industry that the general DSP architectures can be divided into three or four categories or generations and we will look at each of them in turn.

1. Early Single Chip DSP Processors

The first single chip processors were the foundation on which modern DSP processors were built. Although most of them were not commercially successful, manufacturers were quick to learn the pitfalls surrounding each of them. It is also interesting to note that among these early chip vendors, only one has maintained a DSP product line to this day.

2. First Generation Conventional

This class of architecture represented the first widely accepted DSP processors in the market, appearing in the early 1980's. There were a few key manufacturers that offered processors that share many similar traits. The chips were designed around a Harvard architecture with separate data and program buses for the individual data and program memories respectively. The key functional blocks were the multiply, add and accumulator units, but these processors could only perform fixed-point computations. The software that accompanied the chips had specialized instruction sets and addressing modes for DSP with hardware support for software looping.

3. Second Generation Enhanced Conventional

The next stage of development started in the late 1980's/early 1990's, and variants of this architecture have lasted until today. These processors retain much of the design of the first generation but with added features such as pipelining, multiple arithmetic logic units (ALU) and accumulators to enhance performance. The advantage in this is that most processors are code compatible with their predecessors while providing speedup in operations.

Shrinkage of feature sizes also allowed more functional units to be included on the chip. Peripheral device interfaces, counters and timer circuitry, important to data acquisition, are now incorporated in the same die as the DSP. In addition, parallelism could be attained by duplicating key functional units.

4. Third Generation Novel Designs

It is about this time that designers were looking at incorporating GPP architectures into DSPs. This speeds up computations while retaining the functions critical to DSP. Today's DSPs execute single instruction multiple data (SIMD), very long instruction word (VLIW) and superscalar operations. On the software side, more advanced debugging and application development tools have been created to complement multiple instruction hardware loops, modulo addressing and user defined instructions.

SIMD is characteristic of most high performance GPPs that are also capable of multimedia extensions (MMX) and AltiVec algorithms. SIMD allows one instruction to be executed on many independent groups of data. For SIMD to be effective, programs and data sets must be tailored for data parallel processing, and SIMD is most effective with large blocks of data. In DSP, SIMD may require a large program memory for rearranging data, merging partial results and loop unrolling. The two common ways of implementing SIMD are to use split execution units and multiple execution units or data paths depicted in Fig.2-3.

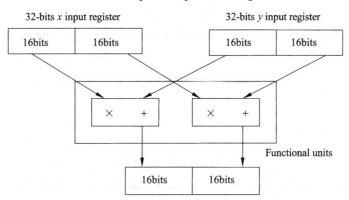

Fig. 2-3 SIMD split execution unit data path.

VLIW processors issue a fixed number of instructions either as one large instruction or in a fixed instruction packet, and the scheduling of these instructions is performed by the compiler. For VLIW to be effective, there must be sufficient parallelism in straight line code to occupy the operation slots. Parallelism can be improved by loop unrolling to remove branch instructions and to use global scheduling techniques, but then a disadvantage of VLIW is low code density if loops cannot be sufficiently unrolled.

Superscalar processors, on the other hand, can issue varying numbers of instructions per cycle and can be scheduled either statically by the compiler or dynamically by the processor itself. As a result, superscalar designs may hold a couple of code density advantages over VLIW. This is because the processor can determine if the subsequent instructions in a program sequence can be issued during execution, in addition to running unscheduled programs.

Recently, we have seen that VLIW has been regaining popularity as a means to improve performance. The latest instruction set architecture co-developed by Intel and Hewlett-Packard, the IA-64, retains much of the VLIW flavor with nuances of CISC and RISC. This hybrid architecture is called explicitly parallel instruction computing (EPIC) and its main purpose is to permit the compiler to group instructions for parallel execution in a flexible fashion. This VLIW-like concept has also been ported to the DSP domain. The joint-venture between Motorola and Lucent Technologies, StarCore, has announced a new DSP architecture known as variable length execution sets (VLES). Like EPIC, VLES combines CISC, RISC and traditional VLIW into an architecture that tries to eliminate VLIW's two major disadvantages: code density and code scalability/compatibility.

The debate between the merits of superscalar and VLIW is not only restricted to the GPP universe. LSI Logic Corp. prefers the superscalar approach and is currently the major manufacturer to champion this architecture. We know that a key difference between superscalar and VLIW lies in the hardware and software complexity respectively. The argument presented by LSI Logic is that the VLIW methodology requires a greater programming effort and is at the mercy of the compiler. A change in the processor hardware will also require a corresponding change in the compiler to preserve efficiency.

It is also common in DSP programming to hand code assembly code instructions for optimization, especially in loop operations. However, because of VLIW's bundling of instructions, it is difficult for programmers to track the multiple instructions for different functional units in a deeply pipelined structure.

5. Power Considerations

Power has been a major concern lately with increased use of DSPs in mobile computing. Fortunately, the architectural concepts we discussed in this subsection help to play a part in reducing power consumption. Power dissipation is lowered as parallelism is increased with the use of multiple functional units and buses. As a result, power usage is reduced when memory accesses is minimized.

Increasing the word size as well as implementing a VLIW-like algorithm allows more data to be fetched per cycle and improves code density. An optimum code density saves power by scaling the instruction size to just the required amount. This is the basic idea of a variable length instruction set processor.

6. Fourth Generation Hybrids

The distinction between a true DSP product and a computer is getting fuzzier, and each day a larger percentage of Internet traffic is composed of audio and video data. The problem lies in processing the audio and video at the users' end. Here lies the dilemma; the need for signal processing in a computer based environment, sometimes simultaneously with general purpose computing. Or in other cases, to be capable of processing some digital signals but not wanting to incur the extra cost of a dedicated DSP chip. Devices such as these process control signals as well as digital data.

Instead of a DSP core, the hybrids in the market now incorporate DSP circuitry with a CPU core. A positive side effect is that printed circuit board (PCB) real estate is saved, thereby reducing the size of the product, costs and more importantly the real savings in the power consumed. In the hybrid processor, the GPP instruction set is retained and the additional DSP instructions offload the processing from the GPP core.

7. Next Generations

Based on the current trends seen in DSP development, we can predict that the manufacturers will be following the path of GPP techniques. We have already seen that superscalar, VLIW and pipelining architectural methods, common in GPP, are in use in the latest DSP processors. Process technologies such as copper interconnect and submicron feature size will reduce chip area to enable smaller handheld devices. Since 1985, there has been an increase of almost 150% in DSP processor performance and this trend will certainly continue for the next few years.

This means that we can expect to see more on-chip peripherals and memory; the system-on-chip (SOC) may not be too far away. Clock speeds will increase to reduce MAC computation times, but supply voltage must also correspondingly drop to reduce power consumption.

New words and phrases

pitfall	['pitfɔ:l]	n. 缺陷
subroutine	[ˌsʌbru:'ti:n]	n. 子程序
coprocessor		n. 协处理器
die	[dai]	n. 钢型，硬模，冲模
multiplier	['mʌltiplaiə]	n. 增效器，乘法器
accumulator	[ə'kju:mjuleitə]	n. 累加器，加法器
counter	['kauntə]	n. 计算器，计数器
timer	['taimə]	n. 定时器
debug	[di:'bʌg]	v. 调试
compiler	[kəm'pailə]	n. 编译器
adder	['ædə]	n. 加法器
shifter	['ʃiftə]	n. 移动装置，转换机构，开关
multiplexer	['mʌltiˌpleksə]	n. 多路（复用）器
unroll	['ʌn'rəul]	v. 解开，打开
fetch	[fetʃ]	vt. 取数，取指令，抽取
dissipation	[ˌdisi'peiʃən]	n. 消散，分散，挥霍，浪费

cache	[kæʃ]	n.	高速缓冲存储器
generator	[ˈdʒenəreitə]	n.	发生器，生成器
generator	[ˈdʒenəreitə]	n.	发生器，生成器
submicron	[ˈsʌbˈmaikrɔn]	adj.	亚微细粒的，亚微型的
copper	[ˈkɔpə]	n.	铜
voltage	[ˈvəultidʒ]	n.	电压，伏特数
floating point	[ˈfləutiŋˈpɔint]	n.	浮点
gigahertz	[ˈgigəhə:ts]	n.	千兆赫

Auxiliary Register Arithmetic Unit (ARAU)	辅助寄存器算术单元
Bit shift	位移
Serial Communications Interface (SCI)	串行通信接口
Synchronous Serial Interface (SSI)	同步串行接口
Parallel Lock Loop (PLL)	锁相环
Multiply and accumulator (MAC)	媒体接入控制器
Arithmetic logic units (ALU)	算术逻辑部件，运算器
Single instruction multiple data (SIMD)	单指令多数据
Very long instruction word (VLIW)	超长指令字
Multimedia extensions (MMX)	多媒体增强指令集
superscalar	n. 超标量体系结构
Complex Instruction Set Computing (CISC)	复杂指令集计算机
Explicitly parallel instruction computing (EPIC)	显示并行指令计算
Variable length execution sets (VLES)	可变长度执行指令集
Printed circuit board (PCB)	印刷电路板

Exercises

Ⅰ. Please answer the following questions according to the text.

1. Please introduce briefly the development of DSP processors.

2. Please describe the differences among SIMD、VLIW and superscalar processors.

3. What should be paid attention to when design a DSP processor?

Ⅱ. Please answer the following questions.
1. Have you ever used a DSP product? Describe its applications and functions.

2. Discuss the future developments of DSP.

C. 数学公式的表示与读法

1. 基本运算符号

$A+B = C$	A plus B equals C
$A-B = C$	A minus B equals C
$A \times B = C$	A multiplied by B equals C
$A/B = C$	A divided by B equals C
$A:B$	The ratio of A to B
$A:B = C:D$	A is to B of A to B as C is to D
0.3 %	Zero point three percent
x^2	x squared
x^3	x cubed
x^4	x to the fourth power
$x^{\frac{1}{2}}$	x to the one-half power
$e = 1.6 \times 10^{-19}$	e equals one point multiplied by ten to minus nineteenth power
$\sqrt{x}$	The square root of x
$\sqrt[3]{x}$	The cube of x
$\sqrt[n]{x}$	The nth root of x
$A = B$	A equals B; A is equal to B
$A \equiv B$	A is identical with B; A is equivalent to B
$A \neq B$	A is not equal to B
$A \approx B$	A be approximately equal to B
$A > B$	A is greater than B
$A < B$	A is less than B
$A \geq B$	A is greater than or equal to B
$A \ll B$	A is far less than B

2. 简单函数

$f(x)$	Function of x
$f(x) = ax^2 + bx + c$	The function of x equals a times the square of x plus b times x plus c
$\lvert a \rvert = b$	The absolute value of a equals that of b
$\text{Max } f(x)$	The maximum value of $f(x)$
$\text{Min } f(x)$	The maximum value of $f(x)$
$a_n \to \infty$	A sub n approaches / tends to infinity
$\lim b$	The limit of b
$\lim\limits_{n \to \infty} S_n = \dfrac{1}{3}$	The limit of S_n as n gets arbitrarily large is one third
$(A+B)C$	The quantity A plus B times C
$\dfrac{x^5 + A}{(x^2 + B)^2}$	x to the fifth power plus A over (divided by) the quantity x squared plus B, to the two-thirds power
$\log x$	Log of x
$\log_2 x$	Log of x to the base two

3. 复杂运算

Δx	Datla x
$\mathrm{d}x$	Differential of x
$\dfrac{\mathrm{d}y}{\mathrm{d}x}$	Derivative of y with respect to x
$\dfrac{\mathrm{d}^2 y}{\mathrm{d}x^2}$	The second derivative of y with respect to x
$\dfrac{\partial y}{\partial x}$	Partial derivative of y with respect to x
$\dfrac{\partial^2 y}{\partial x^2}$	The second partial derivative of y with respect to x
$\dfrac{\partial^2 z}{\partial x \partial y}$	The partial derivation of z with respect to x of the partial derivative of z with respect to y
$\prod\limits_{n=1}^{\infty} a_n$	The product of all a_n from n equals one to infinity
$\sum\limits_{n=1}^{5} S_n$	The capital sigma S_n from n equals one to n equals five
$\sum\limits_{n=1}^{n} x_n$	The sum from a equals one to n of x sub n
$\int ax\,\mathrm{d}x$	The indefinite integral of a times x with respect to x
$\int_a^b f(x)\,\mathrm{d}x$	The integral from a to b of function of x

$$\iint f(x)\mathrm{d}x\mathrm{d}y \qquad \text{The double integral of } f \text{ of } x, y$$

4. 数学问题求解的一般表示

下面以一个简单例子来说明如何表达问题的求解。

Solve the following system of equations

$$\begin{cases} 3x + 3y + z = 7 \\ 3x + y + 3z = 15 \\ x + 3y + 3z = 13 \end{cases} \qquad (1)(2)(3)$$

Solution: multiply equation (1) by (2) and get

$$9x + 9y + 3z = 51 \qquad (4)$$

Subtract equation (2) from equation (4), and get

$$3x + 4y = 3 \qquad (5)$$

Subtract equation (3) from equation (2), and get

$$2x - 2y = 2 \qquad (6)$$

from equations (5) and (6), obtain x and y.

UNIT 8

A. Text

Digit-Serial Approach and Reconfigurable VLSI Architectures

1. Digit-Serial Approach

1.1 Digit-Serial Implementation

Previous architectures have primarily focused on two approaches: bit-serial and bit-parallel implementations. Bit-serial systems process one input bit of a word (or sample) at a time. The advantages of these systems include fewer interconnections, fewer pin-outs, less internal hardware, faster clock speed, and less power consumption. Their main disadvantage is that they are slow because for a word-length of W-bits the bit-serial architectures will require W clock cycles to compute one word or sample[1]. Therefore they are primarily suited for low to medium speed applications. Bit-parallel systems process all input bits of a word in one clock cycle and is the most common implementation style. Their main advantage is that they can compute one word in one clock cycle and therefore can provide high-performance and are ideal for high-speed applications. Their disadvantages include larger chip area, interconnection, pin-out, and they consume more power.

To avoid the disadvantages of the bit-serial and bit-parallel computation, the concept of *digit-serial* implementations has been proposed. These systems process multiple bits of the input word, referred to as the *digit-size*, in one clock cycle. The digit-size can vary from 1 to the word-length to achieve trade-off between speed, area, and the input/output pin limitation. In a digit-serial arithmetic implementation, the W-bit of a data word are processed in units of the digit-size N-bits in W/N clock cycles, and are processed serially one digit at a time with the least significant digit first. For example, if the word-length is 16-bits and the digit-size is 4-bits, then 4-bits are processed in a clock cycle and a word is processed in 4 clock cycles as shown in Fig.2-4[2]. This leads to arithmetic operators that have smaller area than equivalent bit-parallel arithmetic design and have a larger throughput than equivalent bit-serial arithmetic design. For a digit-size of unity, the architecture reduces to a bit-serial system and for a digit-size equal to the word-length; the architecture becomes a bit-parallel system. Architectures based on the digit-serial approach may offer the best overall trade-off between speed, efficient area utilization, throughput, I/O pin limitations and power consumption. By considering a range of values for the digit-size, one can search the design space to find the optimum implementation for a given application.

Time →									
Bit 0	a0	a4	a8	a12	b0	b4	b8	b12	c0	c4
Bit 1	a1	a5	a9	a13	b1	b5	b9	b13	c1	c5
Bit 2	a2	a6	a10	a14	b2	b6	b10	b14	c2	c6
Bit 3	a3	a7	a11	a15	b3	b7	b11	b15	c3	c7
Reset	1	0	0	0	1	0	0	0	1	0

Fig. 2-4 Digit-serial data format (Word-length W=16 bits and digit-size N=4 bits).

Digit-serial approach offers a flexible trade-off between bit-serial and bit-parallel approaches, and between data throughput and the size of arithmetic operators (Fig. 2-5). A system

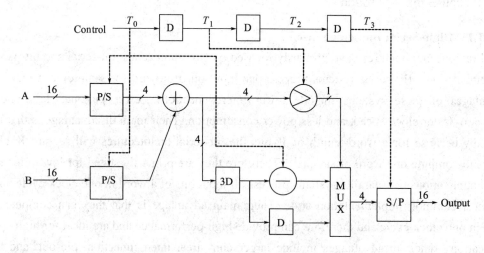

Fig. 2-5 Control scheme for digit-serial circuit.

based on these approaches can combine the advantages of the high throughput of parallel computation and the small operator size of serial computation. The digit-serial formats offer a solution to the interconnection problem in large word-width systems, especially in distributed data flow systems, where the wiring area is usually very large[3]. Digit-serial approach was chosen in this implementation because it has the advantage that by varying the digit-size, the best trade-off of speed and area can be found.

The implementation methods of digit-serial architectures have been proposed in [41]. The first approach is to start with a bit-parallel structure and then use folding to obtain the digit-serial architecture. The second approach is to start with a bit-serial architecture and then uses unfolding to obtain the digit-serial architecture. The major drawback of the architectures based on these approaches is that they cannot be pipelined at the bit-level, which has severely limited their through put. This could be a major obstacle for high-speed applications. The main reason why these structures cannot be pipelined is due to the existence of carry feedback loops, which are impossible to pipeline[4]. Recently, the digit-serial architectures that can be pipelined at the bit-level have been presented in [38]~[40]. The use of carry feed-forward has solved a major bottleneck of the carry feedback loops of conventional digit-serial designs. The possibility of high degree of pipelining increases the throughput rate of the digit-serial architectures.

1.2 Timing of Control Signals

In every digit-serial operator, it is necessary to add some control signal to indicate the word boundary for each digit-serial operator. Since there is no gap between successive words of data, some mechanism is necessary to indicate where one word ends and the next one begins. This is provided by a periodic signal, called control signal, which is passed to the individual operators. The control signal is high for exactly one clock cycle in each sample period, that is, becomes active every W/N cycles. Normally, all of the different delayed versions of the control signal are available in a digit-serial circuit, and operators may be connected to one or more of these control signals for synchronization. Only W/N different control signals are required because of the periodicity. It can be generated by a shift-register ring and broadcast throughout the chip, or distributed by a chain of shift-registers. Fig. 2-5 shows a typical complete control scheme for digit-serial circuit using a digit-size $N = 4$ bits and a word-length $W=16$ bits. This particular circuit accepts two 16-bit wide parallel inputs, A and B, and calculates the absolute value of their sum. Four offset control signals, T_0, T_1, T_2, T_3, are generated by delaying the input control signal. The control signal T_i has a pulse at time i and then every subsequent 4 cycles.

2. Reconfigurable VLSI Architectures

Because of the great proliferation and low cost of VLSI technology, virtually every new digital design produced today consists almost entirely of high-density devices. For high-volume applications, the use of dedicated architectures is almost expected. In the demanding and often constantly changing market of today, the cost (in terms of design time and financial costs) of designing dedicated architectures for prototyping and low-volume applications is becoming prohibitive. For this reason, many prototypes and even production designs are being built using reconfigurable VLSI architecture or programmable logic devices (PLDs). Their primary advantages are the almost instantaneous turn around time, low start-up costs, and ease of incorporating design changes. Today, many kinds of reconfigurable VLSI architectures are available, i.e., FPGAs and CPLDs (Complex Programmable Logic Devices), and they are the keys to constructing reconfigurable system. The time-to-market pressures and low financial risk have made FPGAs and CPLDs increasingly as popular vehicle for prototyping and in many cases actual productions. Almost all reconfigurable systems use commercially available FPGAs/CPLDs, but some utilize custom reconfigurable chips.

Field Programmable Gate Arrays

FPGAs are a form of programmable logic devices which permits the design of many different complex digital circuits. FPGAs were first introduced in 1986 by Xilinx using a memory-based programming technology. Since then there have been many new commercial architectures. A few non-commercial FPGA architectures have been proposed for which the design details are more readily available. The key property of programmable logics that differentiates them from custom hardware is their reconfigurability[5]. Such device cannot compete with a custom hardware implementation in terms of density or speed, but their reconfigurability allows hardware designs to be created and changed rapidly, thus reducing time-to-market and costs over custom hardware. Traditionally, programmable logics have been configured in special programmers that are external to the host system. However, many current FPGAs have SRAM configuration memories, which can be programmed in-system. Thus, a configuration can be loaded into the FPGA and run, just like a soft program, but with performance closer to that of dedicated hardware. FPGAs can be programmed using just a personal computer and simple hardware interface, giving them flexibility and time-to-market advantages over traditional ASICs, which must have all wiring completed in a fabrication plant. FPGAs can all be classified according to the general architecture, the type of logic block and the programming technology. There are a number of different types of FPGAs. The commercially available FPGAs are mainly designed by Xilinx, Altera, Latice, Actel and Lucent Technologies etc.

Although FPGAs provide some support for the implementation of DSP arithmetic circuit, they are still predominantly general purpose devices. Due to the wide range of DSP applications and their computationally intensive nature, there is a clear need for FPGAs which are DSP-specific. Therefore, the application-specific FPGA architectures have been proposed.

New words and Technical Terms

bottleneck ['bɔtl‚nek] n. 瓶颈

boundary ['baundəri] n. 边界, 分界线

successive	[sək'sesiv]	adj. 继承的，连续的
synchronization	[ˌsiŋkrənai'zeiʃən]	n. 同步，同一时刻
offset	['ɔ:fset]	n. 偏移量；vi. 偏移
reconfigurable	['ri:kənfigju'rəbl]	adj. 可重新配置的
feed-forward		n. 前馈
trade-off		n. 交换，协定，交易，平衡
shift-register		n. 移位寄存器
bit-serial		位串行
bit-parallel		位并行
pin-out		引脚
digit-serial		字串行
very large scale integration（VLSI）		超大规模集成电路
programmable logic device（PLD）		可编程逻辑电路
field programmable gate array（FPGA）		现场可编程门阵列
complex programmable logic device（CPLD）		复杂可编程逻辑器件
static random access memory（SRAM）		静态存储器
application specific integrated circuit（ASIC）		专用集成电路
Look-Up-Table（LUT）		查找表

Notes

[1] Their main disadvantage is that they are slow because for a word-length of W-bits the bit-serial architectures will require W clock cycles to compute one word or sample.

它们主要的缺点是速度慢，因为对于一个 W 位字长，位串行结构需要 W 个时钟周期来计算一个字或取样。that 之后引导的是表语。

[2] For example, if the word-length is 16-bits and the digit-size is 4-bits, then 4-bits are processed in a clock cycle and a word is processed in 4 clock cycles as shown in Figure 1.

举例说明，如果一个字长 16 位并且数据位长度是 4 位，那么一个时钟周期处理 4 位，一个字就需要 4 个时钟周期，如图 1 所示。

[3] The digit-serial formats offer a solution to the interconnection problem in large word-width systems, especially in distributed data flow systems, where the wiring area is usually very large.

字串行格式提供了为字长宽的系统所存在的互联问题提供了一种解决方法，特别是配线区域非常大的分布式数据流系统。where the wiring area is usually very large 是非限定性定语从句，修饰的是 distributed data flow systems。

[4] The major drawback of the architectures based on these approaches is that they cannot be pipelined at the bit-level, which has severely limited their through put. This could be a major obstacle for high-speed applications. The main reason why these structures cannot be pipelined is

due to the existence of carry feedback loops, which are impossible to pipeline.

基于这些方法的结构的主要缺点是，它们不能以位传输，这就严重限制了吞吐量。这也是高速应用的主要障碍之一。这种结构不能传输的主要原因是进位反馈环路的存在，因为这种环路是不可能传输的。

注意以上段落中两个 which 的用法。英语中关系代词 which 引导的定语从句（尤其是非限定性的从句），在很多时候并不表示定语意义，而表示原因、结果、条件、时间、顺接等各种逻辑语义关系，视上下文而定。本段中的第一个 which 引导的从句表示顺接关系，第二个 which 引导的从句表示原因，因而翻译时可以加上"因为……"之类的措词。

[5] The key property of programmable logics that differentiates them from custom hardware is their reconfigurability.

可编程逻辑区别于传统硬件的关键特性是它们可以重新配置。differentiate…from…，使……区别于……，使……与……不同。

Exercises

Ⅰ．Please answer the following questions according to the text.

1．Please describe the main advantages and disadvantages of bit-serial systems and bit parallel systems

2．Please describe the digit-serial arithmetic implementation.

3．Why is the control signal necessary?

4．What are FPGAs?

Ⅱ．Please answer the following questions.

1．What are the differences among bit-serial, bit-parallel and digit-serial?

2．Discuss the advantages and applications of FPGA.

Ⅲ．Please translate the Chinese into English.

半导体的电气性质介于导体和绝缘体之间，像锗和硅这样的元素以及氧化铜和硫化镉这样一些化合物，都属于这种类型，其名称正是来源与此。例如，在普通的室温情况下，1cm³ 的纯铜（导体）对电流形成的电阻约为 0.000 001 7Ω。1cm³ 的岩石（绝缘物）具有的电阻约为 100 000 000Ω。1cm³ 的锗（半导体）具有的电阻约为 60Ω。

正如所学过的那样，我们讨论的原子是包含着质子和中子的原子核。原子是被位于一个或多个在同心壳体轨道上电子旋转的一种结构。质子的正电荷被电子的负电荷中和。在中性原子中，轨道上的电子与原子核中的质子数量是相同的。

B. Reading

High-Performance DSP Design Using FPGAs

Recent improvements in FPGA technology have demonstrated that FPGAs are no longer devices simply relegated to handling control and dataflow tasks. As FPGAs have grown in capacity, improved in performance, and decreased in cost, they are becoming a viable solution for performing computationally intensive tasks, with the ability to tackle applications formerly reserved for custom chips and programmable DSP devices. The flexibility of a programmable DSP processor combined with the high speed, density and performance of an ASIC is provided by the reconfigurable logic. Traditionally DSP algorithms are most commonly implemented using programmable DSP devices for low rate applications, and ASICs for higher rates. FPGAs maintain the advantages of high gate density, while avoiding the high development costs and inability to make design modifications after production like ASICs. FPGAs also add design flexibility and adaptability with optimal device utilization conserving both board space and system power which is often not the case with programmable DSP devices. FPGAs can also be partially or completely reconfigured in the system for a modified or completely different algorithm.

The SRAM-based FPGAs are well suited for arithmetic, including Multiply and Accumulate (MAC) intensive DSP functions. A wide range of arithmetic functions (such as convolutions, Fast Fourier Transform's (FFT's), and other filtering algorithms) can be integrated with surrounding peripheral circuitry. FPGAs can also be reconfigured on-the-fly to perform one of many system-level functions. When building a DSP system in an FPGA, the design can take advantage of parallel structures and arithmetic algorithms to minimize general-purpose DSP devices. The key advantage of FPGAs over ASICs and programmable DSPs is their unique combination of performance and flexibility. Researches have shown that FPGAs can significantly outperform programmable DSPs in terms of speed, size, and power requirements in certain applications. In addition, FPGAs also enjoy flexibility far in excess of ASICs. Fig. 2-6 graphically illustrates the merits of FPGAs relative to ASICs and programmable DSPs. We see from this chart that reconfigurable VLSI architectures (or FPGAs) capture in large measure the best of both worlds. They possess DSP-like flexibility far in excess of ASICs, but they also achieve ASIC-like speed, area, and power performance, far outperforming programmable DSPs for certain applications.

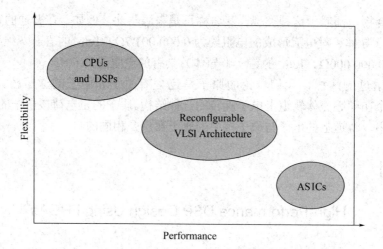

Fig. 2-6 A comparison of FPGAs to ASICs and DSPs in terms of flexibility and performance.

One of the important features in the Xilinx XC4000-series FPGA architecture is the ability to use CLB lookup tables (LUTs) as RAM. Each LUT can be used as a 16×1 RAM. There are two LUTs in each CLB, allowing a single CLB to either implement a 31×1, a 16×2, or two 16×1 RAMs with a shared clock. The abundance of small distributed RAM blocks throughout the chip enables the user to pre-calculate partial products, and to load these into the distributed RAM, thereby eliminating the large amounts of logic needed to compute multiplication results in a non-distributed approach. The most versatile approach using the distributed RAM is an approach called Distributed Arithmetic (DA) techniques, which perform multiplication with lookup table-based schemes. DA-techniques permit computations in the form of sum of products to be decomposed into repetive lookup table procedures, the results from which are then accumulated to produce the final result. Since Xilinx XC4000-series FPGAs are based on lookup tables, DA-techniques are a convenient way to implement the multiply-intensive algorithm like FIR filters, provided that one of the multiplication operands is constant. The bits of the other operand are then used as address lines for looking up a table which is a storage, (i.e., ROM, RAM), where the potential products from the multiplication of the first operand by the potential values of the second operand and stored.

In practical digital signal processing applications, it may be desirable to combine the area-efficiency of a bit-serial architecture with the time-efficiency of a corresponding bit-parallel architecture into a single area-time efficient digit-serial architecture. It has been demonstrated that the area-time efficiency and performance of the digit-serial architectures are considerably above bit-serial / bit-parallel architectures for FPGAs.

New words and Technical Terms

optimal	['ɔptiməl]	adj. 最佳的，最理想的
outperform	[autpə'fɔ:m]	vt. 做得比……好，胜过
versatile	['və:sətail]	adj. 通用的，万能的，多才多艺的，多面手的

convolution	[ˌkɔnvəˈljuːʃən]	n.	卷积
Fast Fourier Transform Algorithm (FFT)		abbr.	快速傅里叶变换算法的首字母缩写

Exercises

Ⅰ. Please answer the following questions according to the text.

1. Please compare FPGAs with ASICs and DSPs.

2. Please describe DA techniques briefly.

3. Do you know the Xilinx XC4000-series FPGA architecture? Please describe simply.

Ⅱ. Please answer the following question.

1. Discuss the advantages of FPGA on DSP design.

2. Talk about some algorithms that you are familiar with and their applications in system design.

C. 英文摘要简介

1. How to write a summary

Today I am going to talk about how to write a summary. I think if you remember one word, it will help you to write a summary. The word is SIMPLE. This word represents six steps to writing a good summary. SIMPLE's first letter is "S". "S" here stands for the first step you should do. That is to study the text carefully. And letter "I" here stands for the second step, to identify the key points while you read the text. "M" here represents the third step of writing a summary, that is to make notes. Then the fourth one is to put points in order.

The next step is to leave out unnecessary detail. The last step is to edit your first draft. Now I will talk about these steps one by one.

Let us start with studying the text. When you get an article, you should read it first fairly quickly to get a sense of the general meaning. Then read it more carefully, following the writer's argument and noticing what fact and what is opinion, what is a general statement and what is a particular example. It is often helpful to summarize each paragraph in a few words at this stage.

Now let's turn to identifying the key points. You must go through the text and mark the places where important information is given. You can underling or highlight with a colored pen or simply make a mark in the margin.

The third step is to make notes. This is a very important stage. You should write down the key points you've identified in note form in your own words. This is also especially important in an exam because the examiner needs to know you understand what you have written and that you are not just copying from the text.

Let's turn to the fourth step, to put points in order. You should look at the list of points you have made and see if there are any which go together. Then decide the best order to put the points in. Number the points in order.

Now let's look at the next stage, leave out unnecessary detail. This stage is much like the tailor who cuts off unnecessary parts for making clothes. You should choose the important facts and get rid of unnecessary details.

The last stage is to edit your first draft. You should check the spelling and grammar, counting the number of words. If you have many fewer than the limit, you should add in something so it is important to check the original text again. If you have more than the limit, look for ways of combining points in one sentence or of "losing" words here and there.

If you follow the word SIMPLE, it may help you to make a good summary in an academic essay.

2. Sample for summary

The following sample for summary is very short, primarily because it was the first draft done by the student (but edited for publication).

Science Shows Us How the World Is

By Min Seok Kim

Eng 3027-5, Advanced Composition, University of Minnesota

"Is Science Dangerous?" by Lewis Wolpert appeared in the March 25, 1999 issue of Nature. In this article, Wolpert insists that scientific knowledge has no moral or ethical value, and that all it does is make a just society.

Wolpert tells us that we do not know the exact difference between science and technology. In actuality, science makes ideas about how the world works; scientists do not cause unethical behaviors. However, technology—such as the genetic engineering feats of human cloning, gene therapy, and genetically modified foods—can do so. Wolpert suggests some guidelines to reduce ethical problems: all scientific ideas should be criticized by others; knowledge should be used to do good, not evil; and government and the media should act correctly in carrying out the applications of science

In the article "Is Science Dangerous?" Lewis Wolpert explains that science itself is not dangerous, and the real danger depends on how safely science is applied—and on how we respond to it.

PART 3

Signal and System

UNIT 9

A. Text

Mathematical Representation of Signals

Anything that bears information can be considered a signal. Signals may describe a wide variety of physical phenomena. For example, speech, music, interest rates, the speed of an automobile are signals. Although signals can be represented in many ways, in all cases the information in a signal is contained in a pattern of variations of some form[1]. For example, consider the human vocal mechanism, which produces speech by creating fluctuations in acoustic pressure[2]. Fig. 3-1 is an illustration of a recording of such a speech signal, obtained using a microphone to sense variations in acoustic pressure, which are then converted into an electrical signal[3]. As can be seen in the figure, different sounds correspond to different patterns in the variations of acoustic pressure, and the human vocal system produces intelligible speech by generating particular sequences of these patterns. Alternatively, for the monochromatic picture, it is the pattern of variations in brightness across the image that is important[4].

The signal represents acoustic pressure variations as a function of time for the spoken words "should we chase." The top line of the figure corresponds to the word "should," the second line to the word "we," and the last two lines to the word "chase."

Signals are presented mathematically as functions of one or more independent variables. For example, a speech signal can be represented mathematically by acoustic pressure as a function of time, and a picture can be presented by brightness as a function of two spatial variables[5]. For convenience, we will generally refer to the independent variable as time, although it may not in fact represent time in specific applications[6]. For example, in geophysics, signals representing variations with depth of physical quantities such as density, porosity, and electrical resistivity are used to study the structure of the earth[7].

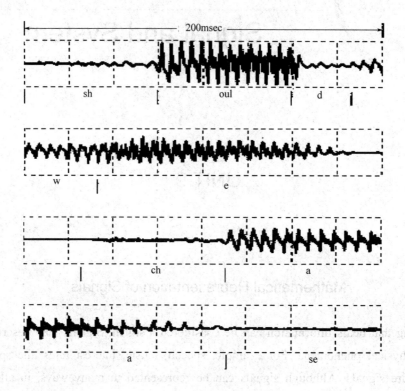

Fig. 3-1 Example of a recording of speech.

Two basic types of signals will be considered: continuous-time signals and discrete-time signals. In the case of continuous-time signals the independent variable is continuous, and thus these signals are defined for a continuum of values of the independent variable. On the other hand, discrete-time signals are defined only at discrete times, for these signals, the independent variable takes on only a discrete set of values. A speech signal as a function of time and atmospheric pressure as a function of altitude are examples of continuous-time signals. The weekly Dow-Jones stock market index is an example of a discrete-time signal. Other examples of discrete-time signals can be found in demographic studies in which various attributes, such as average budget, crime rate, or pounds of fish caught, are tabulated against such discrete variables as family size, total population, or type of fishing vessel, respectively[8].

To distinguish between continuous-time signals and discrete-time signals, we will use the symbol t to denote the continuous-time independent variable and n to denote the discrete-time independent variable. In addition, for continuous-time signals we will enclose the independent variable in parentheses (·), whereas for discrete-time signals we will use brackets[·] to enclose the independent variable. We will also have frequent occasions when it will be useful to represent signals graphically[9]. Illustrations of a continuous-time signal $x(t)$ and a discrete-time signal $x[n]$ are shown in Fig. 3-2. It is important to note that the discrete-time signal $x[n]$ is defined only for integer values of the independent variable[10]. For further emphasis we will on occasion refer to $x[n]$ as a discrete-time sequence.

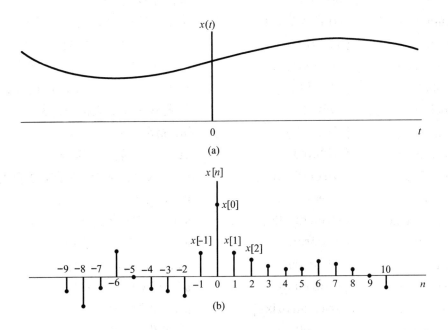

Fig. 3-2 Graphical representations of (a) continuous-time and (b) discrete-time signals.

A discrete-time signal $x[n]$ may represent a phenomenon for which the independent variable is inherently discrete. Signals such as demographic data are examples of this. On the other hand, a very important class of discrete-time signals arises from the sampling of continuous-time signals. In this case, the discrete-time signal $x[n]$ represents successive samples of an underlying phenomenon for which the independent variable is continuous. No matter what source of the data, however, the signal $x[n]$ is defined only for integer values of n. It makes no more sense to refer to the $3\frac{1}{2}$ th sample of a digital speech signal than it does to refer to the average budget of a family with $2\frac{1}{2}$ family members[11].

New words and Technical Terms

    bear   [bɛə]   v. 带给，具有，载有，负担，忍受
    variation   [ˌvɛəriˈeiʃən]   n. 变化，变更，变异

fluctuation	[ˌflʌktjuˈeiʃən]	n. 波动，起伏
acoustic	[əˈkuːstɪk]	adj. 有关声音的，声学的，音响学的
illustration	[ˌiləsˈtreiʃən]	n. 说明，例证，例子，图表，插图
intelligible	[inˈtelidʒəbl]	adj. 可理解的
sequence	[ˈsiːkwəns]	n. 次序，顺序，序列
monochromatic	[ˌmɔnəukrəuˈmætik]	adj. [物]单色的，单频的
spatial	[ˈspeiʃəl]	adj. 空间的
continuum	[kənˈtinjuəm]	n. 连续统一体，闭联集
discrete	[disˈkriːt]	adj. 不连续的，离散的
atmospheric	[ˌætməsˈferik]	adj. 大气的
attribute	[əˈtribju(ː)t]	n. 属性，品质，特征，加于，归结于
tabulate	[ˈtæbjuleit]	v. 把……制成表格，列表
denote	[diˈnəut]	vt. 指示，表示
enclose	[inˈkləuz]	vt. 放入，装入，围绕
parentheses	[pəˈrenθisis]	n. 插入语，附带，插曲，圆括号
bracket	[ˈbrækit]	n. 括弧
demographic	[deməˈgræfik]	adj. 人口统计学的
inherently	[inˈhiərəntli]	adv. 天性地，固有地
successive	[səkˈsesiv]	adj. 继承的，连续的
underlying	[ˈʌndəˈlaiiŋ]	adj. 根本的，潜在的
geophysics	[ˌdʒi(ː)əuˈfiziks]	n. 地球物理学
porosity	[pɔːˈrɔsiti]	n. 多孔性，有孔性
a wide variety of		极为广泛的，各种各样的
convert into		转换，转化
correspond to		相应，符合
take on		呈现，具有，雇用
arise from		起于，由……出身

Notes

[1] Although signals can be represented in many ways, in all cases the information in a signal is contained in a pattern of variations of some form.

虽然信号可以用许多方式来表示，但是在所有情况下，信号所载有的信息总是包含在某种形式变化的波形中。

句中 in all cases 为固定搭配，可译为：在所有情况下。Pattern 原意为：模式、图案，本句可译为：波形。

[2] For example, consider the human vocal mechanism, which produces speech by

PART 3   Signal and System

creating fluctuations in acoustic pressure.

考察人类的发声机制，即是通过声压的起伏波动产生的语音信息。

which…引导的定语从句修饰 vocal mechanism。

[3] Fig. 3-1 is an illustration of a recording of such a speech signal, obtained by using a microphone to sense variations in acoustic pressure, which are then converted into an electrical signal.

图 3-1 是一个语音信号的录音波形，它是通过拾音器来感知声压的变化，然后将这种变化再转化为电信号。

过去分词短语 obtained by…用做后置定语，修饰 signal。which…引导的非限定性定语从句，对先行词 variations 进行补充说明。

[4] Alternatively, for the monochromatic picture, it is the pattern of variations in brightness across the image that is important.

另一个例子是一幅黑白照片，这时照片上各点的亮度变化波形才是重要的。

It is…that…为强调句型。

[5] For example, a speech signal can be represented mathematically by acoustic pressure as a function of time, and a picture can be presented by brightness as a function of two spatial variables.

例如，一个语音信号在数学上可以用声压随时间变化的函数来表示，而一张照片可以表示为亮度随二维空间变量变化的函数。

该句为被动句，翻译成汉语时习惯于用主动语态表达。

[6] For convenience, we will generally refer to the independent variable as time, although it may not in fact represent time in specific applications.

为了方便起见，通常用时间来表示自变量，尽管在某些具体应用中自变量不一定是时间。

句中 refer to…as…是固定搭配，可译为：把……称作……，用……表示……。Although 引导让步状语从句。

[7] For example, in geophysics, signals representing variations with depth of physical quantities such as density, porosity, and electrical resistivity are used to study the structure of the earth.

例如，在地球物理学研究中用于研究地球结构的一些物理量如密度、气隙度和电阻率就是随地球深度变化的信号。

现在分词短语 representing…用作定语，修饰 signals。本句主语是 signals，谓语动词是 are used，动词不定式 to study…作目的状语。

[8] Other examples of discrete-time signals can be found in demographic studies in which various attributes, such as average budget, crime rate, or pounds of fish caught, are tabulated against such discrete variables as family size, total population, or type of fishing vessel,

respectively.

在人口统计学的研究中可以找到其他离散时间信号的例子，例如像平均预算、犯罪率或捕鱼的重量等各种属性都可以分别对家庭大小、总人口数或捕鱼船的类型等离散变量列成表格。

定语从句 in which…修饰 study，两个 such as 引导的部分同位语分别对 attributes 和 discrete variable 作解释说明。

[9] We will also have frequent occasions when it will be useful to represent signals graphically.

我们常常用图解的方法来表示信号。

when…引导的定语从句修饰 occasions。

[10] It is important to note that the discrete-time signal $x[n]$ is defined only for integer values of the independent variable.

值得强调的是，离散时间信号 $x[n]$ 仅仅在自变量的整数值上有定义。

句中动词不定式 to note…作主语，it 是形式主语，that…引导的宾语从句包含在不定式短语中。

[11] It makes no more sense to refer to the $3\frac{1}{2}$ th sample of a digital speech signal than it does to refer to the average budget of a family with $2\frac{1}{2}$ family members.

所谓的一个数字语音信号的第 $3\frac{1}{2}$ 个样本和所谓的具有 $2\frac{1}{2}$ 个家庭成员的家庭平均预算一样都是毫无意义的。

句中 no more…than…为固定搭配，可译为：和……一样都不。

Exercises

Ⅰ. Please answer the following questions according to text.

1. What are signals? Please give some examples of signals.

2. What is the definition of continuous-time signals and discrete-time signals? Please give some examples of continuous-time signals and discrete-time signals respectively.

3. How to represent signals mathematically?

4. What is the difference of mathematical representation between continuous-time signals and discrete-time signals?

II. Please write vocabulary according to corresponding description.

Description	Vocabulary
Something such as sound, image, or message transmitted or received in telegraphy, telephony, radio, television, or radar	
An ordered set of quantities	
Uninterrupted in time, sequence, substance, or extent	
Defined for a finite set of values; not continuous	
A member of the set of positive whole numbers (1, 2, 3,···), negative whole numbers (−1,−2,−3,···), and zero (0)	
Not dependent on other variables	
To arrange in tabular form	
Of or relating to sound, the sense of hearing, or the science of sound	
The act of clarifying or explaining	
Having or appearing to have only one color	

B. Reading

Representation of Digital Signals

A signal is called a digital signal if its time is discretized and its amplitude is quantized. A digital computer can accept only sequences of numbers(discrete-time), and the numbers are limited by the number of bits used. Therefore, all signals processed on digital computers are digital signals.

Messages sent by telegraph are digital signals. They are written using 26 alphabetical characters, 10 numerals, and symbols such as commas and periods. These symbols certainly can be represented by different voltage levels, for example, A by 10 V(volts), B by 9.5V, C by 9V and so forth. This type of representation, however, is not used because it is susceptible to noise, shifting of power supply, and any other disturbances[1].

In practice, these symbols are coded as sequences of dashes and dots or, equivalently, ones and zeros. The symbol 0 can be represented by a voltage from 0 to 0.8V. The symbol 1 can be represented by a voltage from 2.0 to 5.0V. The precise voltage of each symbol is not important, but it is critical that its value lies within one of the two allowable ranges[2]. This type of representation of 1 and 0 is much less susceptible to noise. Furthermore. It is easy to implement. Therefore, digital signals are always coded by ones and zeros in physical implementation. This is called binary coding.

There are many types of binary coding. In this section, we discuss the simplest one, called sign-and-magnitude coding. Consider the following sequences of a_i:

$$
\begin{array}{cccccc}
a_0 & a_1 & a_2 & a_3 & a_4 & a_5 \\
\text{Sign bit} & 2^1 & 2^0 & 2^{-1} & 2^{-2} & 2^{-3}
\end{array}
$$

Each a_i can assume only either 1 or 0 and is called a binary digit or bit. There are six bits in the sequence. The left-most bit is called the sign bit. The sequence represents a positive number if $a_0=0$ and a negative number if $a_0=1$. The remaining five bits represent the magnitude of the number. For example, we have

$$1\ 1\ 0\ 0\ 1\ 1 \leftrightarrow -(1\times2^1+0\times2^0+0\times2^{-1}+1\times2^{-2}+1\times2^{-3}) = -2.375$$

and

$$0\ 0\ 1\ 1\ 1\ 0 \leftrightarrow (0\times2^1+1\times2^0+1\times2^{-1}+1\times2^{-2}+0\times2^{-3}) = 1.75$$

The left-most bit, excluding the sign bit, is the most significant bit (MSB) and the right-most bit is the least significant bit (LSB) [3]. If we use 10 bits to represent the decimal part of a number, then the LSB represents $2^{-10}=1/1024=0.000\ 976\ 5$, which yields the quantization step[4]. Fig.3-3 shows the conversion of a continuous-time signal into a 4-bit digital signal. The digital signal shown in Fig.3-3 © is said to be pulse-code modulated (PCM). The width of a pulse can be in the order of nanoseconds (10^{-9} seconds), and the sampling period can be in the order of microseconds (10^{-6} seconds), or we can take one million samples in one second. The waveform of the digital signal in Fig.3-3 © does not resemble in any way the waveform of the physical variable; thus we may call digital signals nonanalog signals.

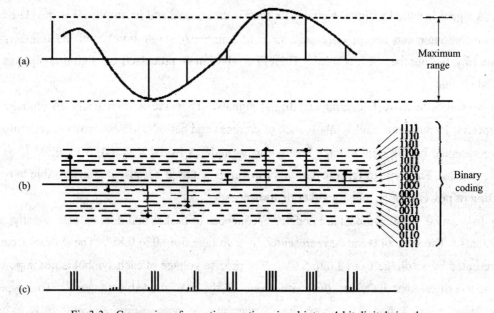

Fig.3-3 Conversion of a continuous-time signal into a 4-bit digital signal.

Signals encountered in practice are mostly continuous-time signals. To process an analog signal digitally, it must first be discretized in time to yield a discrete-time signal and then quantized in amplitude to yield a digital signal. Therefore, in actual digital signal processing, we deal exclusively with digital signals.

An analytical study of digital signals, however, is difficult, because quantization is not a linear process. To simplify the discussion, we use decimal numbers to illustrate this point. Suppose every number is to be rounded to the nearest integer (that is, the quantization step is 1); Then we have

$$Q(2.6+2.7) = Q(5.3) = 5 \neq Q(2.6) + Q(2.7) = 3 + 3 = 6$$

and

$$Q(2.6 \times 2.7) = Q(7.02) = 7 \neq Q(2.6) \times Q(2.7) = 3 \times 3 = 9$$

Where Q stands for quantization. Because of these nonlinear phenomena, analytical study of digital signals is complicated. There are, however, no such problems in studying discrete-time signals. For this reason, in analysis and design, all digital signals will be considered as discrete-time signals. In actual processing or implementation, all discrete-time signals must be convened into digital signals. In quantization, if the amplitude of a discrete-time signal does not fall exactly on a quantization level, then the value must be approximated by a quantization level either by truncation or rounding[5]. In either case, errors will occur. Such errors are called quantization errors. In general, quantization errors are studied separately in digital signal processing. Such a study is important in specialized hardware that uses a small number of bits such as 4 or 8 bits. On digital computers and DSP processors that have 16 or 32 bits, quantization errors are very small and can often be simply ignored. For convenience, we use digital signals and discrete-time signals interchangeably with the understanding that all discrete-time signals must be transformed into digital signals in implementation and all digital signals are considered as discrete-time signals in analysis and design[6].

New words and Technical Terms

discretize	['diskri:taiz]	v. 使离散
amplitude	['æmplitju:d]	n. 广阔，丰富，振幅
quantize	['kwɔntaiz]	v. 使量化
telegraph	['teligrɑ:f]	n. 电报机，电报
alphabetical	[ˌælfə'betikəl]	adj. 依字母顺序的，字母的
susceptible	[sə'septəbl]	adj. 易受影响的，易感动的，容许……的
shift	[ʃift]	v. 转换，移动，转变

disturbance	[dis'tə:bəns]	n. 骚动，动乱，打扰，干扰
implement	['implimənt]	v. 贯彻，实现，执行
binary	['bainəri]	adj. 二进位的，二元的
assume	[ə'sju:m]	v. 假定，设想，采取，呈现
yield	[ji:ld]	v. 产生，出产
conversion	[kən'və:ʃən]	n. 变换，转化
truncation	[trʌŋ'keiʃən]	n. 切断，截断
resemble	[ri'zembl]	v. 像，类似
exclusively	[ɪk'sklu:sɪvlɪ]	adv. 专有地
linear	['liniə]	adj. 线的，线性的，直线的
analytical	[ˌænə'litikəl]	adj. 分析的，解析的
pulse-code modulated(PCM)		脉冲编码调制
stand for		代表，代替
quantization error		量化误差

Exercises

Ⅰ. Please answer the following questions according to text.

1. What is the definition of digital signals? Please give some examples of digital signals.

2. What is binary coding? What are the characteristics of binary coding?

3. Using sign-and-magnitude coding, calculate the magnitude of the following sequence: 0 1 0 0 1 1 1. What is its LSB?

4. What are quantization errors? Can quantization errors be ignored in specialized hardware that uses a small number of bits?

Ⅱ. Please translate the following text into Chinese.

Signals encountered in practice are mostly continuous-time signals. To process an analog signal digitally, it must first be discretized in time to yield a discrete-time signal and then quantized in amplitude to yield a digital signal. Therefore, in actual digital signal processing, we deal exclusively with digital signals.

C. 从句的翻译

英语中的从句有定语从句、状语从句、主语从句、表语从句、宾语从句，以及同位语从句。翻译英语从句时，应弄清原文的句法结构，根据汉语的特点和表达方式，正确地译出原文的意思。下面根据不同的从句结构，来讨论它们的译法。

1. 定语从句翻译法

定语从句的翻译方法较多，一般有三种方法，一是将从句翻译成前置定语，二是将从句单独翻译成一句话，三是将定语从句译成状语分句。对每一种方法的解释及说明都是针对本部分的定语从句的翻译而言的。一般来说，限制性定语从句一般采用第一种译法，非限制性定语从句采用第二种译法。以下是几种典型的方法。

（1）合译法：合译法通常用于句式较短的情况，主要以限制性定语从句为主。翻译时，可采用前置法，把定语从句译成带"的"的定语词组，放在被修饰词之前，从而将复合句译成汉语单句。如

① A discrete-time signal $x[n]$ may represent a phenomenon for which the independent variable is inherently discrete.

一个离散时间信号 $x[n]$ 可以表示一种其自变量变化本来就是离散的现象。

② On digital computers and DSP processors that have 16 or 32 bits, quantization errors are very small and can often be simply ignored.

在 16 位或 32 位的数字计算机和 DSP 处理器中，量化误差很小，通常被忽略。

（2）分译法：分译法是指将主句和从句分开翻译的一种方法，主要用于较长的非限制性定语从句中。采用这种方法可避免句子的冗长和累赘。翻译时，将从句从句子中抽出来单独组成分句，放在主句后面。如

① Such a system will be represented pictorially as in figure 1, where $x(t)$ is the input and $y(t)$ is the output.

这样的系统可用图 1 来表示，图中 $x(t)$ 是输入，$y(t)$ 是输出。

② A similar effect is commonly observed in western movies, where the wheels of a stagecoach appear to be rotating more slowly than would be consistent with the coach's forward motion, and sometimes in the wrong direction.

一个类似的效果也常在西部电影中观察到，电影中马车的轮子看上去转得比马车实际向前运动的速度要慢，偶尔还会向相反的方向转动。

③ Consider the situation depicted in Fig. 3-1, in which we have a disc rotating at a constant rate with a single radial line marked on the disc.

考虑图 3-1 所示的情况，在这里有一个圆盘，以恒定的速度旋转，在圆盘上标一根径向

直线。

（3）转译法：有些非限制性定语从句，从形式上看它们是定语从句，但它们并不表示先行词的特征和属性，而起状语的作用，这时可根据具体情况，采用转译法，把定语从句译成目的、结果、原因、条件、让步等状语从句。如

① The strike would prevent the docking of ocean steamships, which require assistance of tugboats.

罢工会使远洋航船不能靠岸，因为他们需要拖船的帮助。（翻译成原因状语从句）

② He wishes to write an article, which will attract public attention to the matter.

他想写一篇文章，以便能引起公众对这件事的关注。（翻译成目的状语从句）

综上所述，定语从句一般要视其含义，与先行词关系的密切程度、长度的不同而采取不同的翻译方法，一般可以将其译成前置定语，独立成分，与先行词等融合在一起，甚至将其译成各种状语分句。

2. 状语从句翻译法

在复合句中状语从句通常由连词或起连词作用的词引导，用来修饰主句中的动词、形容词或副词。对于状语从句的翻译，一般情况下按正常语序翻译。如

（1）Although signals can be represented in many ways, in all cases the information in a signal is contained in a pattern of variations of some form.

虽然信号可以用多种方式来表示，但在所有情况下，信号所携带的信息总是被包含在某种变化的波形中。（由 although 引导的让步状语从句）

（2）If the hi-fi system has tone controls, we can change the tonal quality of the reproduced signal.

如果高保真的系统具有音调控制功能的话，那么我们就可以改变被录制信号的音调质量。（由 if 引导的条件状语从句）

（3）The flashing strobe acts as a sampling system, since it illuminates the disc for extremely brief time intervals at a periodic rate.

闪光灯可作为一个抽样系统，因为它以某一周期律在一个极短的时间间隔内照亮圆盘。（由 since 引导的原因状语从句）

（4）When the strobe frequency becomes less than twice the rotational frequency of the disc, the rotation appears to be at a lower frequency than is actually the case.

当闪光灯的闪烁频率小于圆盘旋转速度的两倍时，这时圆盘的旋转速度看起来要比真正的旋转速度慢。（由 when 引导的时间状语从句）

（5）I could understand his point of view, in that I'd been in a similar position.

我能理解他的观点，因为我也有过类似的处境。（In that = because）

（6）For all that he seems so bad-tempered, I still think he has a very kind nature.

尽管他好像脾气很坏，我仍然认为他心地善良。（for all that 引导让步状语从句，翻译

为"尽管……","虽然……")

（7）Electricity is such an important energy that modern industry couldn't develop without it.

电是一种非常重要的能量，没有它，现代化工业就不能发展。（由 such…that…引导的结果状语从句，译为汉语的并列句）

3．主语从句翻译法

（1）"主-谓-宾"结构：以 what, how, whether, that, where, when 引导的主语从句，可以译成"主-谓-宾"结构，从句本身做句子的主语，其余部分按原文顺序译出。如

① What someone chooses to observe and the way one observes it must, after all, in part be a reflection of experience and of ideas as to what is significant.

某人选择观察的事物和他观察事物的方式在某种程度上终归反映这个人的经历和他关于重大的事件的看法。（what 引导的主语从句，翻译成名词"……的事（情）"）

② When we will begin to work has not been decided yet.

什么时候开始工作还没决定呢。（when 引的主语从句，直接翻译成"……时候"）

（2）分译法：把原来的主语从句从整体结构中分离出来，译成另一个相对独立的单句。如

① It has been rightly stated that this situation is a threat to international security.

这个局势对国际安全是个威胁，这样的说法是完全正确的。（It 是形式主语，that this situation is a threat to international security 是真正的主语）

② It is my duty that I must teach English well.

我必须教好英语，这是我的职责。

4．表语从句翻译法

大部分情况下可以采用顺译法，间或也可以用逆译法。如

（1）That was how they were defeated.

他们就是这样给打败的。（顺译法）

（2）His view of the press was that the reporters were either for him or against him.

他对新闻界的看法是，记者们不是支持他，就是反对他。（顺译法）

（3）Water and food is what the people in the area badly need.

该地区的人们最需要的是水和食品。（逆译法）

5．宾语从句翻译法

翻译宾语从句时一般按原句的顺序即可。当句中有 it 作形式宾语时，it 一般省略不译。如

（1）Lagrange argued that trigonometric series were of very limited use.

拉格伦日认为三角级数的应用是非常有限的。

（2）I don't believe he has seen the film.

我相信他没看过这部电影。

（3）Scientists have reason to think that a man can put up with far more radiation than 0.1 rem without being damaged.

科学家们有理由认为，人可以忍受远超过 0.1 雷姆的辐射而不受伤害。

（4）I took it for granted that he would sign the document.

我认为他当然会在文件上签字。

6．同位语从句翻译法

同位语从句是用来进一步说明从句前面一个名词的具体内容。常见的带同位语从句的名词有：fact, news, promise, truth, belief, idea, answer, information, knowledge, doubt, hope, law, opinion, plan, suggestion, question 等，同位语从句较短小时，翻译时可考虑将其前置；如果较长，则可考虑后置。如

（1）The question whether we need it has not yet been considered.

我们是否需要它，这个问题还没有考虑。（从句前置）

（2）This is a universally accepted principle of international law that the territory sovereignty does not admit of infringement.

一个国家的领土不容侵犯，这是国际法中人尽皆知的准则。（从句前置）

（3）In this case, the sampling process corresponds to the fact that moving pictures are a sequence of individual frames with a rate (usually between 18 and 24 frames per second) corresponding to the sampling frequency.

在这种情况下，抽样过程就相当于：活动图像是一串单个的画面，帧频（通常每秒 18 到 24 帧）相当于抽样频率。（顺译法）

（4）For convenience, we use digital signals and discrete-time signals interchangeably with the understanding that all discrete-time signals must be transformed into digital signals in implementation and all digital signals are considered as discrete-time signals in analysis and design.

为了方便起见，我们根据以下理解交替使用数字信号和离散时间信号，即在实现过程中，将所有的离散时间信号转化为数字信号来处理，在分析和设计过程中，将数字信号视作离散信号来处理。（顺译法）

（5）His criticism was based on his own belief that it was impossible to represent signals with corners using trigonometric series.

他批评的论据是基于自己的信念，即不可能用三角函数级数来表示具有间断点的信号。

UNIT 10

A. Text

Mathematical Representation of Systems

Physical systems in the broadest sense are an interconnection of components, devices, or subsystems. In contexts ranging from signal processing and communications to electromechanical motors, automotive vehicles, and chemical-processing plants, a system can be viewed as a process in which input signals are transformed by the system or cause the system to respond in some way, resulting in other signals as outputs[1]. For example, a high fidelity system takes a recorded audio signal and generates a reproduction of that signal[2]. If the hi-fi system has tone controls, we can change the tonal quality of the reproduced signal. Similarly, the circuit can be viewed as a system with input voltage $x(t)$ and output voltage $v(t)$, while the automobile can be thought of as a system with input equal to the force $f(t)$ and output equal to the velocity $v(t)$ of the vehicle. An image-enhancement system transforms an input image into an output image that has some desired properties, such as improved contrast[3].

A continuous-time system is a system in which continuous-time input signals are applied and result in continuous-time output signals. Such a system will be represented pictorially as in Fig. 3-4(a), where $x(t)$ is the input and $y(t)$ is the output. Alternatively, we will often represent the input-output relation of a continuous-time system by the notation

$$x(t) \rightarrow y(t)$$

Similarly, a discrete-time system—that is, a system that transforms discrete-time inputs into discrete-time outputs—will be depicted as in Fig.3-4(b) and will sometimes be represented symbolically as

$$x[n] \rightarrow y[n]$$

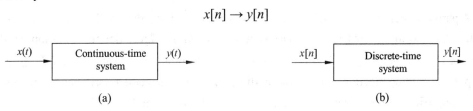

Fig. 3-4　(a) Continuous-time system; (b) Discrete-time system.

Many real systems are built as interconnections of several subsystems. By viewing such a system as an interconnection of its components, we can use our understanding of the component systems and of how they are interconnected in order to analyze the operation and behavior of the overall system. In addition, by describing a system in terms of an interconnection of simpler subsystems, we may in fact be able to define useful ways in which to synthesize complex systems out of simpler, basic building blocks.

While one can construct a variety of system interconnections, there are several basic ones that are frequently encountered. A series or cascade interconnection of two systems is illustrated in Fig. 3-5(a). Diagrams such as this are referred to as block diagrams. Here, the output of System 1 is the input to System 2, and the overall system transforms an input by processing it first by System 1 and then by System 2[4]. An example of a series interconnection is a radio receiver followed by an amplifier. Similarly, one can define a series interconnection of three or more systems.

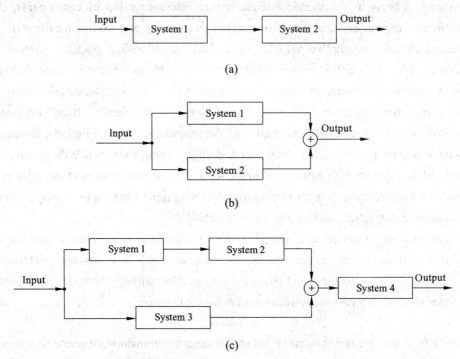

Fig. 3-5 Interconnection of two systems: (a) series (cascade) interconnection; (b) parallel interconnection; (c) series-parallel interconnection.

A parallel interconnection of two systems is illustrated in Fig. 3-5 (b). Here, the same input signal is applied to systems 1 and 2. The symbol "⊕" in the figure denotes addition, so that the output of the parallel interconnection is the sum of the outputs of Systems 1 and 2. An example of a parallel interconnection is a simple audio system with several microphones feeding into a single amplifier and speaker system. In addition to the simple parallel interconnection in Fig.3-5(b), we can define parallel interconnections of more than two systems, and we can combine both cascade and parallel interconnections to obtain more complicated interconnections[5]. An example of such an interconnection is given in Fig. 3-5(c).

Another important type of system interconnection is a feedback interconnection, an example of which is illustrated in Fig. 3-6. Here, the output of system 1 is the input to system 2, while the output of system 2 is fed back and added to the external input to produce the actual input to System 1[6]. Feedback systems arise in a wide variety of applications. For example, a cruise control system on an automobile senses sense the vehicle's velocity and adjusts the fuel flow in order to keep the speed at the desired level.

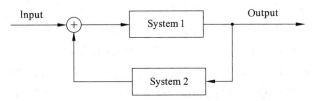

Fig. 3-6 Feedback interconnection.

New words and Technical Terms

interconnection	[ˌintə(ː)kəˈnekʃən]	n. 互相连接
fidelity	[fiˈdeliti]	n. 保真度，重现精度
reproduction	[ˌriːprəˈdʌkʃne]	n. 繁殖，再现，复制品
tone	[təun]	n. 音调，音质，语调
velocity	[viˈlɔsiti]	n. 速度，速率
pictorially	[pikˈtɔːriəli]	adv. 用图示，绘画般地
notation	[nəuˈteiʃən]	n. 符号
depict	[diˈpikt]	vt. 描述，描写
parallel	[ˈpærəlel]	adj. 平行的，并联的
audio	[ˈɔːdiəu]	adj. 音频的，声频的，声音的
cascade	[kæsˈkeid]	n. 小瀑布，[电学]串级
receiver	[riˈsiːvə]	n. 接受者，接收器，收信机
amplifier	[ˈæmpliˌfaiə]	n. 扩音器，放大器
feedback	[ˈfiːdbæk]	n. 回授，反馈
cruise	[kruːz]	n. 巡游，巡航
Fidelity	[fiˈdeliti]	n. 忠实，诚实，忠诚，保真度
hi-fi(High-Fidelity)		n. 高保真
ranging from…to…		从……到……
be viewed as		看作，视为
result in		导致，引起，产生
transform…into…		变换，转化
feed into		输入
in addition to		除……之外
feed back		反馈，反作用

Notes

[1] In contexts ranging from signal processing and communications to electromechanical motors, automotive vehicles, and chemical-processing plants, a system can be viewed as a

process in which input signals are transformed by the system or cause the system to respond in some way, resulting in other signals as outputs.

从信号处理、通信到电机马达、机动车和化学处理设备，一个系统可看作输入信号的变换器或对输入信号做出某种响应而产生出另外的输出信号。

ranging from…to…现在分词短语作定语，修饰 contexts，context 在文中可译为：场合，背景。in which 引导定语从句，修饰 process。

[2] For example, a high fidelity system takes a recorded audio signal and generates a reproduction of that signal.

例如，一个高保真度的系统对输入音频信号进行录制，并重现原输入信号。

过去分词 recorded 作定语，表示被动，修饰 audio signal。

[3] An image-enhancement system transforms an input image into an output image that has some desired properties, such as improved contrast.

某个图像增强系统可把一副输入图像转化成为具有某些所需性质的输出图像，如增强图像对比度。

that…引导的定语从句修饰 output image, such as 引导的短语说明 properties 的部分内容。 an image-enhancement system 作主语，transforms…into…作谓语。

[4] Here, the output of System 1 is the input to System 2, and the overall system transforms an input by processing it first by System 1 and then by System 2.

这里系统 1 的输出是系统 2 的输入，整个系统首先按系统 1，然后按系统 2 来变换输入。

and 引导的一个并列句，by processing…引导的短语作状语，修饰谓语动词 transform，其中 it 指的是 input。

[5] In addition to the simple parallel interconnection in Fig. 10-2 (b), we can define parallel interconnections of more than two systems, and we can combine both cascade and parallel interconnections to obtain more complicated interconnections.

除了图 10-2 (b)所示的简单的并联结构外，系统的并联可以是两个以上的系统的连接，我们还可以将级联与并联结合在一起得到一种更为复杂的系统。

in addition to…引导的短语作状语，…and…引导的是一个并列句；to obtain…不定式短语作目的状语，修饰谓语动词 combine。

[6] Here, the output of System 1 is the input to System 2, while the output of System 2 is fed back and added to the external input to produce the actual input to System 1.

这里系统 1 的输出是系统 2 的输入，而系统 2 的输出反馈回来与外加的输入信号相加，一起组成系统 1 的实际输入。

本句是由表转折的并列连词 while 引导的一个并列句，to produce…不定式短语作目的状语。

Exercises

Ⅰ. Please answer the following questions according to text.

1. What is the definition of the system?

2. How to represent continuous-time systems and discrete-time systems symbolically?

3. What are basic system interconnections?

II. Please write vocabulary according to corresponding description.

Description	Vocabulary
A group of interacting, interrelated, or interdependent elements forming a complex whole	
The degree to which an electronic system accurately reproduces the sound or image of its input signal	
Something put into a system or expended in its operation to achieve output or a result	
A series of components or networks, the output of each of which serves as the input for the next	
A device, such as a part of a radio, television set, or telephone, that receives incoming radio signals and converts them to perceptible forms, such as sound or light	
A device, especially one using transistors or electron tubes, that produces amplification of an electrical signal	
The return of a portion of the output of a process or system to the input, especially when used to maintain performance or to control a system or process	
Something reproduced, especially in the faithfulness of its resemblance to the form and elements of the original	
The quality or character of sound	
To represent in a picture or words	

B. Reading

Comparison of Digital and Analog Techniques

Digital techniques have become increasingly popular and have replaced, in many applications, analog techniques. We discuss some of the reasons in the following.

1. Digital techniques are less susceptible to noise and disturbance. In the transmission and processing of analog signals, any noise or disturbance will affect the signals. Digital signals are coded in 1 and 0, which are represented by ranges of voltages; therefore, small noise disturbance, or perturbation in power supply may not affect the representation. Thus digital techniques are less susceptible to noise and disturbance. This reliability can further be improved by using

error-detecting and error-correcting codes. For example, the transmission of the pictures of the Mars, is taken by a spacecraft, to the ground station on the earth. After traveling over 200×10^6 kilometers, the received signal has a power level in the order of 10^{-18} watts. If the signal is transmitted by analog techniques, the received signal will be severely corrupted by noise and it is not possible to reconstruct the pictures. However, the pictures of the Mars have been transmitted successfully to Earth by using digital techniques.

2. The precision in digital techniques is much higher than that in analog techniques. In analog display, the accuracy of the reading is often limited. Generally, we can achieve only an accuracy of 1% of the full scale. In digital display, the accuracy can be increased simply by increasing the number of bits used. In analog systems, it is difficult or very expensive to have a number of components with identical value. For example, if we buy ten 1kΩ resistor, probably the resistances of the ten resistors will be all different and none exactly equals 1kΩ. Even simple analog voltmeters require constant resetting in their use. Digital systems have no such problem; they can always be exactly reproduced.

3. The storage of digital signals is easier than that of analog signals. Digital signals can be easily stored in shift registers, memory chips, floppy disks, or compact discs for as long as needed without loss of accuracy. These data can be retrieved for use in a few microseconds. This easy storage and rapid access is an important feature of digital techniques. The only convenient way to store analog signals is to tape or film them. Their retrieval is not as convenient and fast as in digital techniques.

4. Digital techniques are more flexible and versatile than analog techniques. In digital display, digital signals can easily be frozen, expanded, or manipulated. A digital system can be easily altered by resetting its parameters. To change an analog system, we must physically replace its components. Using time multiplexing, a digital system can be used to process a number of digital signals: for example, if the sampling period of a digital signal is 0.05 s and if the processing of the signal requires only 0.005 s. Then the digital system will be free in the next 0.045 s and can be used to process other signals. Another example of this type of arrangement is the digital transmission of human voices. On a telephone line, the voice is sampled 8000 times per second; each sample is coded by using eight bits. Thus the transmission of one channel of voices requires the transmission of 64 000 or 64K bits per second. The existing telephone line can transmit 1544K bits per second. Therefore, a single telephone line can be used to transmit 24 voice-band channels. If we use fiber optics, then the number of channels is even larger.

Digital techniques have been advancing rapidly in recent years and have found many applications in almost every field of technology.

The human voice can be transmitted digitally as shown in Fig. 3-7. The voice is sampled and coded by a series of 8-bit words. After transmission, the digital signal is converted back to analog signal by using a D/A convert. This type of transmission is much less sensitive to cross talk, distortion, and noise than direct transmission. Furthermore the faded signal can be readily amplified without any distortion. Digital techniques can also be used to increase the capacity of speech transmission. By analyzing the frequency spectrum of speech, it is possible to extract key features of the speech. At the receiving end, we use these features to synthesize a voice that resembles the original one. Thus the capacity of the transmission can be increased. Digital processing is also useful in speech recognition and in vocal communication between men and computers.

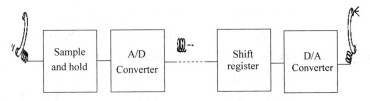

Fig. 3-7 Digital voice communications.

Once music or a picture is transformed and stored in digital form, it is possible to carry out many manipulations. For example, the waveform in Fig. 3-8 (a) is a section of sound track that contains two clicks and dropout due to faulty recording. It is possible to remove the clicks and reconstruct the missing sound as shown in the lower waveform in Fig. 3-8 (b). Once a picture is stored digitally, it can be easily enlarged, enhanced, or sharpened. It is also possible to remove a divorced husband from a family portrait. These techniques are now available commercially.

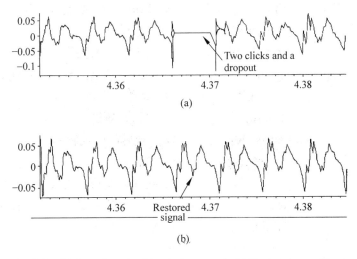

Fig. 3-8 (a) Sound track with missing sound; (b) Restored sound track.

Personal computers are now widely available; so is computer software. This fact speeds considerably the spreading of digital techniques.

From the preceding discussion, it is not surprising to see the avalanche of digital techniques. In many applications digital techniques have almost completely replaced analog techniques such as in analog oscilloscopes and analog computers.

New words and Technical Terms

digital   ['didʒitl]   adj. 数字的 n. 数字

analog	[ˈænəlɔg]	n. 模拟
replace	[ri(:)ˈpleis]	vt. 取代，替换，代替
transmission	[trænzˈmiʃən]	n. 发射，传送，传输
perturbation	[ˌpəːtəːˈbeiʃən]	n. 扰乱，混乱
reliability	[riˌlaiəˈbiliti]	n. 可靠性
corrupt	[kəˈrʌpt]	vt. 破坏，腐蚀，使恶化
reconstruct	[ˈriːkənˈstrʌkt]	v. 重建，改造
precision	[priˈsiʒən]	n. 精确，精密度，精度
accuracy	[ˈækjurəsi]	n. 正确性，准确（度）；精确性，精度
identical	[aiˈdentikəl]	adj. 同一的，完全相同的，丝毫不差的
voltmeter	[ˈvəultˌmiːtə]	n. 伏特计，电压表
reproduce	[ˌriːprəˈdjuːs]	v. 繁殖，再生，复制
storage	[ˈstɔridʒ]	n. 贮藏库，存储
register	[ˈredʒistə]	n. 寄存器
retrieve	[riˈtriːv]	v. 重新得到，恢复
tape	[teip, tep]	vt. 录音 n. 带子，录音带，磁带
film	[film]	vt. 拍成电影 n. 胶卷，影片
convenient	[kənˈviːnjənt]	adj. 便利的，方便的
manipulate	[məˈnipjuleit]	v. （熟练地）操作，巧妙地处理
multiplex	[ˈmʌltipleks]	v. 多路（转接，复用，传输）n. 多重通道
sample	[ˈsæmpl]	vt. 取样，采样
channel	[ˈtʃænl]	n. 信道，频道
sensitive	[ˈsensitiv]	adj. 敏感的，灵敏的，感光的
cross talk	[ˈkrɔstɔːk]	n. 串话
distortion	[distortion]	n. 扭曲，变形，失真
fade	[feid]	v. （声音等）减弱下去，褪色，消失
synthesize	[ˈsinθisaiz]	v. 综合，合成
recognition	[ˌrekəgˈniʃən]	n. 识别
track	[træk]	n. 轨迹，跟踪，途径
click	[klik]	n. 滴答声
sharpen	[ˈʃɑːpən]	v. 削尖，磨快，尖锐
avalanche	[ˈævəˌlɑːnʃ]	n. 雪崩
oscilloscope	[ɔˈsiləskəup]	n. 示波器

Exercises

I. Please answer the following questions according to text.

1. Which features do digital techniques have compared with analog techniques?

2. Why are digital techniques less susceptible to noise and disturbance?

3. Is it easy to have a number of components with identical value in analog system?

4. How are digital signals and analog signals stored?

Ⅱ. Please translate the following text into Chinese.

On a telephone line, the voice is sampled 8000 times per second; each sample is coded by using eight bits. Thus the transmission of one channel of voices requires the transmission of 64,000 or 64K bits per second. The existing telephone line can transmit 1544K bits per second. Therefore, a single telephone line can be used to transmit 24 voice-band channels. If we use fiber optics, then the number of channels is even larger.

C. 被动句的翻译

被动语态被广泛使用于英语中，当着重指出动作的承受者或不必说明谁是动作的执行者时，就用被动语态。尤其是在科技英语中，被动语态用得相当多，常把事物的名称作为主语放在突出的位置上，用被动语态表述有关的动作或状态。而在汉语中被动句却不如英语中使用得频繁。因此，在翻译有关科技英语文章时，英语的被动语态一般都被译成汉语的主动句式，只有在特别强调被动动作或特别突出被动者时才译成汉语被动句式或无主句。很多被动的动作往往借助于主动语态或具有被动意义的单词来表达。英语被动句译为汉语主动句时，主语可以是原句的主语，可以是 by 后面的名词或代词，也可以是原句中隐藏的动作执行者。被动语态的译法主要有以下几种形式。

1. 译成汉语被动句

英译汉时，汉语也有用被动形式来表达的情况。这时通常看重被动的动作。在把英语被动句译成汉语被动句时，常常使用"被"、"受到"、"遭到"、"得到"、"让"、"给"、"把"、"使"、"由"等措词。如

（1）The process is similar to that performed at the transmit end, and the carriers are suppressed within the balanced modulation.

此项过程与发送端所进行的相类似，载波被压制在平衡调制器内。

（2）If the signal is transmitted by analog techniques, the received signal will be severely corrupted by noise.

如果用模拟技术进行信号传输，那么接收到的信号将要受到噪声的严重破坏。

（3）Despite their countless capabilities the miracle chips must be programmed by human beings.

尽管这些神奇的集成线路中有数不清的性能，但还需要由人为它们编制程序。

（4）His many contributions—in particular, those concerned with the series and transform that carry his name—are made even more impressive by the circumstances under which he worked.

他当时进行研究所处的境遇使他的许多贡献（特别是以他的名字命名的级数和变换）给人留下了极深的印象。

2. 译成汉语主动

直接将原文的被动语态按照主动语态译成汉语的主动句。这类句子有的是英语中形式上是被动句，但意义上是主动的句子；有的则是英语从习惯来说要用被动语态来表达，而汉语习惯于用主动语态来表达的句子。如

（1）The machine will be repaired tomorrow.

这台机器明天修理。（不必译作：这台机器明天被修理。）

（2）The experiment will be finished in a month.

这项实验将在一个月后完成。（不必译作：这项实验将在一个月后被完成。）

（3）Using time multiplexing, a digital system can be used to process a number of digital signals.

利用时分复用技术，一个数字系统能处理多路数字信号。

（4）A signal is called a digital signal if its time is discretized and its amplitude is quantized.

时间上离散，幅值上量化的信号称为数字信号。

（5）Signals are presented mathematically as functions of one or more independent variables.

在数学上，信号可以表示为一个或多个变量的函数。

（6）A monochromatic picture can be presented by brightness as a function of two spatial variables.

一张黑白照片可以表示为亮度随二维空间变量变化的函数。

（7）This reliability can further be improved by using error-detecting and error-correcting codes.

利用检错和纠错编码能进一步提高可靠性。

（8）This organ is situated at the base of the brain.

该器官位于脑底。

（9）Digital signals can be easily stored in shift registers, memory chips, floppy disks, or compact discs without loss of accuracy.

数字信号可以在不损失精度的情况下非常容易地存储到移位寄存器、存储器、软盘或硬盘中。

（10）It is well-known that paper was first made in China.

众所周知，纸最初是在中国发明的。

在 it is (has been) +…+ that. 句型中，it 引导的被动语态常有固定的用法。

It is assumed that：人们认为

It is said that：据说

It is learned that：据闻

It is supposed that：据推测

It is considered that：据估计

It is believed that：人们认为

It is reported that：据报道

It is well-known that：众所周知

It is asserted that：有人断言

It can't be denied that：不可否认

It must be admitted that：必须承认

It must be pointed that：必须指出

3．译成汉语的加强语句

当英语被动句不是强调被动的动作，而只是强调或肯定某一事实或行为的存在时，通常可用"是……的"或"为所"等句式来翻译此类句子。如

（1）These computers were made in Xinhua Company.

这些电子计算机是新华公司制造的。

（2）The project was completed last year.

这个项目是去年完成的。

（3）The cakes which have just been cooked are made of corn.

刚做好的蛋糕是玉米做的。

4．译成汉语的无主句

在科技英语中，在讲述什么事情时往往是强调如何去做，而不介意谁去做。对于这一类被动句的翻译，我们可以译为汉语无主句，如

（1）Now the heart can be safely opened and its valves repaired.

现在可以安全地打开心脏，并对心脏瓣膜进行修复。

（2）This instrument must be handled with great care.

必须仔细操作这台仪器。

总之，在翻译英语被动语态语句时，不能固守原句，要灵活地采用多种翻译技巧，使译文既在内容上忠实于原文，又符合汉语的表达方式。

UNIT 11

A. Text

Fourier Transforms and Frequency-Domain Description

Signals encountered in practice are mostly continuous-time signals and can be denoted as $x(t)$, where t is a continuum[1]. Although some signals such as stock markets, savings account, and inventory are inherently discrete time, most discrete-time signals are obtained from continuous-time signals by sampling and can be denoted as $x[n]:=x(nT)$, where T is sampling period and n is the time index and can assume only integers. Both $x(t)$ and $x[n]$ are functions of time and are called the time-domain description. In signal analysis, we study frequency contents of signals. In order to do so, we must develop a different but equivalent description, called the frequency-domain description[2]. From the description, we can more easily determine the distribution of power in frequencies.

In digital processing of a continuous-time signal $x(t)$, the first step is to select a sampling period T and then to sample $x(t)$ to yield $x(nT)$. It is clear that the smaller T is, the closer $x(nT)$ is to $x(t)$. However, a smaller T also requires more computation. Thus an important task in DSP is to find the largest possible T so that all information (if not possible, all essential information) of $x(t)$ is retained in $x(nT)$. Without the frequency-domain description, it is not possible to find such a sampling period. Thus computing the frequency content of signals is a first step in digital signal processing.

The frequency-domain description is developed from the Fourier transform. If the Fourier transform of a signal is defined, the transform is called the frequency spectrum of the signal, that is

$$\text{Fourier transform} \leftrightarrow \text{frequency spectrum}$$

The continuous-time Fourier transform is defined by the following pair of equations:
Forward Continuous-Time Fourier Transform

$$X(j\omega) = \int_{-\infty}^{\infty} x(t) e^{-j\omega t} dt \tag{3-1}$$

and Inverse Continuous-Time Fourier Transform

$$x(t) = \frac{1}{2\pi} \int_{-\infty}^{\infty} X(j\omega) e^{j\omega t} d\omega \tag{3-2}$$

Equation (3-1) and (3-2) are referred to as the Fourier transform pair, with the function $X(j\omega)$ referred to as the Fourier Transform or Fourier integral of $x(t)$ and eq. (3-2) as the inverse Fourier Transform equation[3]. $X(j\omega)$ is commonly referred to as the frequency-domain representation or the spectrum of the signal, as it provides us with the information needed for describing $x(t)$ as a linear combination (specifically, an integral) of sinusoidal signals at different frequencies[4]. Likewise, $x(t)$ is the time-domain representation of the signal. We indicate this relationship between the two domains as

$$\text{Time-Domain} \qquad \text{Frequency-Domain}$$
$$x(t) \xrightleftharpoons{F} X(j\omega)$$

The notation F signifies that it is possible to go back and forth uniquely between the time-domain and the frequency-domain.

If we are given $x(t)$ as a mathematical function, we can determine the corresponding spectrum function $X(j\omega)$ by evaluating the integral in (3-1). In other words, (3-1) defines a mathematical operation for transforming $x(t)$ into a new equivalent representation $X(j\omega)$. It is common to say that we take the Fourier transform of $x(t)$, meaning that we determine $X(j\omega)$ so that we can use the frequency-domain representation of the signal[5].

Similarly, given $X(j\omega)$ as a mathematical function, we can determine the corresponding time function $x(t)$ using (3-2) by evaluating an integral[6]. Thus, (3-2) defines the inverse Fourier transform operation that goes from the frequency-domain to the time-domain.

Armed with the powerful tool of Fourier transform, we will be able to: (1) define a precise notion of bandwidth for a signal, (2) explain the inner workings of modern communication systems which are able to transmit many signals simultaneously by sharing the available bandwidth, and (3) define filtering operations that are needed to separate signals in such frequency-shared systems. There are many other applications of the Fourier transform, so it is safe to say that Fourier analysis provides the rigorous language needed to define and design modern engineering systems.

New words and Technical Terms

inventory	[ˈinvəntri]	n. 详细目录，存货，总量
inherently	[inˈhiərəntli]	adv. 天性地，固有地
equivalent	[iˈkwivələnt]	adj. 相等的，相当的
continuum	[kənˈtinjuəm]	n. 连续统一体，连续区
spectrum	[ˈspektrəm]	n. 光谱，频谱
sample	[ˈsæmpl]	vt. 取样，采样
inverse	[inˈvəːs]	adj. 倒转的，反转的
likewise	[ˈlaikˌwaiz]	adv. 同样地，照样地
indicate	[ˈindikeit]	vt. 指出，显示，简要地说明
sinusoidal	[ˌsainəˈsɔidəl]	adj. 正弦曲线的
signify	[ˈsignifai]	v. 表示，意味
evaluate	[iˈvæljueit]	vt. 评价，估计，求……的值
integral	[ˈintigrəl]	n. 积分
notion	[ˈnəuʃən]	n. 概念，观念，想法
bandwidth	[ˈbændwidθ]	n. 带宽

filter　　　　　　　['filtə]　　　　　　　　n. 滤波器
rigorous　　　　　['rigərəs]　　　　　　　adj. 严密的，精确的，严格的

Notes

[1] Signals encountered in practice are mostly continuous-time signals and can be denoted as $x(t)$, where t is a continuum.

实际遇到的信号大多是连续时间信号，这类信号可以用 $x(t)$ 表示，其中 t 是连续变量。

过去分词短语 encountered in practice 作定语，修饰主语 signals；where 引导定语从句，补充说明与 $x(t)$ 有关的信息。

[2] In order to do so, we must develop a different but equivalent description, called the frequency-domain description.

为了能做到这点，必须开发不同但等效的描述方法，称为频域描述法。

Called 过去分词引导的短语作定语，修饰 description。

[3] Equation (3-1) and (3-2) are referred to as the Fourier transform pair, with the function $X(j\omega)$ referred to as the Fourier Transform or Fourier integral of $x(t)$ and eq. (3-2) as the inverse Fourier Transform equation.

式（3-1）和式（3-2）称为傅里叶变换对，函数 $X(j\omega)$ 称为 $x(t)$ 的傅里叶变换或傅里叶积分，而式（3-2）称为傅里叶反变换。

Equation (3-1) and (3-2)作主语，谓语部分是 are referred to as（译为：称为），the Fourier transform pair 是宾语。with the function $X(j\omega)$ referred to as…这一部分在语法上属过去分词独立结构的用法。在这一独立结构中，the function $X(j\omega)$ 为逻辑主语，referred to as…为逻辑谓语，with 可以略去，保留后结构更为紧凑。在逻辑主语前加上介词 with 可以认为是分词独立结构中的一种特例。

[4] $X(j\omega)$ is commonly referred to as the frequency-domain representation or the spectrum of the signal, as it provides us with the information needed for describing $x(t)$ as a linear combination of sinusoidal signals at different frequencies.

$X(j\omega)$ 通常称为信号的频域表示或信号的频谱，因为 $X(j\omega)$ 告诉我们这样一个信息，就是 $x(t)$ 可以描述成不同频率正弦信号的线性组合。

As 引导原因状语从句，其中 needed for describing 短语作定语，修饰 information。

[5] It is common to say that we take the Fourier transform of $x(t)$, meaning that we determine $X(j\omega)$ so that we can use the frequency-domain representation of the signal.

通常说得到了 $x(t)$ 的傅里叶变换，就意味着确定了 $X(j\omega)$，这样我们就可以运用信号的频域表示方法。

这是一个含有多层从句的句子。首先是 that 引导的宾语从句，其次是 so that 引导的目的状语从句，meaning 后又是 that 引导的宾语从句，meaning that we determine $X(j\omega)$作伴随状语，修饰 we take the Fourier transform of $x(t)$。

[6] Similarly, given $X(j\omega)$ as a mathematical function, we can determine the corresponding time function $x(t)$ using (3-2) by evaluating an integral.

同样，已知函数 $X(j\omega)$，就可以利用式（3-2）通过计算积分值确定相应的时间函数 $x(t)$。

分词作状语时，可以表示时间、原因、条件、伴随状况等，相当于由 when/while, if, as 等引导的状语从句，若主语是动作执行者，则用 doing；若主语是被动的，则用 done。如句中 given $X(j\omega)$ as a mathematical function = if we are given $X(j\omega)$ as a mathematical function，相当于 if 引导的状语从句。using (3-2) by evaluating an integral = when we use (3-2) by evaluating an integral，相当于 when 引导的时间状语从句。该句中 given 的这种用法使用极为频繁，因而人们干脆将 given 视作介词或连词使用，如接从句，后面要用 that 引导。此时的介词（或连词）given 经常译成"如果有……；假定是……；考虑到……；设想到……"等。

Exercises

Ⅰ. Please answer the following questions according to text.

1. Please give the description of the continuous-time Fourier transform.

2. What are referred to as the time-domain representation and the frequency-domain representation of the signal?

3. How to transform $x(t)$ into a equivalent representation $X(j\omega)$?

4. There are many applications of the Fourier transform, please give some examples.

Ⅱ. Please write vocabulary according to corresponding description.

Description	Vocabulary
The number of repetitions per unit time of a complete waveform	
The numerical difference between the upper and lower frequencies of a band of electromagnetic radiation	
A continuous extent, succession, or whole, no part of which can be distinguished from neighboring parts except by arbitrary division	
To ascertain or fix the value or worth of	
Present and ready for use; at hand; accessible	
The rate at which work is done, expressed as the amount of work per unit time and commonly measured in units such as the watt and horsepower	
To send from one person, thing, or place to another	
The distribution of a characteristic of a physical system or phenomenon	
The act of combining or the state of being combined	
Any of various electric, electronic, acoustic, or optical devices used to reject signals, vibrations, or radiations of certain frequencies while passing others	

B. Reading

History of Fourier analysis

The development of Fourier analysis has a long history involving a great many individuals and the investigation of many different physical phenomena[1]. The concept of using "trigonometric sums"—that is, sums of harmonically related sine and cosine or periodic complex exponentials —to describe periodic phenomena goes back at least as far as the Babylonians, who used ideas of this type in order to predict astronomical events. The modern history of the subject begins in 1748 with L.Euler, who examined the motion of a vibrating string. In Fig. 3-9, we have indicated the first few of what are known as the "normal modes" of such a string. If we consider the vertical deflection $f(t, x)$ of the string at time t and at a distance x along the string, then for any fixed instant of time, the normal modes are harmonically related sinusoidal functions of x. What Eular noted was that if the configuration of a vibrating string at some point in time is a linear combination of these normal modes, so is the configuration at any subsequent time. Furthermore, Euler showed that one could calculate the coefficients for the linear combination at the later time in a very straightforward manner from the coefficients at the earlier time. In doing this, Euler performed the same type of calculation as we will see in deriving one of the properties of trigonometric sums that make them so useful for the analysis of LTI systems[2]. Specifically, we will see that if the input to an LTI system is expressed as a linear combination of periodic complex exponentials or sinusoids, the output can also be expressed in this form, with coefficients that are related in straightforward way to those of the input[3].

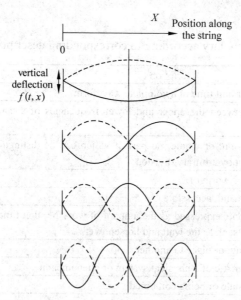

Fig. 3-9 Normal modes of a vibrating string.

The property described in the preceding paragraph would not be particularly useful, unless it were true that a large class of interesting functions could be represented by linear combinations of complex exponentials. In the middle of the 18th century, this point was the subject of heated debate. In 1753, D.Bernoulli argued on physical grounds that all physical motions of a string could be represented by linear combinations of normal modes, but he did not pursue this mathematically, and his ideas were not widely accepted. In fact, Euler himself discarded trigonometric series, and in 1759 J.L.Lagrange strongly criticized the use of trigonometric series in the examination of vibrating string. His criticism was based on his own belief that it was impossible to represent signals with corners (i.e., with discontinuous slopes) using trigonometric series[4]. Since such a configuration arises from the plucking of a string (i.e., pulling it taut and then releasing it), Lagrange argued that trigonometric series were of very limited use[5].

It was in this somewhat hostile and skeptical environment that Jean Baptiste Joseph Fourier presented his ideas half a century later. Fourier was born on March 21, 1768, in Auxerre, France, and by the time of his entrance into the controversy concerning trigonometric series, he had a lifetime of experiences. His many contributions—in particular, those concerned with the series and transform that carry his name—are made even more impressive by the circumstances under which he worked[6]. His revolutionary discoveries, although not completely appreciated during his own lifetime, have had a major impact on the development of mathematics and have been and still are of great importance in an extremely wide range of scientific and engineering disciplines[7].

The physical motivation for Fourier's work was the phenomenon of heat propagation and diffusion. By 1807, Fourier had found series of harmonically related sinusoids to be useful in representing the temperature distribution through a body. In addition, he claimed that "any" periodic signal could be represented by such a series. Fourier's mathematical arguments were still imprecise, and it remained for P.L.Dirichlet in 1829 to provide precise conditions under which a periodic signal could be represented by a Fourier series[8]. In addition, Fourier took this type of representation one very large step farther than any of his predecessors. He obtained a representation for aperiodic signals—not as weighted sums of harmonically related sinusoids—but as weighted integrals of sinusoids that are not all harmonically related. Like the Fourier series, the Fourier transform remains one of the most powerful tools for the analysis of LTI systems.

Four distinguished mathematicians and scientists were appointed to examine the 1807 paper of Fourier. Three of the four—S.F. Lacroix, G.Monge, and P.S. de Laplace—were in favor of publication of the paper, but the fourth, J.L.Lagrange, remained adamant in rejecting trigonometric series, as he had done 50 years earlier[9]. Because of Lagrange's vehement objections, Fourier's paper never appeared. After several other attempts to have his work accepted and published by the Institute de France, Fourier undertook the writing of another version of his work, which appeared as the text "The Analytical Theory of Heat". This book was published is 1822, 15 years after Fourier had first presented his results to the Institute.

Toward the end of his life Fourier received some of the recognition he deserved, but the most significant tribute to him has been the enormous impact of his work on so many disciplines within the fields of mathematics, science, and engineering[10].

New words and Technical Terms

individual	[ˌindiˈvidjuəl]	n. 个人，个体
trigonometric	[ˌtrigənəˈmetrik]	adj. 三角的，三角函数的
harmonical	[hɑːˈmɔnikəl]	adj. 调和的，音乐般的
sine	[sain]	n. 正弦
cosine	[ˈkəusain]	n. 余弦
exponential	[ˌekspəuˈnenʃəl]	adj. 指数的，幂数的
Babylonian	[ˌbæbiˈləunjən]	n. 巴比伦人
vibrate	[vaiˈbreit]	v. (使)振动，(使)摇摆
deflection	[diˈflekʃən]	n. 偏斜，偏转，偏差
configuration	[kənˌfigjuˈreiʃən]	n. 构造，结构，配置，外形
subsequent	[ˈsʌbsikwənt]	adj. 后来的，并发的
derive	[diˈraiv]	v. 得自，起源
discard	[disˈkɑːd]	v. 丢弃，抛弃，放弃
pluck	[plʌk]	v. 拔去，拨动
taut	[tɔːt]	adj. (绳子)拉紧的，紧张的
skeptical	[ˈskeptikəl]	adj. 怀疑性的，好怀疑的
controversy	[ˈkɔntrəvəːsi]	n. 论争，辩论，论战
motivation	[ˌməutiˈveiʃən]	n. 动机
propagation	[ˌprɔpəˈgeiʃən]	n. (声波，电磁辐射等)传播
diffusion	[diˈfjuːʒən]	n. 扩散，漫射
predecessor	[ˈpriːdisesə]	n. 前辈，前任
aperiodic	[ˌeipiəriˈɔdik]	adj. 非周期的
distinguished	[disˈtiŋgwiʃt]	adj. 卓著的，著名的，高贵的
adamant	[ˈædəmənt]	adj. 坚硬的
vehement	[ˈviːimənt]	adj. 激烈的，猛烈的
tribute	[ˈtribjuːt]	n. 礼物，颂词，称赞
normal modes		正常振荡模
trigonometric series		三角级数
in favor of		赞成
Auxerre		(地名) 奥克斯雷

Exercises

I. Please answer the following questions according to text.

1. What did the Babylonians use trigonometric sums to do?

2. What did Euler note in the examination of vibrating string?

3. What was the physical motivation for Fourier's work?

4. What carries Fourier's name in his many contributions?

5. Who provided precise conditions under which a periodic signal could be represented by a Fourier series?

6. Why did Fourier's paper never appear?

Ⅱ. Please translate the following text into Chinese.

The physical motivation for Fourier's work was the phenomenon of heat propagation and diffusion. This in itself was a significant step in that most previous research in mathematical physics had dealt with rational and celestial mechanics. By 1807, Fourier had completed a work, Fourier had found series of harmonically related sinusoids to be useful in representing the temperature distribution through a body. In addition, he claimed that "any" periodic signal could be represented by such a series. Fourier's mathematical arguments were still imprecise, and it remained for P.L.Dirichlet in 1829 to provide precise conditions under which a periodic signal could be represented by a Fourier series.

C. 长句的翻译

英语习惯于用长句表达比较复杂的概念，而汉语则不同，常常使用若干短句，并列表达思想。长句在科技英语文章中出现得极为频繁，一般来说，造成长句的原因有三方面：
（1）修饰语过多；
（2）并列成分多；
（3）语言结构层次多。

在翻译长句时，首先不要因为句子太长而产生畏惧心理，因为无论是多么复杂的句子，它都是由一些基本的成分组成的。其次要弄清英语原文的句法结构，找出整个句子的中心内容及其各层意思，然后分析几层意思之间的相互逻辑关系，再按照汉语的特点和表达方式，正确地译出原文的意思，不必拘泥于原文的形式。

分析长句的结构应考虑以下几个方面：

（1）找出全句的主语、谓语和宾语，从整体上把握句子的结构；

（2）找出句中从句的引导词，分析从句的功能。例如，是否为主语从句、宾语从句、表语从句等，若是状语，它是表示原因、结果，还是表示条件等；

（3）分析词、短语和从句之间的相互关系，例如，定语从句所修饰的先行词是哪一个等；

（4）注意插入语等其他成分；

（5）注意分析句子中是否有固定词组或固定搭配。

在翻译英语长句的时候，要特别注意英语和汉语之间的差异，长句要恰当地分成长度适中、合乎汉语习惯的句子。长句的翻译是难点也是重点，关键是首先找出句子的骨架，即主、谓、宾语，然后再将其他修饰成分嵌入框架。如果英文句子内容符合汉语规则，则可自前而后依序译出；如果句子内容顺序不符合汉语规则，可根据逻辑关系从后向前译出；如果不便用一句话表达，可将句子重新组织，按逻辑关系分成两个或数个短句。只要能完整准确地传达原意，即使没有拘泥于原文结构，也统一正确。下面通过几个例子加以说明。

（1）The concept of using "trigonometric sums"-that is, sums of harmonically related sine and cosine or periodic complex exponentials—to describe periodic phenomena goes back at least as far as the Babylonians, who used ideas of this type in order to predict astronomical events.

结构分析：弄清该句的句法结构是翻译此句的关键，根据句子结构和语意分析，这个句子可分成7段：主语（The concept…）+后置定语（of using…）+同位语（that is 之后引出的内容）+目的状语（to describe…）+谓语（goes back）+宾语（the Babylonians）+定语从句（who…）。首先找出该句的主句，即主谓宾，把握句子的中心内容，然后分析从句和短语的功能。根据汉语的表达习惯，译文的表达顺序与原文相同。

参考译文：利用"三角函数和"（即成谐波关系的正弦和余弦函数或周期复指数函数的和）的概念来描述周期性的现象至少可以追溯到古代巴比伦人时代，他们利用这一想法来预测天体的运动。

（2）If we consider the vertical deflection $f(t, x)$ of the string at time t and at a distance x along the string, then for any fixed instant of time, the normal modes are harmonically related sinusoidal functions of x.

结构分析：翻译此句的关键是必须清楚被修饰词与修饰短语之间的相互关系，把握细节。句中 at time t and at a distance x along the string 修饰 deflection $f(t, x)$，harmonically related 修饰 sinusoidal functions。

参考译文：如果用 $f(t, x)$ 来表示弦在时刻 t 和沿着弦的横向位移 x 处的垂直偏差，那么对于任意的固定时刻 t 来说，正常振荡模均为 x 的正弦函数，并成谐波关系。

（3）What Eular noted was that if the configuration of a vibrating string at some point in time is a linear combination of these normal modes, so is the configuration at any subsequent time.

结构分析：本句含有多个从句。句中 what 引导主语从句，that 引导表语从句，if 引导条件状语从句，嵌套在表语从句中。

参考译文：欧拉注意到，如果振动弦在某一时刻的形状是这些正常振荡模的线性组合，则在其后的任何时刻，振动弦的形状都是这些振荡模的线性组合。

（4）The property described in the preceding paragraph would not be particularly useful, unless it were true that a large class of interesting functions could be represented by linear combinations of complex exponentials.

结构分析：此句 unless 意为："如果不，除非"，根据汉语的表达习惯，译文的表达顺序与原文正好相反。

参考译文：除非很多有用信号都能用复指数函数的线性组合来表示，否则上面所讨论的性质就不是特别有用。

（5）He obtained a representation for aperiodic signals—not as weighted sums of harmonically related sinusoids—but as weighted integrals of sinusoids that are not all harmonically related.

结构分析：此句中的主要结构涉及 not…but…的固定表达，意为："不是……而是……"。

参考译文：他得到了关于非周期信号的表示，即不是成谐波关系的正弦信号的加权和，而是成并非全部谐波关系的正弦信号的加权积分。

（6）After several other attempts to have his work accepted and published by the Institute de France, Fourier undertook the writing of another version of his work, which appeared as the text "The Analytical Theory of Heat".

结构分析：根据句子结构和语意分析，这个句子可分成 4 段：状语（After…）+嵌套在状语中的后置定语（to have…）+主句（Fourier undertook…）+定语从句（which…）。从语意上讲，主句讲的是结果，从句说的是细节。根据汉语的表达习惯，译文的表达顺序与原文相同。

参考译文：为了使研究成果能被法兰西研究院接受并发表，在经过了几次其他的尝试之后，傅里叶把他的成果以另一种方式出现在《热的分析理论》这本书中。

（7）You have all heard it repeated that men of science work by means of induction and deduction, that by the help of these operations, they, in a sort of sense, manage to extract from Nature certain natural laws, and that out of these, by some special skill of their own, they build up their theories.

结构分析：如能看出此句所涉及的并列结构…that…，that…，and that…，即可以说解决了此句的关键疑难点。因此，遇到长句如能查看一下是否有并列结构很重要。

参考译文：人们常说过，科学家基于归纳法和演绎法工作，借助于这些方法，在某种意义上说，设法从自然界找出某些自然规律，然后根据这些规律，用他们自己特殊的技能逐步建立起自己的理论。

（8）Science moves forward, they say, not so much through the insights of great men of genius as because of more ordinary things like improved techniques and tools.

结构分析：此句中的主要结构涉及 not so much…as…的固定表达，意为："与其说……不如说……"。

参考译文：他们说，科学的发展与其说是借助伟大天才的真知灼见，不如说是由于改进了技术和工具等更为普通的事物。

UNIT 12

A. Text

The Sampling Theorem

Under certain conditions, a continuous-time signal can be completely represented by and recoverable from a sequence of its values, or samples, at points equally spaced in time[1]. This somewhat surprising property follows from a basic result that is referred to as the sampling theorem. This theorem is extremely important and useful. It is exploited, for example, in moving pictures, which consist of a sequence of individual frames, each of which represents an instantaneous view (i.e., a sample in time) of a continuously changing scene[2]. When these samples are viewed in sequence at a sufficiently fast rate, we perceive an accurate representation of the original continuously moving scene.

Much of the importance of the sampling theorem also lies in its role as a bridge between continuous-time signals and discrete-time signals. The fact that under certain conditions a continuous-time signal can be completely recovered from a sequence of its samples provides a mechanism for representing a continuous-time signal by a discrete-time signal[3]. In many contexts, processing discrete-time signals is more flexible and is often preferable to processing continuous-time signals[4]. This is due in large part to the dramatic development of digital technology over the past few decades, resulting in the availability of inexpensive, lightweight, programmable, and easily reproducible discrete-time system. We exploit sampling to convert a continuous-time signal to a discrete-time signal, process the discrete-time signal using a discrete-time system, and then convert back to continuous-time signal.

Sampling theorem can be stated as follows:

Let $x(t)$ be a band-limited signal with $X(j\omega) = 0$ for $|\omega| > \omega_m$. Then $x(t)$ is uniquely determined by its samples $x(nT)$, $n = 0, \pm1, \pm2, \cdots$, if

$$\omega_s > 2\omega_m$$

where

$$\omega_s = 2\pi/T$$

Given these samples, we can reconstruct $x(t)$ by generating a periodic impulse train in which successive impulses have amplitudes that are successive sample values. This impulse train is then processed through an ideal lowpass filter with gain T and cutoff frequency greater than ω_m and less than $\omega_s - \omega_m$. The resulting output signal will exactly equal $x(t)$ [5].

The frequency $2\omega_m$, which, under the sampling theorem, must be exceeded by the sampling frequency, is commonly referred to as the Nyquist rate.

In previous discussion, it was assumed that the sampling frequency was sufficiently high that the conditions of sampling theorem were met[6]. As illustrated in Fig.3-10, with $\omega_s > 2\omega_m$, the spectrum of the sampled signal consists of scaled replications of the spectrum of $x(t)$, and this forms the basis for the sampling theorem. When $\omega_s < 2\omega_m$, $X(j\omega)$, the spectrum of $x(t)$, is no longer replicated in $X_p(j\omega)$ and thus is no longer recoverable by lowpass filtering. The reconstructed signal will no longer be equal to $x(t)$. This effect is referred to as aliasing.

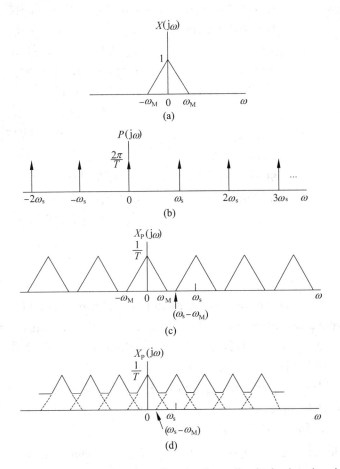

Fig.3-10 Effect in the frequency domain of sampling in the time domain.

(a) spectrum of original signal; (b) spectrum of sampling function; (c) spectrum of sampled signal with $\omega_s > 2\omega_m$; (d) spectrum of sampled signal with $\omega_s < 2\omega_m$.

Sampling has a number of important applications. One particularly significant set of applications relates to using sampling to process continuous-time signals with discrete-time systems, by means of minicomputers, microprocessors, or any of a variety of devices specifically oriented toward discrete-time signal processing.

New words and Technical Terms

theorem   [ˈθiərəm]   n. 定理，定律，法则

exploit	[iksˈplɔit]	vt. 开拓，开发，利用
sequence	[ˈsi:kwəns]	n. 次序，顺序，序列
frame	[freim]	n. 帧，画面，框架
instantaneous	[ˌinstənˈteinjəs]	adj. 瞬间的，即刻的，即时的
availability	[əˌveiləˈbiliti]	n. 可用性，有效性，实用性
programmable	[ˈprəugræməbl]	adj. 可设计的，可编程的
reproducible	[ˌri:prəˈdju:səbl]	adj. 能繁殖的，可再生的，可复写的
gain	[gein]	n. 增益，利润，收获
cutoff	[ˈkʌtɔ:f]	n. 截止，中止，切掉
replication	[ˌrepliˈkeiʃən]	n. 复制，重现
view	[vju:]	n. 景色，风景　vt. 观察，观看
perceive	[pəˈsi:v]	v. 感知，感到，认识到
mechanism	[ˈmekənizəm]	n. 作用过程，机理
spectrum	[ˈspektrəm]	n. 频谱，光谱
aliasing	[ˈeiliəsiŋ]	n. 混淆现象，混叠
Nyquist rate		n. 奈奎斯特抽样率

Notes

[1] Under certain conditions, a continuous-time signal can be completely represented by and recoverable from a sequence of its values, or samples, at points equally spaced in time.

在一定的条件下，一个连续时间信号完全可以由该信号在时间等间隔点上的瞬时值或样本值来表示，并且能用这些样本值恢复出原信号来。

本句中过去分词短语 equally spaced in time 作定语，修饰 points，译为：在时间上等分的点。can be completely represented by and recoverable from 这一结构中，and 与 recoverable 之间省略了 be 动词，翻译时可分开翻译。

[2] It is exploited, for example, in moving pictures, which consist of a sequence of individual frames each of which represents an instantaneous view (i.e., a sample in time) of a continuously changing scene.

例如，抽样定理在电影里得到了利用。电影由一组按时序排列的单个画面所组成，其中每一个画面都代表着连续变化景象中的一个瞬时画面（即时间样本）。

句中有两个定语从句，第一个 which 引导的定语从句修饰 moving pictures，第二个 which 引导的定语从句修饰 individual frames，这一定语从句嵌套在第一个定语从句之中。本句中的主语是 it，指前面提到的 sampling theorem，谓语是 is exploited，其余的作状语。

[3] The fact that under certain conditions a continuous-time signal can be completely recovered from a sequence of its samples provides a mechanism for representing a continuous-time signal by a discrete-time signal.

在一定的条件下，可以用信号的时序样本值完全恢复出原连续时间信号，这就提供了用一个离散时间信号来表示一个连续时间信号的机理。

本句中主语是 the fact，谓语是 provides，that 引导的同位语从句解释 fact 的内容。

[4] In many contexts, processing discrete-time signals is more flexible and is often preferable to processing continuous-time signals.

在许多方面，处理离散时间信号要更加灵活些，因此往往比处理连续时间更为可取。

句中 is preferable to 为固定搭配，意思是"比……更为可取"。

[5] Given these samples, we can reconstruct $x(t)$ by generating a periodic impulse train in which successive impulses have amplitudes that are successive sample values. This impulse train is then processed through an ideal lowpass filter with gain T and cutoff frequency greater than ω_m and less than $\omega_s - \omega_m$. The resulting output signal will exactly equal $x(t)$.

已知这些样本值，我们可以用以下方法重新构造 $x(t)$：产生一个周期的冲激串，其冲激的强度就是依次而来的样本值，然后将冲激串通过一个增益为 T，截止频率大于 ω_m，而小于 $\omega_s - \omega_m$ 的理想低通滤波器，该滤波器的输出就等于 $x(t)$。

by generating…作状语，修饰谓语动词 reconstruct，该状语中定语从句 in which…修饰 impulse train，该定语从句中又有一个定语从句 that are successive sample values，修饰 amplitudes。

[6] In previous discussion, it was assumed that the sampling frequency was sufficiently high that the conditions of sampling theorem were met.

在前面的讨论中，假设抽样频率足够高，因而满足抽样定理的条件。

句中 that the sampling frequency was sufficiently high 是 that 引导的主语从句，it 是形式主语。that the conditions of sampling theorem were met 中 that 相当于 so that，引导目的状语从句。

Exercises

Ⅰ. Please answer the following questions according to text.

1. How is the sampling theorem exploited in moving picture?

2. Why does the sampling theorem lie in its role as a bridge between continuous-time signals and discrete-time signals?

3. Please state the sampling theorem and tell what is the Nyquist rate.

4. What is the spectrum of the sampled signal when $\omega_s > 2\omega_m$ and when $\omega_s < 2\omega_m$, where ω_s is sampling frequency and ω_m is bandwidth of original signal?

Ⅱ. Please translate the following text into Chinese.

英 文 解 释	词 汇
the process of reading the value of a signal at evenly spaced points in time	
the degree to which a system or resource is ready when needed to process data	
an increase in signal power, voltage, or current by an amplifier, expressed as the ratio of output to input	
a designated limit or point of termination	
the act or process of duplicating or reproducing something	
with a function that can be established or changed by means of a program	

Ⅲ. Please translate the following text into Chinese.

The circuit consists of a transistor switch, a capacitor with a large capacitance, and two voltage followers. The voltage followers are used to shield the capacitor to eliminate the loading problem. The switch is controlled by control logic. When the switch is open, the capacitor voltage remains roughly constant. Thus the output of the sampled-and-hold circuit is stepwise. Using this circuit, the problem due to the conversion time can be eliminated. Therefore, a sample-and-hold circuit is often used, either internally or externally, with an A/D converter.

B. Reading

A/D and D/A Conversions

In many applications, there is a significant advantage offered in processing an analog signal by first converting it to a digital signal and, after digital signal processing, converting back to an analog signal. The digital signal processing can be implemented with a general—or special-purpose computer, with microprocessors, or with any of the variety of devices that are specifically oriented toward digital signal processing. The theoretical basis for converting an analog signal to a digital signal and reconstructing an analog signal from digital signal lies in the sampling theorem. This section discusses how these convertions are carried out.

We discuss first the digital-to-analog (D/A) converter, or DAC. Fig.3-11 shows the basic structure of a 4-bit D/A converter. It consists of 4 latches, 4 transistor switches, a number of precision resistors, an operational amplifier, and a precision voltage reference. The 4-bit input denoted by $\{x_1\ x_2\ x_3\ x_4\}$, latched in the register, controls the closing or opening of the switches. The switch is closed if $x_i=1$, open if $x_i=0$. The input remains unchanged until the next string of x_i arrives. The signal v_0 in Fig. 3-12 denotes the output voltage of the operational amplifier. Because the current and voltage at the inverting terminal are zero as shown, we have

$$i_f = \frac{v_0}{R} \qquad i_1 = \frac{x_1 E}{2R} \qquad i_2 = \frac{x_2 E}{4R} \qquad i_3 = \frac{x_3 E}{8R} \qquad i_4 = \frac{x_4 E}{16R}$$

And

$$i_f = i_1 + i_2 + i_3 + i_4$$

Thus we have

$$v_0 = R\left(\frac{x_1 E}{2R} + \frac{x_2 E}{4R} + \frac{x_3 E}{8R} + \frac{x_4 E}{16R}\right) = (2^{-1}x_1 + 2^{-2}x_2 + 2^{-3}x_3 + 2^{-4}x_4)E$$

For example, if $X_1 X_2 X_3 X_4 = 1011$ and $E=10$, then

$$v_0 = (1\times 2^{-1} + 0\times 2^{-2} + 1\times 2^{-3} + 1\times 2^{-4})\times 10 = (0.5 + 0.125 + 0.0625)\times 10 = 6.875$$

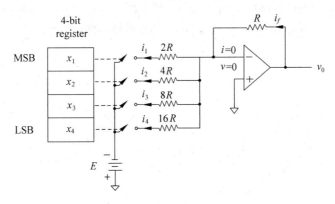

Fig.3-11   4-bit D/A converter.

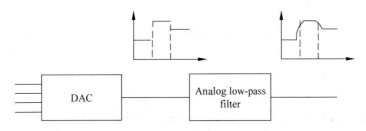

Fig.3-12   Smoothing the output of a D/A converter.

The output of the operational amplifier will hold this value until the next set of binary numbers arrives. Thus the output of the D/A converter is stepwise, as shown in Fig.3-12. This discontinuous signal can be smoothed by passing it through an analog low-pass filter as shown in Fig. 3-12.

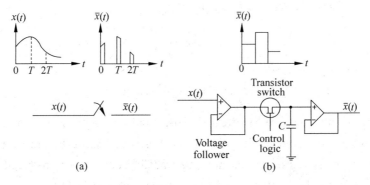

Fig.3-13   (a) Sampler; (b) Sample-and-hold circuit.

Next we discuss the analog-to-digital (A/D) converter or ADC. An analog signal can be discretized by using a switch or sampler as shown in Fig. 3-13(a). The switch is closed for a short period of time every T seconds to yield the signal $\bar{x}$ shown. This signal is then applied to an A/D converter as shown in Fig.3-14 (a). The A/D converter consists of an operational amplifier that acts as a comparator, a D/A converter, a counter and output registers, and control logic. In the conversion, the counter starts to drive the D/A converter. The output $\hat{x}$ of the converter is compared with $\bar{x}$. The counter stops as soon as $\hat{x}$ exceeds $\bar{x}$, as shown in Fig.3-14 (b). The value of the counter is then transferred to the output registers and is the digital representation of the analog signal. This completes the A/D conversion.

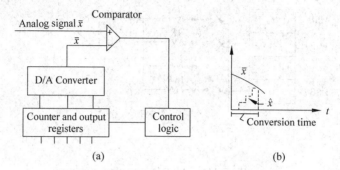

Fig. 3-14　(a) A/D converter; (b) Conversion time.

We see from Fig. 3-14 (b) that the A/D conversion takes a small amount of time, called the conversion time, to achieve the conversion. A 12-bit A/D conversion may take $1\mu s=10^{-6}s$ to complete a conversion. Because of this conversion time, if an analog signal changes very rapidly, the value converted may not be the value intended for conversion. This problem can be resolved by using a sample-and-hold circuit, as shown in Fig.3-13 (b). The circuit consists of a transistor switch, a capacitor with a large capacitance, and two voltage followers. The voltage followers are used to shield the capacitor to eliminate the loading problem. The switch is controlled by control logic. When the switch is open, the capacitor voltage remains roughly constant. Thus the output of the sampled-and-hold circuit is stepwise as shown in Fig.3-13. Using this circuit, the problem due to the conversion time can be eliminated. Therefore, a sample-and-hold circuit is often used, either internally or externally, with an A/D converter.

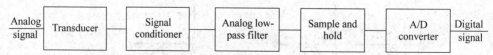

Fig. 3-15　Conversion of analog signals into digital signals.

Inputs of A/D converters are electrical signals, usually ranging from 0 to 10 volts or from −5 to +5 volts. To process nonelectrical signals such as sound (acoustic pressure), temperature, displacement, or velocity, these signals must be transformed, using transducer, into electrical signals. A transducer is a device that transforms a signal from one form to another. Microphones, thermocouples, potentiometers, and tachometers are transducers; they transform acoustic pressure, temperature, displacement, and velocity into electrical voltage signals. Therefore, the transformation of a physical analog signal into a digital signal may require the steps shown in Fig.3-16. The left-most block is a transducer. The output of the transducer may be in millivolt levels and must be amplified to drive the A/D converter. To improve the accuracy of the digital representation of the analog signal, the analog signal may also require scaling so that it will utilize the full range of the converter. Some transducers may exhibit nonlinearities and can be compensated in conversion. These operations (matching signal levels, scaling to improve accuracy, and compensation for nonlinearities) are called signal conditioning. After conditioning, the signal is generally applied to an analog low-pass filter. This filter will eliminate high-frequency noise that may be introduced by transducers. It is also introduced to reduce the effect of aliasing. Therefore the analog low-pass filter is also called an antialiasing filter. Thus the conversion of a physical analog signal to a digital signal generally requires the five operations shown in Fig.3-15. We mention that in addition to analog transducers, there are digital transducers that can transform an analog signal directly into a digital signal. Examples of such transducers are shown in Fig.3-16. They transform, respectively, the angular velocity and angular position of the motor shaft into digital signals. In these cases, the intermediate steps in Fig. 3-16 become unnecessary. At present, data acquisition devices are widely available commercially for achieving the operations in Fig.3-15. Thus conversions of analog signals to digital signals or conversely can be readily achieved in practice.

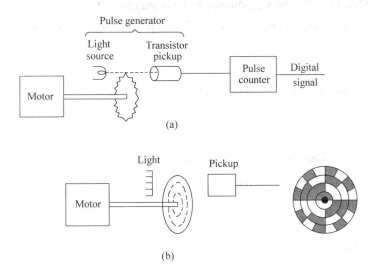

Fig. 3-16   (a) Digital speed transducers; (b) Digital position transducer.

New words and Technical Terms

microprocessor	[maɪkrəʊˈprəʊsesə(r)]	n. 微处理器
converter	[kənˈvɜːtə(r)]	n. 转换器
latch	[lætʃ]	n. 锁存器

switch	[swɪtʃ]	n. 开关
terminal	['tə:mɪnl]	n. 终点站，终端，接线端
comparator	['kɔmpəreitə]	n. 比较器
counter	['kauntə]	n. 计数器
transistor	[træn'zistə]	n. 晶体管
follower	['fɔləuə]	n. 跟随器
shield	[ʃi:ld]	v. 保护，防护，遮蔽
volt	[vəult]	n. 伏特
transducer	[trænz'dju:sə]	n. 传感器，变换器
thermocouple	['θə:məu,kʌpl]	n. 热电偶
potentiometer	[pə,tenʃi'ɔmitə]	n. 电位计，分压计
tachometer	[tæ'kɔmitə]	n. 转速计，流速计
nonlinearity	[,nɔnlini'æriti]	n. 非线性（特性）
conditioning	[kən'diʃəniŋ]	n. 调理，条件作用，训练

Exercises

Ⅰ. Please answer the following questions according to text.

1. Which conversion will be involved in digital processing of analog signals?

2. How is a discontinuous signal smoothed?

3. Which operations should be required in the transformation of a physical analog signal into a digital signal by using analog transducers?

4. What is the digital transducer?

Ⅱ. Please translate the following text into Chinese.

The circuit consists of a transistor switch, a capacitor with a large capacitance, and two voltage followers. The voltage followers are used to shield the capacitor to eliminate the loading problem. The switch is controlled by control logic. When the switch is open, the capacitor voltage remains roughly constant. Thus the output of the sampled-and-hold circuit is stepwise. Using this circuit, the problem due to the conversion time can be eliminated. Therefore, a sample-and-hold circuit is often used, either internally or externally, with an A/D converter.

C. 英汉语序的对比与翻译

英译汉、汉译英的翻译方法和技巧是建立在英汉两种语言语句结构和语序的对比之上的。翻译的本质是不同思维方式的转换，思维的方式决定着语言的表达形式。西方民族的思维形式是重在分析，这种思维形式使西方人惯于用"由一列多"的思维形式，句子结构以主语和谓语为核心，包含各种短语和从句，结构复杂，形成了"树杈形"的句式结构；而东方民族思维形式是重在综合，这种思维形式使中国人注重整体和和谐，强调"从多而一"的思维形式，句子结构以动词为中心，以时间顺序为语序链，形成"流水型"的句式结构。

例如：He had flown yesterday from Beijing where he spent his vocation after finishing the meeting he had taken part in in Tianjin.

他本来在天津开会，会议一结束，他就上北京去度假了，昨天才坐飞机回来。

从以上句子来看，汉语句子以动词为关键词，以时间顺序为语序链；而英语句子则以主要动词为谓语，以分词、不定式、动名词或介词等短语（或从句）表示汉语中相应动词的语义和动作的先后顺序。汉语的几个短句往往可以译成一个由英语关联词及各种短语连接在一起的一个英语长句。因此翻译时，必须按照东西方民族思维方式的特点，调整语句结构，以符合英汉语的表达习惯。

从语言上看，英语句子结构复杂，多长句；汉语多短句。英语多用被动，汉语多用主动。英语多变化，汉语多重复。英语较抽象，汉语较具体。如

There is no race of men anywhere on earth so backward that it has no language, no set of speech sounds by which the people communicate with one another.

在世界上的任何种族，不论其多么落后，都有自己的语言，都有人们用以交流的语言体系。

从语序上看，英汉语句中的主要成分主语、谓语、宾语或表语的词序基本上是一致的，但各种定语的位置，各种状语的次序和从句的次序在英、汉语言中则有同有异。下面分别加以说明。

1. 定语语序的对比

（1）形容词、分词作定语。英语中，形容词和分词作定语通常放在所修饰的名词之前，但在有些情况下，如修饰 some，any，every，no 和 body，thing，one 组成的合成词时，形容词必须后置。而在汉语中形容词作定语一般都前置。例如：

We were pleased at the inspiring news.（前置）
听到这个鼓舞人心的消息我们很高兴。（前置）
The excited people rushed into the building.（前置）
激动的人们冲进了这幢大楼。（前置）
I've got something important to tell you.（后置）

我有重要的事要告诉你。（前置）

He was the only person awake at the moment.（后置）

他是那时唯一醒着的人。（前置）

（2）短语作定语。英语中，修饰名词的短语一般放在名词之后，而汉语则往往反之，例如：

The next train to arrive was from New York.（不定式作定语，后置）

下一列到站的火车是从纽约开来的。（前置）

There was no time to think.（不定式作定语，后置）

已经没有时间考虑了。（后置）

The man standing by the window is our teacher.（分词短语作定语，后置）

站在窗户旁的那位男士是我们的老师。（前置）

2. 状语语序的对比

英语中状语短语可放在被修饰的动词之前或之后，译成汉语时则大多数放在被修饰的动词之前。例如：

He is sleeping in the bedroom.（位于动词之后）

他正在卧室里睡觉。（位于动词之前）

英语中时间状语、地点状语的排列一般是从小到大，而汉语中则是从大到小。例如：

Fourier was born on March 21, 1768, in Auxerre, France.

傅里叶 1768 年 3 月 21 日生于法国奥克斯雷市。

3. 从句语序的对比

英语复合句中，从句的位置比较灵活，可以放在主句之前，也可以放在主句之后。而汉语中，通常是偏句在前，正句在后。如对于时间状语从句，一般是按时间的先后来描述，对于原因状语从句，一般是原因在前，结果在后。例如：

I went out for a walk after I had my dinner.（后置）

After I had my dinner, I went out for a walk.（前置）

我吃了晚饭后出去散步。（前置）

I will go on with the work when I come back tomorrow.（后置）

我明天回来时会继续干这份工作的。（前置）

I haven't seen him since I came here.（后置）

我来这儿后还没见过他呢。（前置）

He had to stay in bed because he was ill.（后置）

因为他病了，他只好呆在床上。（前置）

根据汉英句子语序特点和表达习惯，采取一些必要的手段来调整语句的顺序，在翻译当中是必要的，因此，只有了解汉英两种语言语序的不同，才能在汉英互译时，以符合汉英语言的表达形式来进行翻译。

PART 4

Communication Technology

UNIT 13

A. Text

Mobile Wireless

Mobile Communications Evolution

During the 1970s, Bell Telephone Laboratories, which was then part of AT&T Corporation developed the first wireless transmission system to provide service to mobile subscribers. That system consisted of three major components that continue to form the infrastructure for more modem mobile systems to this day. Those components include base stations, a Mobile Telephone Switching Office (MTSO), and cellular phones.

Although significant technological developments have occurred in the field of mobile wireless communications since the 1970s, the basic components of a cellular system retain the same infrastructural relationship. In addition, the basic concept behind cellular systems has remained the same.

Basic Mobile Communications Infrastructure

In a mobile communications environment, a geographic area is subdivided into cells that support operations on distinct frequencies. To prevent interference between cells, the first type of mobile wireless communications system, which is referred to as the Analog Mobile Phone System(AMPS), employed a seven-cell pattern, as illustrated in Fig.4-1. The cell pattern shown in Fig.4-1 ensures that no adjacent cells operate on the same frequency.

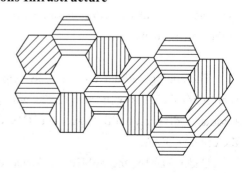

Fig. 4-1 A seven-cell pattern.

In actuality, each cell consists of a base station and an antenna that supports operations over a wide range of frequencies.

However, only one call can occur at one of the frequencies supported in a cell at any given time; the cell pattern is used to ensure that two adjacent cells do not use the same frequency at the same time[1].

Cellular Component Relationship

Each cell consists of a base station housing applicable electronics to support the wireless transmission method used and an antenna. As indicated in Fig. 4-2, each base station is connected to an MTSO. The MTSO, in turn, is connected to the public switched telephone network and provides the interconnection mechanism.

As a mobile subscriber begins to leave the area of coverage of a particular cell, the base station notes a decrease in the level of signal strength of the subscriber. The base station of one or more other cells notes an increase in the level of power as the subscriber moves toward a new cell. Both the serving cell's base station and base stations adjacent to the serving base station communicate this information to the MTSO, which, in effect, functions as a traffic cop, selecting the base station with the strongest increase in signal power to receive a handoff of the subscriber from the existing cell's base station.

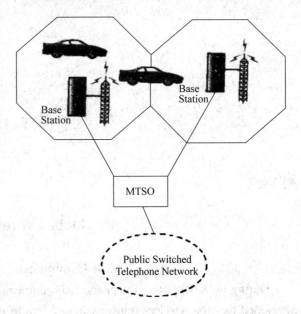

Fig. 4-2 The three component of a mobile wireless system.

In performing the handoff operation, the MTSO checks its database to determine what frequencies are available in the cell the subscriber is entering. The MTSO then communicates this information to the base station that the subscriber is entering, referred to as the "gaining" cell. The base station in the gaining cell then adjusts its transmit and receive frequencies, and sends a message to the subscriber on its old receive frequency that informs the cell phone to adjust itself to the new frequency pair.

AMPS

The analog cellular telephone system invented by Bell Laboratories can be considered to represent the first-generation of wireless mobile communications. This system uses frequency-division multiple access (FDMA) as the network access technique. Fig. 4-3 illustrates the use of FDMA.

Under FDMA, the 50MHz of frequency spectrum allocated by the Federal Communications Commission in the 800MHz band for AMPS operation was subdivided into distinct subchannels of 30kHz bandwidth, with each subchannel capable of supporting a single conversation. When the FCC allocated frequency to AMPS, it permitted two companies to 25MHz, which results in 832 cellular channels available per call. However, each 25MHz is subdivided into forward (base station to subscriber) and reverse (subscriber to base station) operations, referred to as transmit and receive operations. This action was required to provide support for full-duplex communications; however, it limits the number of full-duplex conversations that can occur within a cell to 416.

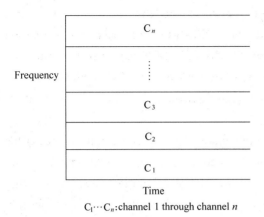

Fig. 4-3 The frequency band allocated for AMPS.

As an analog technology, it is relatively easy to transmit data over AMPS. You can simply connect a modem to an AMPS-compatible cell phone. However, due to potential interference, you normally require a modem designed for over-the-air transmission that supports adjustable packet lengths and error correction[2]. Because the 25kHz channel used by AMPS includes frequencies preassigned for special purposes, a data rate at 9.6kbps is usually the highest that you can expect to achieve.

Until the turn of the millennium, AMPS had by far the most widespread coverage of all mobile wireless systems. Unfortunately, its success also resulted in the search for other network access technologies. As mere users purchased AMPS-compatible cell phones, they began to experience an inability to make calls, especially in urban areas. This situation, referred to as blocking, occurs when call 417 is attempted with a cell whose maximum capacity is the support of 416 simultaneous calls. A second problem encountered by AMPS subscribers occurred when a cell lacked the capacity to assign a channel to a mobile user arriving in its area of coverage. This situation resulted in dropping a call in progress. Noting that fixed-cell analog couldn't support the growing base of subscribers, cellular developers introduced two new access methods. Those access methods are referred to as time-division multiple access (TDMA) and code-division multiple access (CDMA). Each access method supported an increase in the number of simultaneous subscribers that could use the transmission capacity of a cell.

TDMA

Time-division multiple access (TDMA) subdivides the frequency allocation of AMPS into time slots. Each AMPS channel is divided into a repeating sequence of three time slots, with a subscriber allocated to a frequency and time slot, as illustrated in Fig. 4-4.

In North America, TDMA-based

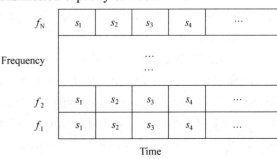

Fig. 4-4 Under time-division multiple access (TDMA).

cellular systems operate at 800MHz or 1900MHz. When operating at 800MHz, TDMA can normally coexist with analog channels on the same network. This enables subscribers with a dual-mode phone to take advantage of AMPS or digital TDMA as they move about, a situation referred to as roaming. A second difference between TDMA and AMPS concerns the manner by which voice is transmitted. Under AMPS, which is an analog system, the 30~20000Hz range of human voice is first filtered to remove very low and high frequencies that are not important for understanding a conversation.

Next, the remaining frequencies are frequency modulated using a carrier in the center of the channel. In comparison, under TDMA voice is first encoded digitally at a low bit rate, typically using a hybrid coder that codes voice at a fraction of the 64kbps PCM rate. Then the resulting digital data stream is modulated onto a radio signal. As a result of the digital coding of speech, the first of TDMA that operated at 800 MHz was also referred to as Digital Advanced Mobile Phone Services (D-AMPS).

PCS

A second version of TDMA that operates at 1900MHz is referred to as the Personal Communications System (PCS). PCS systems operate at higher frequency than D-AMPS, and wavelength is proportional to the reciprocal of frequency, which results in the use of a shorter wavelength. The shorter wavelength associated with PCS results in a smaller cell diameter, which means that a 1900MHz system requires more cells per geographic area than an 800MHz System. This also explains why it's relatively easy to place a call using a PCS cell phone in urban areas or along an interstate highway. When you get into a rural area, however, your dual-mode phone more than likely uses AMPS to communicate.

Several types of PCS systems are in operation around the world. Examples of PCS systems include D-AMPS 1900 when it operates at 1900MHz, Global System for Mobile (GSM), and CDMA. GSM is similar to D-AMPS 1900 in that it is based on the use of TDMA, whereas CDMA uses a completely different access technology.

The key advantage associated with PCS is the fact that a TDMA frame can be modified to support two calls instead of three for a specified period of time. When this occurs, time slots can be used to support what is referred to as a digital control channel (DCC)[3]. Through the use of the DCC, it becomes possible to transmit alphanumeric messages to and from PCS phones, a capability referred to as short message service (SMS). This permits a PCS-compatible cell phone to function as a pager.

The use of TDMA for D-AMPS and GSM permits cell phones to obtain an extended battery life in comparison to AMPS phones. The Key reason for the extended battery life is the fact that the use of TDMA normally results in only one-third of the transmission time used in comparison to that of an AMPS phone. A second reason is based on the capability of a PCS phone in idle mode to periodically check the control channel to see if it has an incoming call. If a signal on the control channel is not found, the phone performs another Rip Van Winkle operation and goes back to sleep.

GSM

GSM dates to the 1980s, when analog cellular systems in Nordic countries experienced rapid growth that resulted in the development of a new digital cellular standard[4]. After five years of effort, 13 network operators and administrators signed a charter for the standardization of GSM. At that time, GSM was referred to by Its French name. Group Special Mobile, but it is now known on a worldwide basis as Global System for Mobile Communications.

The European version of GSM operates in the 900MHz bands, which was available in countries that are members of the European commission. Unfortunately, the 900MHz band in the United States was not available, so the 1900MHz band is used by GSM personal communications system in the United States.

GSM represents a TDMA version of PCS. As a digital technology, voice is first compressed using a hybrid coder at approximately 13kbps before the data is modulated. With this digital technology, you can connect a data source directly to a GSM cell phone without the use of a modem. However, the highest data rate that you can expect to obtain will be approximately 14.4 kbps.

CDMA

A third mobile wireless access technology is CDMA. Unlike AMPS and TDMA, which occur at one frequency, CDMA signals occur over an extended frequency band, referred to as broadband or spread spectrum communications. The key advantage associated with spreading a signal is that, from Shannon's Law, channel capacity can be maintained at a lower power level. Thus, CDMA supports low-power operations.

Under CDMA, spreading occurs through the use of a pseudo random (PN) digital code that spreads each bit. The PN signal is referred to as a code of chips, with each chip representing a data bit in the PN code. Each data bit to be transmitted under CDMA is first modulo-2 added to the PN code. The sequence of extended bits then is modulated over a 1.23MHz channel.

Fig. 4-5 illustrates an example of the direct sequence spreading process. In this example, a 5 bit PN spreading code is used to spread a 3-bit message. This results in each data bit being transmitted five times, or once per chip operation. At the receiver, a modulo-2 subtraction process occurs to restore the data to its original composition. If a sequence of 5 bits (in this example) representing 1 data bit were corrupted because of transmission impairments, the receiver would select the most popular bit setting in the sequence[5]. For example, if 4 bits were set to 1 and 1 bit was set to 0. The receiver would assume that the correct value of the data bit is 0.

Data bits	101		
Spreading code	10110		
Transmitted data	01001	10110	01001

Fig. 4-5 Under direct sequence spread-spectrum transmission.

Under CDMA, 1.23MHz of frequency spectrum accommodates one channel. Although this is significantly higher than with AMPS and TDMA, all available frequency spectrums under CDMA can be reused in each cell. In addition, by varying the PN code, it becomes possible for a CDMA system to support several times the capacity of a TDMA system. According to some studies, CDMA can support 10 times the capacity of a TDMA system, which, in turn, can support 3 times the capacity of an AMPS cell.

New words and Technical Terms

cell	[sel]	n.	（移动通信）蜂窝区，小区
pattern	[ˈpætən]	n.	模式，式样
cop	[kɔp]	n.	警官，巡警
handoff	[ˈhændɔf]	n.	切换
preassign	[ˌpriːəˈsain]	n.	预先指定，预先分配
blocking	[ˈblɔkiŋ]	n.	阻塞
roam	[rəum]	v.	漫游；n. 漫游
hybrid	[ˈhaibrid]	adj.	混合的
alphanumeric	[ˌælfənjuːˈmerik]	adj.	包括文字与数字的
pager	[ˈpeidʒə(r)]	n.	呼机，寻呼机
Nordic	[ˈnɔːdik]	n.	北欧人；adj. 北欧人的

MTSO (mobile telephone switching office)　　移动电话交换局
FDMA (frequency-division multiple access)　　频分多址
FCC (Federal Communications Commission)　　联邦通信委员会
full-duplex　　全双工
over-the-air　　无线广播的
TDMA (time-division multiple access)　　时分多址
CDMA (code-division multiple access)　　码分多址
DCC (digital control channel)　　数字控制信道
SMS (short message service)　　短消息服务
GSM (Global System for Mobile)　　全球移动通信系统
PN (pseudo random)　　伪随机

Notes

[1] However, only one call can occur at one of the frequencies supported in a cell at any given time; the cell pattern is used to ensure that two adjacent cells do not use the same frequency at the same time.

然而，对任意给定的时刻，一个小区中的一个频率上只能存在一个呼叫，蜂窝模式用来确保相邻的蜂窝不会同时使用同一频率。

[2] However, due to potential interference, you normally require a modem designed for

over-the-air transmission that supports adjustable packet lengths and error correction.

然而，由于潜在干扰，通常需要一个支持可调分组长度和纠错功能的无线调制解调器。

over-the-air 无线广播的，例如：over-the-air programming 无线电广播节目。

[3] When this occurs, time slots can be used to support what is referred to as a digital control channel (DCC).

出现这种情况时，可用时隙来支持称为 DCC 的数字控制信道。

time slots 表示时隙，what is referred to as a digital control channel (DCC) 作 support 的宾语从句。

[4] GSM dates to the 1980s, when analog cellular systems in Nordic countries experienced rapid growth that resulted in the development of a new digital cellular standard.

GSM 可以追溯到 20 世纪 80 年代，当时模拟蜂窝系统在北欧国家快速发展促成了新的数字蜂窝标准的发展。

Date 可以翻译为"源自……"。例如：This statue dates from 500 B.C. 这座雕像可以追溯到公元前 500 年。

[5] If a sequence of 5 bits (in this example) representing 1 data bit were corrupted because of transmission impairments, the receiver would select the most popular bit setting in the sequence.

如果代表 1 个数据位的 5 比特序列（在本例中）由于传输受损而遭破坏，接收机将选择序列中最常见的比特。

transmission impairment 传输受损，传输质量降低。

Exercises

Ⅰ. Please translate the following words and phrases into Chinese.

1. transmission impairment

2. dual-mode

3. a base station

4. CDMA

Ⅱ. Fill in the blanks with the missing word(s).

1. Each cell consists _____ a base station housing applicable electronics to support the wireless transmission method used and an antenna.

2. GSM is now known on a worldwide basis _____ Global system for Mobile Communications.

3. Each carrier was allocated 25MHz, which results _____ 832 cellular channels available per call.

4. The key advantage associated _____ spreading a signal is that, from Shannon's Law, channel capacity can be maintained _____ a lower power level.

B. Reading

Technologies on Fourth-Generation Mobile Communication

Fourth-generation mobile communications involves a mix of concepts and technologies in the making. Some can be recognized as deriving from 3G, and are called evolutionary (e.g. evolutions of WCDMA and CDMA2000), while others involve new approaches to wireless mobile, and are sometimes labeled revolutionary. What is important, though, is the common understanding that technologies beyond 3G are of fundamental relevance in the movement toward a wireless world, a term introduced by the WWRF), all of these terms are meant to signify fundamentally better wireless mobile communications in the future.

Fourth-generation mobile includes concepts and technologies for innovations in spectrum allocation and utilization, radio communications, networks, and services and applications. These four major areas are intertwined, and innovations in one will inevitably call for changes in the others. In all cases, it is the interplay of these approaches, technologies, and services/applications with the market, user needs and desires, and even unrecognized future uses that could drive a major technological movement and provides the potential for revolutionary, or very rapid and profound change. It is the belief that we are at the beginning of that process, and that the rest of the first decade of the 21st century will provide the underlying basis for making wireless as useful and ubiquitous in the future as computers are today. These four major areas are providing innovations that will drive this process.

Spectrum allocation and utilization are just at the beginning of a possible paradigm change. Research in adaptive spectrum and bandwidth allocation is underway, as is research in dynamic utilization of spectral resources. The idea of having a spectral resource allocated, assigned, or used in a way that is not fixed is under investigation in Europe, Asia, and the United states, and is beginning to be considered as a possibility by regulators. Spectrum is too precious a resource for us not to do the best we can. Advances in understanding spectral needs and usage, along with physical, MAC link, and network layer approaches to optimize the use of that spectrum, and also including the processing resources to control them, can be used to provide the right services and QoS. Regulatory and system changes will also be necessary.

Radio communications technology innovations will truly be the engine of any major change. The ability to provide large data rates, up to 100Mbps or 1 Gbps, has been mentioned. This is largely determined by the ability of the multiple access, modulation and coding, and radio resource technologies to provide these data rates efficiently in a mobile wireless environment. Going to higher-speeds means that the channels are truly wideband, and the waveform processing rnust thus account for the larger number of resolvable but random, multiple paths. Improved multiple access and channel coding are also needed. MC-CDMA and OFDM are under investigation as are improved coding schemes, as well as combinations of various multiple access multi-user modulations and coding schemes. Also included is space-division multiple access, smart, antennas, and space-time coding techniques. In all cases, fast adaptation to the channel and traffic conditions is key to providing the needed QoS.

Two additional aspects of the radio access area are also critical, as is the network area. One is reconfigurable radio access points and technologies. Those are needed to allow the hardware and software to adopt the beat radio access technique suited to each case (i.e. to adapt to the available spectrum channel conditions, and network). Fortunately, there are software reconfigurable radio technologies under investigation, and in some cases, in very rudimentary form, deployed. More will be needed. But more than reconfigurable radios are needed; reconfigurable networks are also required, since the convergence of the various access technologies will require the networks to provide access to a number of radio technologies, and in fact to be a part of the adaptation process.

The network changes will be apparent in two major aspects. One is the almost certain evolution toward more of an IP, or packet switch, approach, and away from circuit switching, or even a packet switch overlay on circuit switch technology as is the case in 3G. Thus, physical layer techniques for fast acquisition and other needs of burst-type communications will be needed. Also needed are the MAC/link and network layer technologies to implement all IP networks, and to control and optimize radio and network operation in a highly variable environment. A second and related aspect, requiring major network changes, involves the possible convergence of various technologies and services, such as WLAN and mobile. As these strive toward serving users who wish to communicate data, voice, and possibly video and other applications for a variety of services, there will be both a drive for convergence as well as a need for new technologies.

In the end it will be whether these, and possibly other technologies, can meet the challenge of providing new and effective services and applications to a future wireless market that wants more, but is not quite sure what it wants, that will determine what the wireless world will look like. Research in fourth-generation mobile is one key toward this.

New words and Technical Terms

evolutionary	[ˌiːvəˈluːʃənərɪ]	adj. 进化的
intertwine	[ˌintə(ː)ˈtwain]	v. （使）纠缠，（使）缠绕
underlying	[ˈʌndəˈlaiiŋ]	adj. 根本的，优先的
ubiquitous	[juːˈbikwitəs]	adj. 普遍存在的
paradigm	[ˈpærədaim]	n. 范例
resolvable	[riˈzɔlvəbl]	adj. 可分解的
rudimentary	[ruːdɪˈmentərɪ]	adj. 基本的；初步的，未来发展的
overlay	[ˌəuvəˈlei]	n. 覆盖，覆盖图

Exercises

Please answer the following questions according to text.

1. Is fourth-generation mobile communications a mix of new concepts and technologies? Give your reasons.

2. Please look at the second sentence in the second paragraph, what does "These four major areas" refer to?

3. Why do we need reconfigurable networks in the radio access area?

C. 文献检索简介

文献信息检索是指从任何文献信息集合中查出所需信息的活动、过程和方法。广义的文献信息检索还包括文献信息存储,两者又往往合并称为"文献信息存储与检索"。当然,对于信息用户来说,信息检索仅指信息的查找过程。

1. 文献检索的意义

(1) 充分利用已有的文献信息资源,避免重复劳动。

科学研究具有继承和创造两重性,科学研究的两重性要求科研人员在探索未知或从事研究工作之前,应该尽可能地占有与之相关的资料、情报。研究人员在开始研究某一课题前,必须利用科学的文献信息检索方法来了解课题的进展情况,在前人的研究基础上进行研究。可以说一项科研成果中 95% 是别人的,5% 是个人创造的。科研人员只有通过查找文献信息,才能做到心中有数,防止重复研究,将有限的时间和精力用于创造性的研究中。

(2) 缩短查找文献信息的时间,提高科研效率。

目前文献信息的数量和类型增加十分迅速,科研人员不可能将世界上所有的文献都阅读完。据美国科学基金会统计,一个科研人员花费在查找和消化科技资料上的时间占全部科研时间的 51%,计划思考占 8%,实验研究占 32%,书面总结占 9%。由上述统计数字可以看出,科研人员花费在科技出版物上的时间为全部科研时间的 60% 左右。如果科研人员掌握好科学的文献信息检索方法,就可以缩短查阅文献的时间,获取更多的文献信息,从而提高科研效率。

(3) 促进专业学习,实现终身学习。

掌握了科学的文献信息检索方法,可以把学生引导到超越教学大纲的更广的知识领域中去,促进学生的专业学习。在当代社会,人们需要终生学习,不断更新知识,才能适应社会发展的需求,掌握了科学的文献信息检索方法,在研究实践和生产实践中根据需要查找文献信息,就可以无师自通,很快找到一条吸取和利用大量新知识的捷径。

2. 国内检索系统

目前我国高校和科研机构一般根据自己的专业设置和科研需要购置了不同的数据库,下面是常见和常用的一些数据库。

《中国期刊网全文数据库》(http://www.cnki.edu.cn);
《万方数据资源系统》(http://www.wfdata.com.cn);
《重庆维普中文科技期刊数据库》(http://www.cqvip.com.cn);
《中国专利数据库》(http://www.sipo.gov.cn);
《中国生物医学文献数据库》(http://cbm.imicams.ac.cn);
《中国科技论文在线》(http://www.paper.edu.cn);
《国家科技成果网》(http://www.nast.org.cn);
《国家科技图书文献中心》(http://www.nstl.gov.cn)。

3. 国际著名的六大检索系统

(1) 美国《科学引文索引》(Science Citation Index, SCI)。
(2) 美国《工程索引》(Engineering Index, EI)。
(3) 美国《化学文摘》(Chemical Abstracts, CA)。CA 报道的化学化工文献量占全世界化学化工文献总量的 98% 左右,是当今世界上最负盛名、收录最全、应用最为广泛的查找化学化工文献大型检索工具。
(4) 英国《科学文摘》(Science Abstracts, SA;或 INSPEC)
　　——《物理文摘》(Section A-Physics Abstracts, PA);
　　——《电子与电气文摘》(Section B-Electrical Engineering & Electronics Abstracts, EEA);
　　——《计算机与控制文摘》(Section C-Computers and Control Abstracts, CCA);
　　——《信息技术》(Information Technology, IT)。
(5) 俄罗斯《文摘杂志》(Abstract Journals, AJ)。
(6) 日本《科学技术文献速报》,现扩充为大型数据库"日本科学技术情报中心"(Japan Information Center Science and Technology, JICST)。

UNIT 14

A. Text

Fiber Optic

Optical fiber transmission has come of age as a major innovation in telecommunications.

Such systems offer extremely high bandwidth, freedom from external interference, immunity from interception by external means, and cheap raw materials (silicon, the most abundant material on Earth).

Fundamentals of Fiber Optic Systems

Optical fibers guide light rays within the fiber material. They can do this because light rays bend or change direction when they pass from one medium to another. They bend because the speed of propagation of light in each medium is different. This phenomenon is called refraction. One common example of refraction occurs when you stand at the edge of a pool and look at an object at the bottom of the pool. Unless you are directly over the object, it appears to be farther away than it really is. This effect occurs because the speed of the light rays from the object increases as the light rays pass from the water to the air. This causes them to heed, changing the angle at which you perceive the object. You can obtain an appreciation for the manner by which light flows by focusing upon Snell's Law.

Snell's Law

How optical fibers work can be explained by Shell's Law, which states that the ratio of the sine of the angle of incidence to the sine of the angle of refraction is equal to the ratio of the propagation velocities of the wave in the two respective media[1]. This is equal to a constant that is the ratio of the refractive index of the second medium to that of the first. Written as an equation, Snell's Law looks like this:

$$\frac{\sin A_1}{\sin A_2} = \frac{V_1}{V_2} = K = \frac{n_2}{n_1} \tag{4-1}$$

In this equation, A_1, and A_2 are the angles of incidence and refraction, respectively V_1 and V_2 are the velocities of propagation of the wave in the two media, n_1 and n_2 are the indices of refraction of the two media.

The parameters are demonstrated graphically in Fig. 4-6. In each case, A_1 is the angle of incidence, and A_2 is the angle of refraction. The index of refraction of material 1, n_1, is greater than the index of refraction of material 2, n_2. This means that the velocity of propagation of light is greater in material 2 than in material 1.

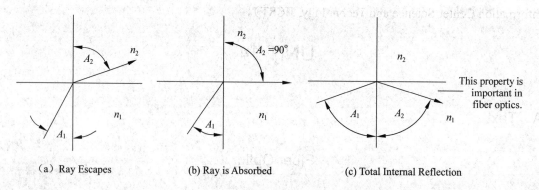

(a) Ray Escapes (b) Ray is Absorbed (c) Total Internal Reflection

Fig. 4-6 The index of refraction ($n_1 > n_2$).

Fig. 4-6 (a) demonstrates how a light ray passing from material 1 to material 2 is retracted in material 2 when A_1 is less than the critical angle. Fig. 4-6 (b) demonstrates the condition that exists when A_1 is at the critical angle and the angle A_2 is at 90[dg] [2]. The light ray is directed along the boundary between the two materials.

As shown in Fig. 4-6 (c), any light rays that are incident at angles greater than A_1 of Fig. 4-6 (b) will be reflected back into material 1 with angle A_2 equal to angle A_1. The condition in Fig. 4-6 (c) is the one of particular interest for optical fibers.

Fiber Composition

An Optical fiber is a dielectric (nonconductor of electricity) waveguide made of glass or plastic. It consists of three distinct regions: a core, the cladding, and a sheath or jacket. The sheath or jacket protects the fiber but does not govern the transmission capability of the fiber.

The index of refraction of the assembly varies across the radius of the cable, and the core has a constant or smoothly varying index of refraction called n_c. The cladding region has another constant index of refraction called n. The core possesses a high refractive index, whereas the cladding is constructed to have a lower refractive index. The result of the difference in the refractive indices keeps light flowing through the core after it gets into the core, even if the fiber is bent or tied into a knot. For a fiber designed to carry light in several modes of propagation at the same time (called a multimode fiber), the diameter of the core is several times the wavelength of the light to be carried. Wavelength is a measure of the distance between two cycles of the same wave measured in nanometers (nm), or billionths of a meter, and the cladding thickness will be greater than the radius of the core[3]. Following are some typical values for a multimode fiber:

- An operating light wavelength of 0.8 micrometers (/~m)
- A core index of refraction n_c of 1.5
- A cladding index of refraction n of 1.485 (=0.99 n_c)
- A core diameter of 50, 62.5, or 100μm
- A cladding thickness of 37.5μm

The clad fiber would have a diameter of 125μm, and light would propagate as shown in Fig. 4-7.

A light source emits light at many angles relative to the center of the fiber. In Fig. 4-7, light ray A enters the fiber perpendicular to the face of the core and parallel to the axis. Its angle of incidence A_1 is 0; therefore, it is not refracted, and it travels parallel to the axis. Light ray B enters the fiber core from air at an angle of incidence of A_{1B} and is refracted at an angle A_{2B} because n_2 is greater than n_1. When light ray B strikes the boundary between the core and the cladding, its angle of incidence, $A_{1'B}$, is greater than the critical angle. Therefore, the angle of refraction, $A_{2'B}$, is equal to $A_{1'B}$, and the light ray is refracted back into the core. The ray propagates in this zigzag fashion down the core until it reaches the other end.

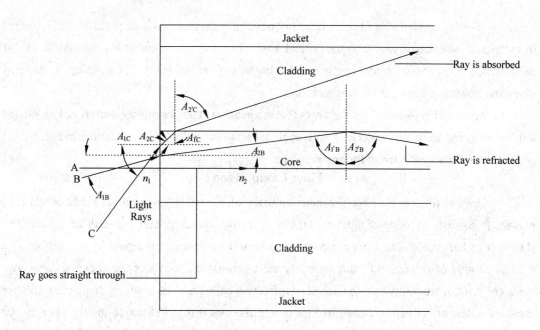

Fig. 4-7　Light ray paths in multimode fiber.

If the angle of incidence, A_{1C}, is too large, as it is for light ray C, the light ray strikes the boundary between the core and the cladding with an angle of incidence, A_{1C}, less than the critical angle. The ray enters into the cladding and propagates into, or is absorbed into, the cladding and jacket (which is opaque to light).

Modal Delay

For optical fibers in which the diameter of the core is many times the wavelength of the light transmitted, the light beam travels along the fiber by bouncing back and forth at the interface between the core and the cladding. Rays entering the fiber at differing angles are refracted varying numbers of times as they move from one end to the other and consequently do not arrive at the distant end with the same phase relationship as when they started[4]. The differing angles of entry are called modes of propagation (or just modes), and a fiber carrying several modes is called a multimode fiber. Multimode propagation causes the rays leaving the fiber to interfere both constructively and destructively as they leave the end of the fiber. This effect is called modal delay spreading.

Because most optical communications systems transmit information in digital form consisting of pulses of light, the effect of modal delay spreading limits the capability of the fiber to transport recognizable pulses[5]. This is because modal delay spreading broadens the pulses in the time domain, as illustrated in Fig. 4-8. The effect of pulse spreading is to make it difficult or impossible for an optical receiver to differentiate one pulse from another after a given transmission distance. Thus, after a predefined transmission distance, a multimode fiber either causes a very high error rate or precludes the capability of the pulse to be recognized and terminates the capability of the cable to de used for communications.

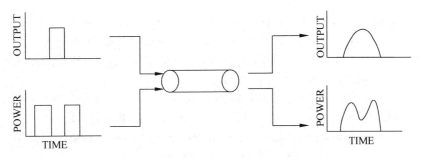

Fig. 4-8 Pulse spreading.

If the diameter of the fiber core is only a few times the wavelength of the transmitted light (say, a factor of 3), only one ray or mode will be propagated, and no destructive interference between rays will occur[6]. These fibers, called single-mode fibers, are the media that are used in most transmission systems. Fig. 4-9(a) and Fig. 4-9(b) show the distribution of the index of refraction across, and typical diameters of, multimode and single-mode fibers[7]. One of the principal differences between single-mode and multimode fibers is that most of the power in the multimode fiber travels in the core, whereas, in single-mode fibers, a large fraction of the power is propagated in the cladding near the core. At the point where the light wavelength becomes long enough to cause single-mode propagation, about 20 percent of the power is carried in the cladding, but if the light wavelength is doubled, more than 50 percent of the power travels in the cladding.

Refractive Index

Fiber can also be classified by its type of refractive index. Fig.4-10. Illustrates a few of the classifications, which are outlined here:

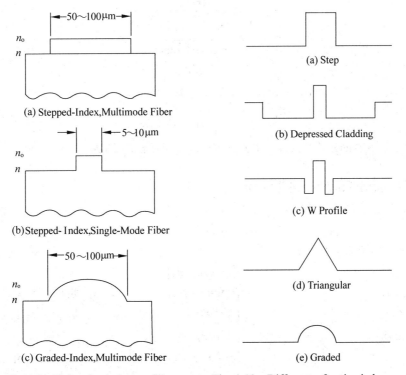

Fig. 4-9 Refractive index profiles.　　Fig. 4-10 Different refractive index profile.

- Stepped-index fiber—The fiber core has a uniform refractive index throughout with a sudden change of the refractive index at the core-cladding boundary.
- Graded-index fiber—The fiber core has a refractive index that gradually decreases as the distance from the center of the fiber increases.
- Single-mode fiber—Also known as monomode, this has a uniform refractive index. This type of fiber permits only a single light ray to pass through the cable.
- Graded-index multimode fiber—The index of refraction varies smoothly across the diameter of the core but remains constant in the cladding. This treatment reduces the intermodal dispersion by the fiber because rays traveling along a graded-index fiber have nearly equal delays.

Other refractive index profiles have been devised to solve various problems, such as reduction of chromatic dispersion. Some of these profiles are shown in Fig.4-10; the step and graded profiles are repeated for comparison.

Fig.4-11. Compares the flow of light through stepped-index, graded-index, and single-mode fiber. A stepped-index fiber typically has a core diameter between 100μm and 500μm. A graded-index fiber commonly has a core diameter of 50μm or 62.5μm, while single-mode fibers have core diameters between 8μm and 10μm. Both stepped-index and graded-index fiber support multimode transmission.

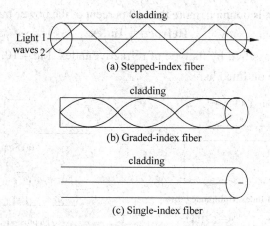

Fig. 4-11 Light flow through different refractive index fibers.

New words and Technical Terms

fiber	['faibə]	n.	纤维
fiber optic (optical fiber)			光纤（光纤电缆）
propagate	['prɔpəgeit]	v.	传播
refraction	[ri'frækʃən]	n.	折射，折射度
refract	[ri'frækt]	v.	折射
refractive	[ri'fræktiv]	adj.	折射的
interception	[ˌintə(:)'sepʃən]	n.	截取，窃听，监听
incidence	['insidəns]	n.	入射

critical	['kritikəl]	adj. 临界的	
dielectric	[ˌdaiiˈlektrik]	n. 电介质，绝缘材料	
waveguide	['weivgaid]	n. 波导，波导管	
core	[kɔ:]	n.（光纤）纤芯	
cladding	['klædiŋ]	n. 包层	
perpendicular	[ˌpə:pən'dikjulə]	adj. 垂直的	
zigzag	['zigzæg]	adj. 之字形的，Z 字形的	
opaque	[əu'peik]	adj. 不传导的，不透明的	
mono-	['mɔnəu]	（前缀）单，单一，一	
dispersion	[dis'pə:ʃən]	n. 色散	
profile	['prəufail]	n. 曲线，分布图	
chromatic	[krə'mætik]	adj. 有色的，彩色的	
chromatic dispersion		色散	
Snell's law		斯涅尔（折射）定律	
multimode fiber		多模光纤	
clad fiber		包层光纤，涂层纤维	
single mode fiber(single-mode fiber)		单模光纤	
error rate		误码率	
optical receiver		光接收器	
destructive interference		破坏性干扰，相消性干扰	
graded-index fiber		渐变折射率光纤	
stepped-index fiber		阶跃折射率光纤	
intermodal dispersion		模间色散	

Notes

[1] How optical fibers work can be explained by Snell's Law, which states that the ratio of the sine of the angle of incidence to the sine of the angle of refraction is equal to the ratio of the propagation velocities of the wave in the two respective media.

光纤的工作原理可用斯涅尔折射定律来解释，入射角正弦值与折射角正弦值之比等于光波在两种媒介中的传输速度之比。

Which 引导非限定性定语从句；the ratio of A to B 表示 A 与 B 之比。

[2] Fig.4-6(b) demonstrates the condition that exists when A_1 is at the critical angle and angle A_2 is at 90[dg].

图 4-6 (b)表示当 A_1 为临界角，A_2 为 90 度时的情况。

[dg] 表示角度单位，dg=degree 度。

[3] Wavelength is a measure of the distance between two cycles of the same wave measured in nanometers (nm), or billionths of a meter, and the cladding thickness will be greater than the radius of the core.

波长是同一个光波 2 周之间距离的量度标准，以纳米即一米的十亿分之一来表示，光纤包层厚度要大于光纤纤芯的半径。

nanometer 纳米，简写为 nm；

nana- （前缀）纳（诺）、毫微（10^{-9}），这种单位前缀在科技文中很常见，例如本课中还出现了 micrometers（微米）、gigabit（吉比特）等。

[4] Rays entering the fiber at differing angles are refracted varying numbers of times as they move from one end to the other and consequently do not arrive at the distant end with the same phase relationship as when they started.

当光线从光纤的一端传到另一端时，光线进入光纤的角度不同，所产生折射的次数就不同，因此到达远端时，其相位关系也与开始时不同。

[5] Because most optical communications systems transmit information in digital form consisting of pulse of light, the effect of modal delay spreading limits the capability of the fiber to transport recognizable pulses.

因为大多数光纤通信系统都是以光脉冲这种数字方式传输信息的，所以模式延迟扩展限制了光纤传输可识别脉冲的容量。

[6] If the diameter of the fiber core is only a few times the wavelength of the transmitted light (say, a factor of 3), only one ray or mode will be propagated, and no destructive interference between rays will occur.

如果光纤纤芯的直径仅仅是传输光波波长的几倍（比如说 3 倍），那么只有一种光或传输模式可以传输，并且在光线之间不会产生破坏性干扰。

Factor 表示"因数、倍"。

[7] Fig.4-9（a）and Fig.4-9（b）show the distribution of the index of refraction across, and typical diameters of, multimode and single-mode fibers.

图 4-9（a）和图 4-9（b）给出了折射率沿多模光纤和单模光纤的分布，以及它们典型的直径值。

Exercises

Ⅰ. Please translate the following words and phrases into Chinese.

1. propagation mode

2. refractive index profile

3. optical receiver

4. dielectric

5. destructive interference

6. stepped-index fiber

Ⅱ. Fill in the blanks with the missing word (s).

1. Optical fiber transmission has com _____ age as a major innovation in

telecommunications.

 2. Light ray A enters the fiber perpendicular _____ the face of the core and parallel _____ the axis.

 3. This is because modal delay spreading broadens the pulses _____ the time domain.

 4. The effect of pulse spreading is to make it difficult or impossible for an optical receiver to differentiate one pulse _____ another after a given transmission distance.

 5. Because most optical communications systems transmit information _____ digital form consisting of pulses of light, the effect of modal delay spreading limits the capability of the fiber _____ recognizable pulse.

B. Reading

Optical Fiber Communications

 Communication may be broadly defined as the transfer of information from one point to another. When the information is to be conveyed over any distance a communication system is usually required. Within a communication system the information transfer is frequently achieved by superimposing or modulating the information on to an electromagnetic wave which acts as a carrier for the information signal. This modulated carrier is then transmitted to the required destination where it is received and the original information signal is obtained by demodulation. Sophisticated techniques have been developed for this process by using electromagnetic carrier waves operating at radio frequencies as well as microwave and millimeter wave frequencies. However, "communication" may also be achieved by using an electromagnetic carrier which is selected from the optical range of frequencies.

 Typical optical fiber communications system is shown in Fig. 4-12. In this case the information source provides an electrical signal to a transmitter comprising an electrical stage which drives an optical source to give modulation of the lightwave carrier. The optical source which provides the electrical-optical conversion may be either a semiconductor laser or light emitting diode (LED). The transmission medium consists of an optical fiber cable and the receiver consists of an optical detector which drives a further electrical stage and hence provides demodulation of the optical carrier. Photodiodes(P-N, P-I-N or avalanche) and, in some instances, phototransistor and photoconductors are utilized for the detection of the optical signal and the optical-electrical conversion . Thus there is a requirement for electrical interfacing at either end of the optical link and at present the signal processing is usually performed electrically.

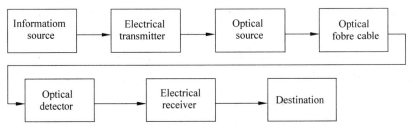

Fig. 4-12 Optical Fiber Communication System.

The optical carrier may be modulated by using either an analog or digital information signal. Analog modulation involves the variation of the light emitted from the optical source in a continuous manner. With digital modulation, however, discrete changes in the light intensity are obtained (i.e. on-off pulses). Although often simpler to implement, analog modulation with an optical fiber communication system is less efficient, requiring a far higher signal to noise ratio at the receiver than digital modulation. Also, the linearity needed for analog modulation is not always provided by semiconductor optical source, especially at high modulation frequencies. For these reasons, analog optical fiber communications link are generally limited to shorter distances and lower bandwidths than digital links.

Initially, the input digital signal from the information source is suitably encoded for optical transmission. The laser drive circuit directly modulates the intensity of the semiconductor laser with the encoded digital signal. Hence a digital optical signal is launched into the optical fiber cable. The avalanche photodiode detector (APD) is followed by a front-end amplifier and equalizer or filter to provide gain as well as linear signal processing and noise bandwidth reduction. Finally, the signal obtained is decoded to give the original digital information.

New words and Technical Terms

electromagnetic wave	[ilektrəu'mægnitik]	n. 电磁波
photodiode	[,fəutəu'daiəud]	n. 光敏二极管，光电二极管
avalanche	['ævə,lɑ:nʃ]	n&v. 雪崩
avalanche photodiode(APD)		雪崩光电二极管
front-end amplifier	['æmpli,faiə]	n. 前置放大器
equalizer	['i:kwəlaizə]	n. 均衡器

Exercises

Ⅰ. Write T (True) or F (False) beside the following statements about the text.

1. This modulated carrier is then transmitted to the required destination where it is received and the original information signal is obtained by modulation.

2. The information source provides an electrical signal to a transmitter comprising an electrical stage which drives an optical source to give modulation of the lightwave carrier.

3. The optical carrier is modulated by using neither an analog nor digital information signal.

4. Analog modulation with an optical fiber communication system is more efficient, requiring a far lower signal to noise ratio at the receiver than digital modulation.

5. The input digital signal from the information source is not suitably encoded for optical transmission.

Ⅱ. Fill in the missing words according to the text.

1. Within a communication system the information transfer is _____ by superimposing

or modulating the information on to an electromagnetic wave which acts as a carrier.

2. The laser drive circuit directly modulates the intensity of the semiconductor laser with the encoded digital. Hence a _____ is launched into the optical fiber cable.

3. There is a requirement for electrical interfacing at either end of the optical link and at present the _____ is usually performed electrically.

C. 文献检索方法简介

文献检索是科学研究工作中的一个重要步骤，它贯穿研究的全过程。文献不仅仅是选题依据，选题确定以后，必须围绕选题广泛地查阅文献资料，能否正确的掌握文献检索方法，关系到研究的过程、质量，以及能否出成果，因此必须掌握文献检索的技能。了解和掌握文献的分类及其特点，是迅速有效地查找所需信息的必要前提。

1. 文献的类型

一级文献，即原始文献，是由亲自经历事件的人所提供的各种形式的材料和各种原著。这种文献是我们搞好研究的第一手资料，对研究工作有很大的价值。

二级文献，指对一级文献加工整理而成的系统化、条理化的文献资料。如索引、书目、文摘，以及类似内容的各种数据库等。

三级文献，指在二级文献的基础上对一级文献进行分类后，经过加工、整理而成的带有个人观点的文献资料。如数据手册、年鉴、动态综述述评等。

2. 检索文献的步骤

（1）分析研究课题。在检索之前先要分析检索的课题，一要分析主题内容，弄清课题的关键问题所在，确定检索的学科范围；二要分析文献类型，不同类型的文献各具特色，根据自己的检索需要确定检索文献类型范围；三要确定检索的时间范围；四要分析已知的检索线索，逐步扩大。

（2）确定检索工具。正确地确定检索工具，能使我们在浩瀚的文献海洋中畅游无阻，从而以最简捷的方法，迅速、准确地获得研究所需的文献信息。几种检索工具如下。

索引：把文献的一些特征，如书目、篇名、作者，以及文献中出现的人名、地名、概念、词语等组织起来，按一定的顺序（字母或笔画）排列，供人检索。

文摘：它概括地介绍原文献的内容，简短的摘要，使人们不必看全文就可以大致了解文章的内容，是一种使用广泛的检索工具。如《新华文摘》、《教育文摘》等。

书目： 它将各种图书按内容或不同学科分类所编制的目录，如《全国总书目》。

参考性与资料性工具书：它的范围很广，如辞典、百科全书、年鉴等。

计算机和互联网：可以通过搜索引擎等对文献进行查询。

（3）确定检索方法。常用的检索方法如下。

顺序查找法：从课题研究的起始年代开始往后顺时查找，直到近期为止，这种方法查全率高，但费时。

回溯查找法：这是利用某一篇论文（或专著）后面所附的参考资料为线索，跟踪追查的方法。这种查找方法针对性更强、直接、效率高。

计算机检索：计算机以其强大的数据处理和存储能力成为当今最为理想的信息检索工具。计算机检索有以下优点，检索速度快，检索范围大。它可以同时对跨越几年甚至几十年的数据做检索；检索途径多。计算机的数据库能提供十几种甚至几十种的检索工具，还可以使用逻辑的方法把它们组合起来使用，非常灵活；可以同时检索多个数据库。计算机可以把几个数据库同时打开供检索，并且可以去掉其中重复的数据；可以立刻得到原文。由于早期的检索系统大多提供索引、文摘等二级文献，有时我们不得不再去寻找原文即一级文献。现在使用计算机全文检索系统，当场就能看到全文，并且根据需要还可以打印出来。

3. 计算机的检索方式

当前广泛使用的计算机检索包括：联机检索、光盘检索和国际互联网检索。

联机检索（online retrieval）是指用户利用计算机终端设备，通过通信线路，从信息中心的计算机（主机）数据库中检索出所需要的信息的过程。它允许用户以人机对话、联机会话这样交互的方式（interactive）直接访问系统及数据库，检索是实时（real time）、在线（online）进行的。用户的提问一旦传到主机被接收后，机器便立刻执行检索运算，很快将检索结果传送到用户终端，用户可反复修改检索式，最后获得较满意的检索结果。联机检索能远程登录到国内外检索系统。大型检索系统不仅数据库多，而且数据库的文献报道量大，高达数以百万条记录，数据更新及时，系统检索点多，组合方式多样，输出形式、输出方式多样。用户容易得到最新、最准确和最完全的检索效果。

基于 Web 方式的联机检索使用 WWW 浏览器在 Windows 界面下交互作业，给用户揭示到一篇篇文章的信息，有很强的直观性，也可以检索多媒体信息。Web 版数据库检索大量采用超文本。超文本（hypertext）的内容排列是非线性的，它按知识(信息)单元及其关系建立起知识结构网络，如具有图形、画面的信息又称做超媒体（hypermedia），超文本（媒体）的检索是通过超文本链接（hyperlink）来实现的。其形式有的在网页的文字处有下划线，或以图标方式标志，用户点击（point-and-click）这些标志便能进入到与此信息相关的下一页，在该页面上通过超文本链接进入下一个页面，超文本起信息导向作用。这样，用户从一个页面转向另一个页面的控制过程中获取自己所需要的信息。

Web 版文献数据库检索在采用超文本的基础上又将命令检索、菜单检索方式融合其中，交互使用，集各种检索机制为一体。许多大型国际联机检索系统在互联网上开设了自己的站点，提供用户检索服务。

UNIT 15

A. Text

Satellites

1. Satellite Fundamentals

Satellite communication has become a part of everyday life in the late 1980s. An international telephone call is made as a local call to a friend who lives down the block. We also see international events, such as an election in England and a tennis match in France, with the same regularity as local political and sporting events. In this case, television news programs bring the sights and sounds of the world into our homes each night.

This capability to exchange information on a global basis, be it a telephone call or a news story, is made possible through a powerful communication tool—the satellite. For those of us who grew up at a time when the space age was not a part of everyday life, satellite-based communication is the culmination of a dream that stretches back to an era when the term satellite was only an idea conceived by a few inspired individuals. These pioneers included authors such as Arthur C. Clarke, who fostered the idea of a worldwide satellite system in 1945. This idea has subsequently blossomed into a sophisticated satellite network that spans the globe.

The first generation of satellites was fairly primitive when compared with contemporary spacecraft. These early satellites embodied active and passive designs.

A passive satellite, such as the Echo I spacecraft launched in 1960, was not equipped with a two-way transmission system. Rather, Echo was a huge aluminized mylar balloon that functioned as a reflector. After the satellite was placed in a low earth orbit, signals relayed to Echo reflected or bounced off its surface and returned to different locations on the earth.

In contrast with the Echo series, the Telstar I active communication satellite launched in 1962 carried receiving and transmitting equipment. It was an active participant in the reception-transmission process. As the satellite received a signal from a ground or earth station, a communications complex that transmitted and/or received satellite signals, it relayed its own signal to earth[1]. Telstar also paved the way for today's communications spacecraft since it created the world's first international satellite television link.

During the span of years that separates Telstar I from today's satellites, there have been a number of improvements. For example, spacecraft such as Telstar and Echo were placed in low earth orbits. In this type of orbital position, a satellite traveled at such a great rate of speed that it was visible, and hence usable, to an individual ground station for only a limited period of time each day. The satellite appeared from below the horizon, raced across the sky, and then disappeared below the opposite horizon.

Since the ground station was cut off from the now invisible satellite, a station situated below the horizon had to be activated to maintain the communication link. In a different scenario, it would have been necessary to launch a series of satellites to create a continuous satellite-based relay for any given earth station. As one satellite disappeared, it would have been replaced by the next satellite in the series.

The latter type of satellite system would have entailed the development of a very complex and cumbersome earth and space-based network. Fortunately though, this problem was eliminated in 1963 and 1964 through the launching of the Syncom satellites, rather than circling the earth at a rapid rate of speed, the spacecraft appeared to be stationary or fixed in the sky. Today' communications satellites, for the most part, have followed suit and are now placed in what are called geostationary orbital positions or "slots"[2].

Simply stated a satellite in a geostationary orbital position appears to be fixed over one portion of the earth. At an altitude of 22 300 miles above the earth's equator, a satellite travels at the same speed at which the earth rotates, and its motion is synchronized with the earth's rotation. Even though the satellite is moving at an enormous rate of speed, it is stationary in the sky in relation to an observer on the earth.

The primary value of satellite in a geostationary orbit is its ability to communicate with ground stations in its coverage area 24 hours a day. This orbital slot also simplifies the establishment of the communications link between a station and the satellite. Once the station's antenna is properly aligned, only minor adjustments may have to be made in the antenna's position over a period of time. The antenna is repositioned to a significant degree only when the station establishes contact with a satellite in a different slot. Prior to this era, a ground station's antenna had to physically track a satellite as it moved across the sky.

Based on these principles, three satellites in equidistant positions around the earth can create a world-wide communications system in that almost every point on the earth can be reached by satellite. This concept was the basis of Arthur Clarke's original vision of a globe-spanning communications network.

2. Uplinks and Downlinks

According to the FCC, an uplink is the "transmission power that carries a signal from its earth station source up to a satellite", while a downlink "includes the satellite itself, the receiving earth station, and the signal transmitted downward between the two". To simplify our discussion, however, the uplink, for our purposes, will refer to the transmission from the earth station to the satellite, while the downlink is the transmission from the satellite to the earth station.

This two-way information stream, the uplink and the downlink, is conducted with special equipment. The station that relays the signal must possess an antenna or dish that is usually parabolic in shape and a transmitter that produces a high-frequency microwave signal. It should also be noted that some ground stations both receive and transmit signals, while others operate in a receive-only mode.

The communication satellite, for its part, operates as a repeater in the sky. After the satellite receives a signal from the ground station, a signal is relayed back to earth. This process is analogous to the function of an earth-based or terrestrial repeater, but in the case of the satellite, the repeater is located more than 22 000 miles above the earth's surface.

This relay between the ground station and satellite is comprised of the following events:

1. The satellite receives a signal from the earth station.

2. The signal is amplified since it has lost a good part of its strength during its 22 300 miles journey.

3. The satellite changes the signal's frequency to avoid interference between the uplinks and downlinks.

4. The signal is relayed back to earth where it is received by one or more earth stations.

PART 4   Communication Technology

In order to create this communications link, the satellite uses transponders, the satellite equipment that conducts the two-way relays. A communications satellite carries multiple transponders, and as is illustrated by the Intelsat family, the number of transponders per satellite class has increased over the years. This design evolution has led, in turn, to the development of a new generation of satellites that can handle an enormous volume of information via their transponders and related electronic systems[3].

For example, the original Intelsat satellite, Early Bird, was equipped with 2 transponders that supported either a single television channel or 240 voice (telephone) circuits. The later Intelsat IV satellites improved upon this initial development. Each satellite, which was launched in the early-to-mid 1970s, carried 12 transponders that provided the satellite with a total average transmission capacity of 4,000 voice circuits and 2 television channels.

The newer Intelsat V spacecraft are equipped with 27 transponders, while the latest of the Intelsat family, Intelsat VI, will be equipped with 48 transponders. Intelsat VI will accommodate well over 100,000 simultaneous telephone calls and possibly 3 television channels.

New words and Technical Terms

aluminize	[əˈljuːmənaiz]	vt. 镀铝，以铝覆盖，以铝处理
antenna	[ænˈtenə]	n. 天线
dish	[diʃ]	v. 提出；
		n. 盘，碟；盘装菜；碟形卫星天线，接收天线盘
downlink	[ˈdaunliŋk]	n. 下行线路，下链路
repeater	[riˈpiːtə]	n. 转发器，中继器
uplink	[ˈʌpˌliŋk]	n. 上行线路，上链路

Notes

[1] As the satellite received a signal from a ground or earth station, a communications complex that transmitted and/or received satellite signals, it relayed its own signal to earth.

地面站是传送/接收卫星信号的通信设备，卫星接收来自地面站发送的信号后，再将其信号传送给地球。

a communications complex that transmitted and/or received satellite signals 是 a ground or earth station 的同位语。

[2] Today's communications satellites, for the most part, have followed suit and are now placed in what are called geostationary orbital positions or "slots".

对于当今的通信卫星，就绝大部分而言，都遵循此道，而且放置在被称为相对地面静止轨道的位置上。

[3] This design evolution has led, in turn, to the development of a new generation of satellites that can handle an enormous volume of information via their transponders and related

electronic systems.

反过来，这种设计的改进又可引导研制新一代的卫星，这些卫星能够通过其转发器及相关电子系统处理大量的信息。

Exercises

Ⅰ. Fill in the blanks with words and phrases found in the context.

1. This capability to exchange information on a global basis, be it a telephone call or a news story, is made possible through a powerful communications tool _____ .

2. For those of us who grew up at a time when the space age was not a part of everyday life, satellite-based communication is the _____ of a dream that stretches back to an era when the term satellite was only an idea conceived by a few _____ individuals.

3. In a different scenario, it would have been necessary to launch _____ satellites to create a continuous satellite-based relay for any given _____ .

4. Today's communications satellites, for the most part, have followed suit and are now placed in what are called _____ orbital positions or " _____ ".

Ⅱ. Write T (True) or F (False) beside the following statements according to the text.

1. Spacecraft such as Telstar and Echo were placed in earth orbits.

2. The antenna is repositioned to a minor degree when the station establishes contact with a satellite in a different slot.

3. If an earth station pointed its receiving dish toward a specific satellite, it could not intercept a different satellite's signal.

4. The FCC's decision has had serious repercussions for organizations that use satellites.

B. Reading

Basic Knowledge of Communication

Communication System

A generalized communication system has the following components (as shown in Fig. 4-13):

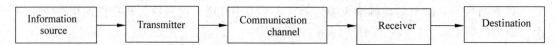

Fig. 4-13 Communication System.

PART 4 Communication Technology

(1) Information Source. This produces a message which may be written or spoken words, or some form of data.

(2) Transmitter. The transmitter converts the message into a signal, the form of which is suitable for transmission over the communication channel.

(3) Communication Channel. The communication channel is the medium used transmit the signal, from the transmitter to the receiver. The channel may be a radio link or a direct wire connection.

(4) Receiver. The receiver can be thought of as the inverse of the transmitter. It changes the received signal back into a message and passes the message on to its destination which may he a loudspeaker, teleprinter or computer data bank.

An unfortunate characteristic of all communication channels is that noise is added to the signal. This unwanted noise may cause distortions of sound in a telephone, or errors in a telegraph message or data.

Frequency Division Multiplexing

Frequency Division Multiplexing (FDM) is a one of analog techniques. A speech signal is 0~3kHz, Single sideband amplitude (SSB) modulation can be used to transfer speech signal to new frequency bands, four similar signals, for example, moved by SSB modulation to share the band from 5 to 20kHz. The gaps between channels are known as guard spaces and these allow for errors in frequency, inadequate filtering, etc in the engineered system.

Once this new baseband signal, a "group" of 4 channels, has been formed it is moved around the trunk network as a single unit. A hierarchy can be set up with several channels forming a "group", several groups a "supergroup" and several "supergroup" either a "mastergroup" or "hypergroup".

Groups or supergroups are moved around as single units by the communications equipment and it is not necessary for the radios to know how many channels are involved. A radio can handle a supergroup provided sufficient bandwidth is available. The size of the groups is a compromise as treating each channel individually involves far more equipment because separate filters, modulators and oscillators are required for every channel rather than for each group. However the failure of one module will lose all of the channels associated with a group.

Time Division Multiplexing

It is possible, with pulse modulation systems, to use the between samples to transmit signals from other circuits. The technique is known as time division multiplexing (TDM). To do this it is necessary to employ synchronized switches at each end of the communication link to enable samples to be transmitted in turn, from each of several circuits. Thus several subscribers appear to use the link simultaneously. Although each user only has periodic short time slots, the original analog signals between samples can be reconstituted at the receiver. Typical TDM system is shown in Fig. 4-14.

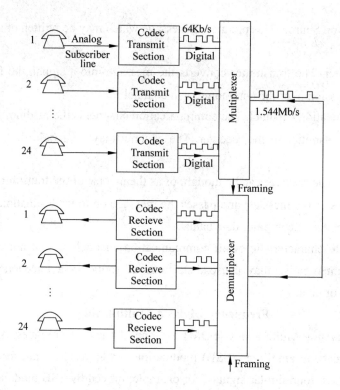

Fig. 4-14 Time Division Multiplexing (TDM) System.

Pulse Code Modulation

In analog modulation, the signal was used to modulate the amplitude or frequency of a carrier, directly. However in digital modulation a stream of pulses, representing the original, is created. This stream is then used to modulate a carrier or alternatively is transmitted directly over a cable. Pulse Code Modulation (PCM) is one of the two techniques commonly used.

All pulse systems depend on the analog waveform being sampled at regular intervals. The signal created by sampling our analog speech input is known as pulse amplitude modulation (as shown in Fig. 4-15). It is not very useful in practice but is used as an intermediate stage towards

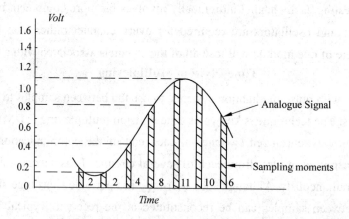

Fig. 4-15 Sampling.

forming a PCM signal. It will be seen later that most of the advantages of digital modulation come from the transmitted pulses having two levels only, this being known as a binary system. In PCM the height of each sample is converted into a binary number. There are three steps in the process of PCM: sampling, quantizing and coding.

New words and Technical Terms

teleprinter	['teli,printə]	n. 电传打字机
multiplexing	['mʌltipleksiŋ]	n. 多路技术
hierarchy	['haiərɑːki]	n. 层次，层级
synchronize	['siŋkrənaiz]	n. 同步
reconstitute	[riːˈkɔnstitjuːt]	v. 重组，重任命

Exercises

Ⅰ. Write T (True) or F (False) beside the following statements about the text.

1. There is no noise added to the signal in all of the communication channels.
2. Groups or supergroups are moved around as single units by the communications equipment and it is necessary for the radios to know how many channels are involved.
3. A radio can not handle a supergroup but provided sufficient bandwidth.
4. The failure of one module will not lose all of the channels associated with a group.
5. Noise may cause distortions of sound in a telephone.
6. In digital modulation the signal was used to modulate the amplitude or frequency of a carrier.
7. Pulse Code Modulation (PCM) is one of the two techniques commonly used.
8. Pulse amplitude modulation is very useful in practice but is used as an intermediate stage towards forming a PCM signal.

Ⅱ. Translate the following into Chinese.

It is possible, with pulse modulation systems, to use the between samples to transmit signals from other circuits. The technique is known as time division multiplexing (TDM). To do this it is necessary to employ synchronized switches at each end of the communication link to enable samples to be transmitted in turn, from each of several circuits. Thus several subscribers appear to use the link simultaneously. Although each user only has periodic short time slots, the original analog signals between samples can be reconstituted at the receiver.

C. SCI 与 EI 简介

1. SCI 简介

美国《科学引文索引》（Science Citation Index，SCI）于 1957 年由美国科学信息研究所（Institute for Scientific Information，ISI）在美国费城创办。40多年来，SCI（或称ISI）数据库不断发展，已经成为当代世界最为重要的大型数据库，被列在国际六大著名检索系统之首。它不仅是一部重要的检索工具书，而且也是科学研究成果评价的一项重要依据。它已成为目前国际上最具权威性的，用于基础研究和应用基础研究成果的重要评价体系。它是评价一个国家、一个科学研究机构、一所高等学校、一本期刊，乃至一个研究人员学术水平的重要指标之一。

（1）SCI 来源期刊的两个档次。

SCI：是 SCI 的核心库，产品代码 K（内圈）。

SCI-Expanded（SCI-E）：是 SCI 的扩展库，产品代码 D（外圈）。

内圈与外圈都是精选的，同等重要。其区别在于：影响因子、地区因素、学科平衡等。

（2）SCI 产品的 6 种版本。

① SCI Print 印刷版。1961 年创刊至今。双月刊。现在拥有 3 700 余种期刊，全为内圈。

② SCI-CDE 光盘版。季度更新。现在拥有 3 700 余种期刊，全为内圈。

③ SCI-CDE with Abstracts 带有摘要的光盘版。逐月更新。现在拥有 3 700 余种期刊，全为内圈。

④ Magnetic Tape 磁带数据库。每周更新。现在拥有 5 700 余种期刊，外圈。

⑤ SCI Search Online 联机数据库。每周更新。现在拥有 5 700 余种期刊，外圈。

⑥ The Web of Science SCI 的网络版。每周更新。现在拥有 5 700 余种期刊，外圈。

（3）SCI 数据库的分类。

目前，SCI 数据库分为两类。

① 引文索引数据库（Citation Index，CI）。包括 4 类学术领域。

- 科学引文索引（Science Citation Index，SCI（产品代码为 K））3500 种期刊。
- 社会科学引文索引（Social Science Citation Index，SSCI（J））1700 种期刊。
- 艺术与人文引文索引（Art & Humanities Citation Index，AHCI）1150 种期刊。
- 其他专业引文索引：

    ◇ 计算数学引文索引 CompuMath Citation Index。

    ◇ 生物化学与生物物理引文索引 Biochemistry & Biophysics Citation Index (BB)。

    ◇ 生物技术引文索引 Biotechnology Citation Index (HI)。

    ◇ 化学引文索引 Chemistry Citation Index (CD)。

    ◇ 神经科学引文索引 Neuroscience Citation Index (MD)。

    ◇ 材料科学引文索引 Materials Science Citation Index (MS)。

② 现刊题录数据库 （Current Contents，CC）。主要包括如下内容。

- 科学技术会议录索引（Index to Scientific & Technical Proccedings，ISTP）。
- 社会及人文学会议录索引（Index to Social Sciences & Humanities Proccedings，ISSHP）。

（4）SCI 对稿件内容和学术水平的要求。

① 主要收录数学、物理、化学等学术理论价值高并具有创新的论文。

② 国家自然科学基金资助项目、科技攻关项目、"八六三"高技术项目等。

③ 论文已达到国际先进水平。

2. EI 简介

美国《工程索引》(Engineering Index, EI),于 1884 年由美国工程信息公司(Engineering Information Inc.)创办,是一个主要收录工程技术期刊文献和会议文献的大型检索系统。

(1) EI 把它收录的论文分为两个档次。

① EI Compendex 标引文摘:它收录论文的题录、摘要、主题词和分类号,进行深加工;有没有主题词和分类号是判断论文是否被 Ei 正式收录的唯一标志。

② EI PageOne 题录:不列入文摘,没有主题词和分类号,不进行深加工。有的 PageOne 也带有摘要,但未进行深加工,没有主题词和分类号。所以带有文摘不一定算做正式进入 EI。

(2) EI 发展的几个阶段。

① 创办初,月刊、年刊的印刷本(EI Compendex),1884 年至今。

② 20 世纪 70 年代,电子版数据库(EI Compendex),并通过 Dialog 等大型联机系统提供检索服务。

③ 20 世纪 80 年代,光盘版(CD-ROM)形式(EI Compendex)。

④ 20 世纪 90 年代,提供网络版数据库(CPX Web),推出了工程信息村(Engineering Village: EI Compendex + PageOne)。

⑤ 1999 年,中国 18 所高等学校联合购买网络版数据库的使用权,镜像在清华大学图书馆。

⑥ 2000 年 8 月,EI 推出 Engineering Village 2 新版本,于 2000 年底出版。

(3) EI 对稿件内容和学术水平的要求。

① 具有较高的学术水平的工程论文,如:机械工程、机电工程、船舶工程、制造技术等,矿业、冶金、材料工程、金属材料、有色金属、陶瓷、塑料及聚合物工程等,土木工程、建筑工程、结构工程、海洋工程、水利工程等,电气工程、电厂、电子工程、通信、自动控制、计算机、计算技术、软件、航空航天技术等,化学工程、石油化工、燃烧技术、生物技术、轻工纺织、食品工业,工程管理。

特别需要指出的是,EI 不收录数理化、生物学、医药、农林等学术理论论文。

② 国家自然科学基金资助项目、科技攻关项目、"八六三"高技术项目等。

③ 论文达到国际先进水平,成果有创新。

UNIT 16

A. Text

Introduction to Computer Networks

During the 1950s, most computers were similar in one respect. They had a main memory, a central processing unit (CPU), and peripherals. The memory and CPU were central to the system. Since then a new generation of computing has emerged in which computation and data storage need not be centralized. A user may retrieve a program from one place, run it on any of a variety of processors, and send the result to a third location.

A system connecting different devices such as PCs, printers, and disk drives is a network. Typically, each device in a network serves a specific purpose for one or more individuals. For example, a PC may sit on your desk providing access to information or software you need. A PC may also be devoted to managing a disk drive containing shared files. We call it a file server. Often a network covers a small geographic area and connects devices in a single building or group of buildings. Such a network is a local area network (LAN). A network that covers a larger area such as a municipality, state, country, or the world is called a wide area network (WAN).

Generally speaking, most networks may involve many people using many PCs, each of which can access any of many printers or servers. With all these people accessing information, their requests inevitably will conflict[1]. Consequently, the devices must be connected in a way that permits an orderly transfer of information for all concerned. A good analogy is a street layout in a large city. With only one person driving it matters little where the streets are, which ones are one-way, where the traffic signals are, or how they are synchronized. But with thousands of the cars on the streets during the morning rush hour, a bad layout will create congestion that causes major delays. The same is true of computer networks. They must be connected in a way that allows data to travel among many users with little or no delay. We call the connection strategy the network topology. The best topology depends on the types of devices and user needs. What works well for one group may perform dismally for another.

Some common network topologies are described as following.

Fig. 4-16 shows a common bus topology (or simply bus topology) connecting devices such as workstations, mainframes, and file servers. They communicate through a single bus (a collection of parallel lines). A common approach gives each device an interface that listens to the bus and examines its data traffic. If an interface determines that data are destined for the device it serves, it reads the data from the bus and transfers it to the device. Similarly, if a device wants to transmit data, the interface circuit sense when the bus is empty and then transmit data. This is not unlike waiting on a freeway entrance ramp during rush hour. You sense an opening and either quickly dart to it or muscle your way through, depending on whether you're driving a subcompact or a large truck.

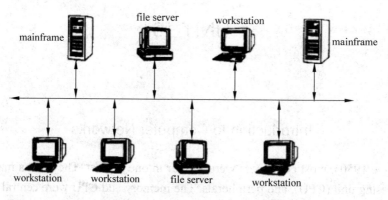

Fig. 4-16 A common bus topology.

Sometimes, two devices try to transmit simultaneously. Each one detects an absence of traffic and begins transmitting before becoming aware of the other device's transmission. The result is a collision of signals. As the devices transmit they continue to listen to the bus and detect the noise resulting from the collisions. When a device detects a collision it stops transmitting, waits a random period of time, and tries again. This process, called Carrier Sense, Multiple Access with Collision Detection (CSMA/CD) will be discussed later.

One popular common bus network is an Ethernet. Its common bus typically is Ethernet cable, which consists of copper, optical fiber, or combinations of both. Its design allows terminals, PCs, disk storage systems, and office machines to communicate. A major advantage of an Ethernet is the ability to add new devices to the network easily.

Another common connecting arrangement is the star topology, shown in Fig. 4-17. It uses a central computer that communicates with other devices in the network. Control is centralized; if device wants to communicate, it does so only through the central computer. The computer, in turn, routes the data to its destination. Centralization provides a focal point for responsibility, an advantage of the star topology. The bus topology, however, has some advantages over a star topology. The lack of central control makes adding new devices easy because no device needs to be aware of others. In addition, the failure or removal of a device in a bus network does not cause the network to fail. In a star topology, the failure of the central computer brings down the entire network.

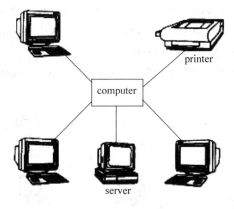

Fig. 4-17 The star topology.

Star topologies often involve a single mainframe computer that services many terminals and secondary devices. With appropriate terminal emulation software, PCs can communicate with the mainframe. Data transfers between terminals or between terminals and storage devices occur only through the main computer.

In a ring topology shown in Fig. 4-18, devices are connected circularly. Each one can communicate directly with either or both of its neighbors but nobody else[2]. If it wants to communicate with a device farther away, it sends a message that passes through each device in between.

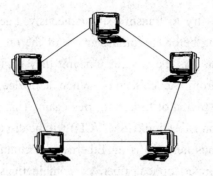

Fig. 4-18 A ring topology.

A ring network may be either unidirectional or bidirectional. Unidirectional means that all transmissions travel in the same direction. Thus, each device can communicate with only one neighbor. Bidirectional means that data transmissions travel in either direction, that is, a device can communicate with both neighbors.

Ring topologies such as IBM's token ring network often connect PCs in a single office or department. Applications from one PC thus can access data stored on others without requiring a mainframe to coordinate communications[3]. Instead, communications are coordinated by passing a token among all the stations in the ring. A station can send something only when it receives the token.

A disadvantage of the ring topology is that when one station sends to another, all stations in between are involved. More time is spent relaying messages meant for others than in, for example, a bus topology[4]. Moreover, the failure of one station causes a break in the ring that affects communications among all the stations.

Many computer networks are combinations of various topologies. Fig. 4-19 shows a possible combination.

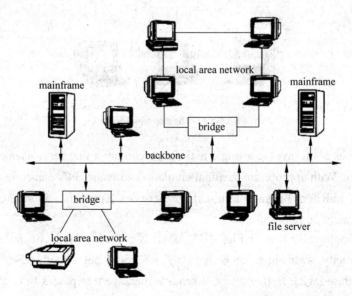

Fig. 4-19 Combinations of various topologies.

New words and Technical Terms

peripheral	[pəˈrifərəl]	n.	外围设备
congestion	[kənˈdʒestʃən]	n.	充满，拥塞
topology	[təˈpɔlədʒi]	n.	拓扑
dismally	[ˈdizməli]	adv.	忧郁地；无力地
mainframe	[ˈmeinfreim]	n.	大型机
bus	[bʌs]	n.	总线
dart	[dɑːt]	v.	猛冲
muscle	[ˈmʌsl]	v.	强行侵入
Ethernet		n.	以太网
terminal	[ˈtəːminl]	n.	终端
circularly	[ˈsəːkjuləli]	adv.	圆形地，循环地
bidirectional	[ˌbaidiˈrekʃənəl]	adj.	双向的
token	[ˈtəukən]	n.	令牌

Notes

[1] With all these people accessing information, their requests inevitably will conflict.

在这么多人存取信息的情况下，不可避免地会产生冲突。

本句中的 With 表示"在……的情况下"，而 accessing information 是现在分词短语，修饰前面的 these people。

[2] Each one can communicate directly with either or both of its neighbors but nobody else.

每一个设备只能与它相邻的一边或两边之间进行的通信，而不能与此外其他设备直接通信。

[3] Applications from one PC thus can access data stored on others without requiring a mainframe to coordinate communications.

一个 PC 上的应用程序可以访问其他机器上的数据，而用不着大型机对通信进行协调。

stored on others 是过去分词短语，作定语修饰它前面的名词"数据"，而 without requiring a mainframe to coordinate communications 表示条件。

[4] More time is spent relaying messages meant for others than in, for example, a bus topology.

这样，比起总线拓扑来，要花更多的时间来为其他的站点转发数据。

本句中，relaying messages 是一个现在分词短语作状语，表示原因；而 meant for others 是一个过去分词短语，修饰 messages。

Exercises

Ⅰ. Please translate the following phrase into Chinese.

1. Central processing unit

2. Local area network

3. Network topology

4. Token ring network

II. Choose the one that best suits the sentence according to the text.

1. During the 1950s, most computers were _____ in one respect. They had a main memory, a central processing unit (CPU), and peripherals.

  A. same   B. different   C. similar   D. the same as

2. A PC may also be devoted to managing a disk drive containing shared _____ . We call it a file server.

  A. files   B. devices   C. printer   D. peripherals

3. With all these people accessing information, their requests _____ will conflict.

  A. usually   B. often   C. sometimes   D. inevitably

4. Sometimes, two devices try to transmit simultaneously. Each one detects an absence of traffic and begins _____ before becoming aware of the other device's transmission.

  A. transmit   B. to send   C. transfer   D. transmitting

5. Star topologies often _____ a single mainframe computer that services many terminals and secondary devices.

  A. evolve   B. covers   C. involve   D. revolve

B. Reading

Where Do Security Threats Come from

  Imagine you work for an organization. You produce goods and/or services. They have value in the marketplace, or you would not be doing it. Your organization took the risks, did the research, and made the investments. You are entitled to the fruits of your labor.

  Unfortunately, there is always a human element eager to take advantage of the work done by you and others, yet without the customary quid pro quo: payment for services rendered or for product provided.

  Direct theft of products or services is a simple motivation. More complex is the theft of information for a variety of nefarious purposes: to improve a competitor's position; to further a political aim; to deny you timely access to correct information that you need to survive; to give the perpetrator an ego high.

  Security is entirely a people issue. It is people who cause security problems, not machines or systems. Fortunately, our high-technology tools can also serve to thwart people who would do us harm, just the way we lock our doors against intruders. That security is a people problem must be borne in mind as an underlying constant theme in any discussion of security.

Even well-intentioned people are a weak point. Well-meaning people write down passwords or let others use theirs. While we try to use social "engineering" internally to modify behavior so that people will keep security in mind, outsiders try to use the same principle of social engineering to talk users out of passwords. In a sense, they are taking advantage of our incomplete or ineffective social engineering, trying to replace it with their own.

Now we are mentally prepared to begin to think like our adversaries. If we can put ourselves in their place, then we can do some role-playing and begin to view our security precautions not just from the inside, but from the outside. Such a dual perspective is essential to effective security management.

1. What Can People Do to Our Information?

- They can destroy:
  Information
  Executable programs
  Operating systems
  Other computing or system resources

Destruction includes both logical damage (to the system involved) and/or physical damage to the equipment itself. More subtle and short of destruction, tamperers can alter any of the above, presenting the appearance of legitimacy though the reality is false.

- They can steal:
  Information
  Service
  Hardware
  Software

Theft includes simply taking information not belonging to them, whether acted on or not. It includes the unauthorized use of system resources and is exemplified by the theft of telephone service. Theft plainly includes removal (such as deletion of information) as well as physical transport off the premises.

- They can disclose:
  Information to which they have no right or need
  Information to unauthorized personnel for other motivations
  How to let others use resources not intended for outside use
- They can cause service disruptions or interruptions:
  By causing physical or logical damage to the system
  By improperly denying access to legitimate users

It is important to note that motivation is not always relevant. Any of the above losses can be caused accidentally. Furthermore, the above can be caused as of omission (such as failing to do a backup) or commission (such as deliberately causing a malfunction).

2. Classifying Threat Sources

A threat is first classified as originating from outside or inside the organization. From there, we proceed to more specific subcategories:

- External threats include:

    Hackers

    Commercial espionage

    Government-sanctioned espionage

    Vendors

    Former employees

- Internal threats include:

    Disgruntled employees

    Unintentional losses or security breaches

    Hackers

The bulk of the case evidence shows that it is the internal and not the external threat that must concern us the most. Kenneth Weiss, the founder and chairman of Security Dynamics, says that 78 percent of computer abuse originates with a company's own employees. Even so, instances of external interference are growing.

New words and Technical Terms

adversary	[ˈædvəsəri]	n. 敌手，对手
disgruntled	[dɪsˈgrʌnt(ə)ld]	adj. 不满的，不高兴的
espionage	[ˈespiənidʒ]	n. 间谍，侦探
nefarious	[niˈfɛəriəs]	adj. 邪恶的，穷凶极恶的
perpetrator	[ˈpəːpitreit]	n. 犯罪者，作恶者
quid	[kwid]	n. 咀嚼物；[英俚]一镑，20 先令
quid pro quo	[kwid prəu ˈkwəu]	n. 补偿物，交换物，相等物，代用品
tamper	[ˈtæmpə]	vi. 干预，损害，削弱，篡改
		vt. 篡改
tamperer		n. 填塞者，干涉者
thwart	[θwɔːt]	adj. 横放的；vt. 反对，阻碍，横过

Exercises

Translate the following into Chinese.

Direct theft of products or services is a simple motivation. More complex is the theft of information for a variety of nefarious purposes: to improve a competitor's position; to further a political aim; to deny you timely access to correct information that you need to survive; to give the perpetrator an ego high.

C. 信息类国内、外重要学术期刊

一般认为，信息学科主要包括电工、电机、电子、通信、计算机、自动化等学科，下面列出了国内、外信息类主要的学术期刊。

1. 国内信息类学术期刊

国内重要学术期刊一般由中国科学院、科技部、教育部以及各专业学会主办，如《自动化学报》由中国自动化学会主办，《计算机学报》由中国计算机学会主办等，国内各行业主要学术期刊如表4-1～表4-4所示。

表 4-1　电工类国内主要学术期刊

1 中国电机工程学报	2 电工技术学报
3 电力系统自动化	4 电网技术
5 电气自动化	6 电气传动
7 中小型电机	8 电工技术杂志
9 微电机	10 微特电机
11 高电压技术	12 电测与仪表

表 4-2　电子、通信类国内主要学术期刊

1 电子学报	2 通信学报
3 中国激光	4 电子与信息学报
5 半导体学报	6 红外与微米波学报
7 电子技术应用	8 电波科学学报
9 电路与系统学报	10 微电子学
11 微波学报	12 固体电子学研究与进展
13 真空科学与技术学报	14 量子电子学报
15 激光与光电子学进展	16 红外与激光工程

表 4-3　自动化、控制类国内主要学术期刊

1 自动化学报	2 控制理论与应用
3 控制与决策	4 信息与控制
5 系统工程与电子技术	6 机器人
7 系统仿真学报	8 系统工程学报
9 模式识别与人工智能	10 仪器仪表学报
11 电机与控制学报	12 电力系统及其自动化学报
13 数据采集与处理	14 传感器学报

表 4-4 计算机类国内主要学术期刊

1 计算机学报	2 软件学报
3 计算机研究与发展	4 小型微型计算机系统
5 计算机辅助设计与图形学学报	6 中国图像图形学报
7 计算机集成制造系统-CIMS	8 计算机科学
9 遥感学报	10 计算机工程
11 计算机应用	12 计算机应用研究
13 计算机工程与设计	14 计算机应用与软件
15 计算机工程与应用	16 微型计算机

2. 国外信息类学术期刊

国外信息类学术期刊众多，除鼎鼎大名的《科学》与《自然》外，主要以美国 IEEE 会刊、ACM 会刊、英国 IET 会刊（英国著名的学会 IEE 已于 2006 年 4 月 1 日起正式更名为 Institution of Engineering and Technology，简称 IET，中文译名为英国工程技术学会）为主，国际各行业学术期刊如表 4-5～表 4-8 所示。

表 4-5 电信类国外主要学术期刊

1 IEEE Transactions on Communications
2 IEEE Transactions on Wireless Communications
3 IEEE Transactions on Circuits and Systems
4 IEEE Transactions on Signal Processing
5 European Transactions on Telecommunications
6 European Transactions on Telecommunications and Related Technologies
7 IEEE Transactions on Mobile Computing
8 IEEE Wireless Communications
9 IEEE Communications Letters
10 IEEE Communications Magazine
11 IEEE Signal Processing Magazine
12 IET – Communications

表 4-6 自动化、控制类国外主要学术期刊

1 IEEE Transactions on Automatic control
2 Automatic
3 International Journal of Control
4 System & Control Letters
5 IEEE Transactions on Control Systems Technology
6 IEEE Control Systems Magazine
7 IEEE Transactions on Systems Man and Cybernetics Part B-Cybernetics
8 IET-Control Theory and Applications
9 IEEE Transactions on Robotics and Automation
10 IEEE Transactions on Industrial Electronics
11 IEEE Transactions on Fuzzy Systems
12 IEEE Intelligent Systems

表 4-7　计算机类国外主要学术期刊

1 Computers & Structures
2 IEEE Software
3 Computers
4 IEEE Transactions on Computers
5 IEEE Transactions on Software Engineering
6 ACM Computing Surveys
7 ACM Transactions on Computers Systems
8 ACM Transactions on Database Systems
9 ACM Transactions on Information Systems
10 ACM Transactions on Mathematical Software
11 ACM Transactions on Programming Languages and Systems
12 ACM Transactions on Software Engineering and Methodology

表 4-8　电工、电子类国外主要学术期刊

1 IEEE Electron Device Letters
2 IEEE Transactions on Instrumentation and Measurement
3 IEEE Transactions on Microwave Theory and Techniques
4 IEEE Transactions on Electron Devices
5 IEEE Transactions on Power Delivery
6 IEEE Transactions on Power Systems
7 IEEE Microwave and Wireless Components Letters
8 IEEE Transactions on Antennas and Propagation
9 IET-Radar and Navigation
10 IET-Vision Image and Signal Processing
11 IET-Microwaves Antennas and Propagation
12 IET-Electric Power Applications
13 IET-Circuits Devices and Systems
14 IEEE - Electronics Letters

应用篇

PART 1 科技论文的结构与写作初步

科技资料主要包括科技图书与科技论文。一般而言，图书的篇幅比论文要长得多，通常可分为两大类：专著和普及性读物。专著通常是对某一问题或某一类问题进行深入的探论，所包含的内容往往比较难。普及性读物则是对某一问题较为全面、实用的论述，通常注重实践性。两类图书具有相同的结构：前言、目录、正文、附录、索引和参考文献。本章主要讨论科技论文的结构与写作问题。

科技论文一般包括报刊科普论文、学术论文、毕业论文和学位论文。科技论文是在科学研究、科学实验的基础上，对自然科学和专业技术领域里的某些现象或问题进行专题研究、分析和阐述，揭示出这些现象和问题的本质及其规律性而撰写成的文章。也就是说，凡是运用概念、判断、推理、论证和反驳等逻辑思维手段，来分析和阐明自然科学原理、定律和各种问题的文章均属科技论文的范畴。科技论文主要用于科学技术研究及其成果的描述，是研究成果的体现。运用它们进行成果推广、信息交流、促进科学技术的发展。它们的发表标志着研究工作的水平，为社会所公认，载入人类知识宝库，成为人们共享的精神财富。科技论文还是考核科技人员业绩的重要标准。

1. 科技论文的特点

科技论文一般具备以下 5 个特点。

（1）学术性。科技论文是科学研究的成果，是客观存在的自然现象及其规律的反映。它要求运用科学的原理和方法，对自然科学领域新问题进行科学分析，严密论证，抽象概括。学术论文的科学性，要求作者在立论上不得带有个人好恶的偏见，不得主观臆造，必须切实地从客观实际出发，从中引出符合实际的结论。在论据上，应尽可能多地收集资料，以最充分的、确凿有力的论据作为立论的依据。在论证时，必须经过周密的思考，进行严谨的论证。可见，学术性是科技论文最基本的特征。

（2）创造性。科技论文不同于教科书和综述性的科学报告，后者的主要任务在于传授知识，能否提出新的内容并不起决定作用，而科技论文则必须有新的内容，科学研究是对新知识的探求。创造性是科学研究的生命。学术论文的创造性在于作者要有自己独到的见解，能提出新的观点、新的理论。这是因为科学的本性就是"革命的和非正统的"，"科学方法主要是发现新现象、制定新理论的一种手段，旧的科学理论就必然会不断地被新的理论推翻。"因此，没有创造性，学术论文就没有科学价值。

（3）理论性。学术论文在形式上是属于议论文的，但它与一般议论文不同，它必须是有自己的理论系统的，不能只是材料的罗列，应对大量的事实、材料进行分析、研究，使感性认识上升到理性认识。一般来说，学术论文具有论证色彩，或具有论辩色彩。论文的内容必须符合历史唯物主义和唯物辩证法，符合"实事求是"、"有的放矢"、"既分析又综合"的科学研究方法。

（4）专业性。不同的专业的科技论文的内容和表示形式不尽相同。可将科技论文分为理论型、实验型和描述型三种。理论型论文的主要研究方法是理论分析；实验型论文的主要研究方法是设计实验、实验过程研究和实验结果分析；描述型论文的主要研究方法是描述说明，目的是介绍新发现的事物或现象及其所具有的科学价值，重点说明这一新事物是什么现象或不是什么现象。

（5）平易性。指的是要用通俗易懂的语言表述科学道理，不仅要做到文从字顺，而且要准确、鲜明、和谐、力求生动。即为人所用，不要让别人看不懂。

2．科技论文的一般结构

随着科学技术的飞速发展，科技论文的大量发表，越来越要求论文作者以规范化、标准化的固定结构模式（即通用型格式）来表达他们的研究过程和成果。这种通用型结构形式，是经过长期实践，人们总结出来的论文写作的表达形式和规律。这种结构形式是最明确、最易令人理解的表达科研成果的好形式，并逐步形成了科学技术报告、学位论文和学术论文的编写格式国家标准（GB 7713—87），其通用型基本结构如下。

```
1. 标题
2. 作者及其工作单位
3. 摘要
4. 引言
5. 正文
6. 结论
7. 致谢
8. 参考文献
9. 附录
```

3．英文科技论文的理解

英文科技论文的阅读是迅速了解科技与工程动态的必要手段，而英文科技论文的写作是进行国际学术交流必须掌握的技能，也是科技成果得到世界同行认可的最佳方式。在撰写英文科技论文时，除了遵循科技论文的基本要求之外，还需要注意英文国际论文的写作风格。究其原因主要在于中国人和西方人思维方式、文化习惯等方面上的差异，这一点突出的表现在于文章的结构与表达上的不同。比如说，中国人行文比较含蓄，因此文章各段之间可能存在不明显的内在关联；而西方人则比较直截了当，他们的文章结构往往一目了然。因此，即使已有一篇现成的中文论文，在其基础上写英文论文时，也不能采用"拿来主义"逐字逐句地翻译。

理解与撰写英文科技论文的第一步就是要了解英文科技论文的分类。英文科技论文一般分为如下 5 个方面。

（1）综述文章（Review paper）。综述文章一般是对一类问题在自己研究的基础上的总结，不是情况的罗列，除了对文献的理解之外，对这个问题自己的分析与看法是不可缺少的。究其原因是，已经发表的研究报告，有些是重要的，但大多数是无关紧要的，综述必须能够根据自己的研究经验去粗取精，以便追随研究者参考。如何去粗取精，这就需要比较，在理论的进展、技术的有效，以及应用的条件等方面都需要考虑。此外，问题的演变与发展也是综述必须包括的内容。因此，一般而言，只有在该领域内有较大影响的学者才可能写出较好的综述。

（2）研究论文（Research paper）。研究论文通常是指对科学领域中的某些现象和问题进行比较系统的研究，以探讨其本质特征及其发展规律等的理论性文章。英文研究论文通常又分为长论文与短论文。本章主要讨论研究论文的结构与写作问题。

（3）简报（brief / Note/ Short article）。简报是传递某方面信息的小论文，具有简洁、精悍、快速、新颖和连续性等特点，一般是某项科学研究的初步进展与新的发现。

（4）评论/回复（Comments / Reply）。评论通常是针对该杂志先前发表的某篇研究论文或简报所做出的评论性文章，且一般是评判性地指出该论文存在的问题与错误之处；而回复则是原论文作者就评论文章指出的问题给出的回复。

（5）书评（Book Review）。书评通常是某领域类有较大影响的学者对新出版的科技专著作出的评论，一般都是推荐性的评论。

理解与撰写英文科技论文的第二步就是要了解推敲科技论文的结构，使之成为西方人利于理解的形式。尽管目前中文科技论文与英文科技论文在论文整体结构上已经趋于一致，但东西方文化的表达与逻辑思维上存在不小差异，特别是科技论文本身的严肃性，即使西方本土大学生也需要科技论文的正规训练。

本章以研究论文为主，简述科技论文的结构与规范。研究论文一般结构如下。

```
标题（Title）
摘要（Abstract）
关键词（KeyWords）
正文
    引言（Introduction）
    主体（Body）
    结论（Conclusion）
致谢（Acknowledgment）
参考文献（Reference）
```

A. Title

标题是论文特定内容最恰当、最简明的逻辑组合，即应"以最少数量的单词来充分表述论文的内容"。标题主要有两个作用：

① 吸引读者，题名相当于论文的"标签"（label），读者通常根据标题来考虑是否需要阅读摘要或全文，因此，标题表达不当，就会失去其应有的作用，使读者错过阅读论文的机会。

② 帮助文献追踪或检索。文献检索系统多以题名中的主题词作为线索，因而标题必须准确反映论文的核心内容，否则就有可能产生漏检与错误。因此，不恰当的标题很可能会导致该论文的"丢失"，从而失去科技论文本身的意义与潜在价值。

1. 基本要求

（1）准确（accuracy）。标题要准确地反映论文的内容，不能过于空泛和一般化，也不宜过于烦琐。为确保标题的含义准确，应尽量避免使用非定量的、含义不明的词；并力求用词专业性与专指性。

（2）简洁（brevity）。标题的用词应该简短、明了，以最少的文字概括尽可能多的内容。题名最好不超过10～12个单词，或100个英文字符；若能用一行文字表达，则尽量不用2行（超过2行可能会削弱读者的印象）。当然，在撰写题名时不能因为追求形式上的简短而忽视对论文内容的反映。题名过于简短，常起不到帮助读者理解论文的作用。另外，还要注意避免题名中词意上的重叠；在内容层次很多的情况下，如果难以简短化，最好采用主、副题名相结合的方法。

（3）清楚（clarity）。标题要清晰地反映文章的具体内容和特色，明确表明研究工作的独到之处，力求简洁有效、重点突出。为使表达直接、清楚，以便引起读者的注意，应尽可能地将表达核心内容的主题词放在标题开头。题名中应慎重使用缩略语，尤其对于有多个解释的缩略语，应严加限制，必要时应在括号中注明全称。对那些全称较长，缩写后已得到科技界公认的才可使用，并且这种使用还应得到相应期刊读者群的认可。

2. 标题的结构

（1）标题的构成。标题常分为词组型标题、动宾型标题、陈述句标题、问句型标题，以及带副标题或破折号标题等几种。标题通常由名词、分词与动名词等短语所构成。如果确实需要用一个句子表达时，大部分编辑和学者一般都认为标题不应由陈述句构成。一般认为，陈述句容易使标题具有判断式的语意。有时可以用问句作为标题，尤其是在评论论文中，使用具探讨性的疑问句型标题显得比较生动，易引起读者的兴趣，生动且切题。

（2）标题的句法规则。由于标题比句子简短，且无需主、谓、宾，因此词序显得尤为重要。题名最好由最能反映论文核心内容的主题词扩展而成，如果词语间的修饰关系使用不当，就会影响读者正确理解标题的真实含意。如 Cars blamed for pollution by scientist（科学家造成的污染归罪于汽车），正确的写法应为 Cars blamed by scientist for pollution（科学家将污染归罪于汽车）。

（3）标题中介词的用法。with 是标题中常用到的介词。一般而言，汉语中是以名词作形容词的，英语中用对应的名词作形容词就不适合。如当名词用作形容词来修饰另一个名词时，如果前者是后者具有的一部分或者是后者所具有的性质、特点时，常需要前置词 with+名词组成的前置词短语，作形容词放在所要修饰的名词之后。如"具有中国特色的新型机器"应译为 New types of machines with the Chinese characteristics 而不用 Chinese characteristics machines"。

在标题中,常常会遇到"××的××",此处"的"在英语有两个前置词相对应,即 of 和 for。其中 of 主要表示所有关系,for 主要表示目的、用途。如 A design method of sliding mode robust controller for uncertain system is presented 可以翻译为"提出了一种针对不确定系统的滑模鲁棒控制器设计方法"。

(4) 题名中单词的大小写。题名中字母主要有全大写、首字母大写、每个实词首字母大写等三种形式。作者应遵循相应期刊的习惯,对于专有名词首字母、首字母缩略词、德语名词首字母与句号后单词的首字母等在一般情况下均应大写。

3. 实例分析

根据上述结构与特征,下面以实例形式简要分析论文标题的命名。

(1) 翻译标题"中国高炉炼钢技术发展"。

较为合理的翻译为:Technical progress of blast furnace iron-making in China.

分析:这是一种偏正结构多词组的标题,作者按词组的组成关系翻译了(blast furnace iron-making)高炉炼钢,重点强调技术进步。该标题重点突出,内容准确、清晰,且相当简洁。

(2) 翻译标题"关于电子信息工程课程改革的几个问题"。

原译为 Some Problems on Curriculum Reform of Electronics & Information.

分析:problems 与 with 属习惯搭配,有"对于"之意,此外,Reform 应变为复数 Reforms。改译:Some problems with curriculum reforms on Electronics & Information.

(3) 翻译标题"立足科研和教学实际提高教学质量"。

原译为 Basing on science and research and teaching, raising teaching quality.

分析:应用 based 而非 basing;此外,结构不合理。改译:Raising teaching quality based on scientific research and teaching quality.

(4) 翻译标题"基于分数阶傅里叶变换的正交频分复用系统同步分析"。

原翻译为:Synchronization analysis of OFDM system based on fractional Fourier transform.

经分析,该翻译结构合理,表述简洁,是一种合理的翻译;但从西方文化的观点来看,该文主要提出的是一种基于分数阶傅里叶变换的同步分析,重点强调的是基于分数阶傅里叶变换,因而更准确的翻译可以改进为:Synchronization analysis based on fractional Fourier transform for OFDM system.

(5) 翻译标题"多层卫星通信网络自适应路由策略"。

原翻译为:Adaptive routing strategy on multi-layer satellite networks by communication.

经分析,该翻译结构合理,表述简洁,但存在用词不当;"多层卫星通信网络"是一个具有较多修饰语的词组,而在英文中常采用名词修饰名词的结构,故可以翻译成 multi-layer satellite communication networks;此外,on 更换成 in 更合理,即:Adaptive routing strategy in multi-layer satellite communication networks.

(6) 翻译标题"基于 DSP 的实时图像压缩软件优化技术研究"。

原翻译为:The study on software optimizing technology of real-time image compression system based on DSP.

经分析，该翻译结构合理，表述简洁，重点突出；但作者讨论的是某一种技术研究，一般应把 The 改为 A 更加合理。

（7）翻译标题"SAR 图像压缩的多尺度自回归滑动平均模型方法"。

原翻译为：A new method for compression of SAR imagery based on multi-scale autoregressive moving average model（MARMA）.

经分析，该标题的重点应在于"多尺度自回归滑动平均模型方法"，因此此部分应该在前；此外，科技论文中，new 与 novel 等词语的使用要特别谨慎，不是创新性工作，最好不要附加这些词汇。因此，更合理的翻译为：A method based on multi-scale autoregressive moving average model（MARMA）for compression of SAR imagery.

（8）翻译标题 On the addition to the method of microscopic research by a new way of producing color contrast between an object and its background or between definite parts of the object itself 成中文。

较为准确的翻译为《关于在显微镜研究中增加一种能在物体和其背景之间或物体本身各确定部分之间产生色差的新方法》，长达43个字，念起来很费劲。其中有一大半是废话，可以缩短成：A new way of producing color-contrast in microscopic examination（一种能在显微镜检查中产生色差的新方法）。

（9）翻译标题 CLUSTAL-W: improving the sensitivity of progressive multiple sequence alignment through sequence weighting, position-specific gap penalties and weight matrix choice. Nucleic Acid Research。

较为合理的翻译为：CLUSTAL-W，通过序列加权、位点特异性空位罚分和加权矩阵选择来提高渐进的多序列对比的灵敏度。作者用20个词（计163个字符）准确地表达了论文的多层意思：以最重要的词 CLUSTAL-W 作为题名的开头，紧接着在冒号后解释 CLUSTAL-W 的目的是 improving the sensitivity of progressive multiple sequence alignment，达到该目的的手段是 through sequence weighting, position-specific gap penalties and weight matrix choice。该标题重点突出，内容准确，结构清晰，但不够简洁。

总之，科技论文标题撰写的 ABC 是 Accuracy 准确、Brevity 简洁与 Clarity 清楚，此外，要特别注意中英文句法的正确性，尤其是动词分词和介词的使用。对于题名的长度、缩写与字母的大小写等，应注意参考相关期刊的"读者须知"及其近期发表的论文。

B. Abstract

摘要是全文的精华，是对一项科学研究工作的研究目的、方法和研究结果的概括与总结。摘要写得好与坏直接关系到论文是否被录用。一般来说，摘要必须回答"研究什么"、"怎么研究"、"得到了什么结果"、"结果说明了什么"等问题。此外，简短精练是其主要特点，只需简明扼要地将目的、方法、结果和结论分别加以概括即可。

1. 基本要求

摘要首先必须符合格式规范。语言必须规范通顺，准确得体，用词要确切、恰如其分，而且要避免非通用的符号、缩略语、生偏词。另外，摘要的语气要客观，不要作出言过其实的结论。

有相当数量的作者和审稿人认为，科技论文的撰写应使用第三人称、过去时和被动语态。但调查表明，科技论文中被动语态的使用在 1920 年～1970 年曾比较流行。由于主动语态的表达更为准确，且更易阅读，因而目前大多数期刊都提倡使用主动语态。国际著名科技期刊《Nature》、《Cell》等尤其如此，其中第一人称和主动语态的使用十分普遍。

（1）时态以简练为佳。

一般现在时：用于说明研究目的、叙述研究内容、描述结果、得出结论、提出建议或讨论等；公认事实、自然规律、永恒真理等也要用一般现在时。

一般过去时：用于叙述过去某一时刻的发现、某一研究过程（实验、观察、调查、医疗等过程）。用一般过去时描述的发现、现象，往往是尚不能确认为自然规律、永恒真理，只是当时情况；所描述的研究过程也明显带有过去时间的痕迹。

现在完成时把过去发生的或过去已完成的事情与现在联系起来，而过去完成时可用来表示过去某一时间以前已经完成的事情，或在一个过去事情完成之前就已完成的另一过去行为。一般较少使用。

（2）语态要合适。

采用何种语态，既要考虑摘要的特点，又要满足表达的需要。一篇摘要很短，尽量不要随便混用，更不要在一个句子里混用。

主动语态：摘要中谓语动词采用主动语态，有助于文字简洁、表达有力。

被动语态：以前强调多用被动语态，理由是科技论文主要是说明事实经过，至于那件事是谁做的，无须一一证明。为强调动作承受者，采用被动语态为好；被动者无关紧要，也必须用强调的事物做主语。

英文摘要的人称：原来摘要的首句多用第三人称 This paper…等开头，现在倾向于采用更简洁的被动语态或原形动词开头。如：To describe…，To study…，To investigate…，To assess…，To determine…，行文时最好不用第一人称。

（3）注意事项。

冠词：主要是定冠词 the 易被漏用。the 用于表示整个群体、分类、时间、地名、独一无二的事物、形容词最高级等情况时较易掌握，用于特指时常被漏用。这里有个原则，即当用 the 时，听者或读者已经明确所指的是什么。

数词：避免用阿拉伯数字作首词。

单复数：一些名词单复数形式不易辨认，从而造成谓语形式出错。

使用短句：长句容易造成语意不清，但要避免单调和重复。

2．内容与结构

从结构与内容来看，摘要一般包括如下内容。

（1）目的（objectives，purposes）：包括研究背景、范围、内容、要解决的问题及解决这一问题的重要性和意义。一般有"论文导向"与"研究导向"两类。

论文导向多使用现在式，如 This paper presents…；研究导向则使用过去式，如 This study investigated…。

（2）研究方法（methods and materials）：包括研究的材料、手段和过程。

介绍研究或试验过程，常用词汇有：test, study, investigate, examine, experiment, discuss, consider, analyze, analysis 等。

说明研究或试验方法，常用词汇有：measure, estimate, calculate 等。

介绍应用、用途，常用词汇有：use, apply, application 等。

（3）结论（conclusions）：主要结论，研究的价值和意义等。

介绍结论时常用词汇有 summary, introduce, conclude 等。

展示研究结果时常用词汇有 show, result, present 等。

陈述论文的论点和作者的观点，常用词汇有 suggest, report, present, explain, expect, describe 等。

阐明论证，常用词汇有 support, provide, indicate, identify, find, demonstrate, confirm, clarify 等。

推荐和建议，常用词汇有 suggest, suggestion, recommend, recommendation, propose, necessity, necessary, expect 等。

另外，在摘要中不要用到公式、参考文献等。要始终记住一点，Abstract 是一个独立的部分，换句话说，别人不看你的文章，只看你的 Abstract 就能了解你的研究工作。

3. 实例分析

根据上述内容与要求，下面以实例形式加以说明。

（1）This paper presents some of the most common Chinese-English habits observed from over two hundred English technical papers by Chinese writers. The habits are explained and in most cases, example text from an actual paper is given along with preferred text. An attempt is made to explain how to correct and prevent such mistakes. In some cases a possible explanation of why the habit occurs is also given. This paper can serve as an individual guide to editing technical papers especially when a native English-speaking editor is unavailable.

分析：本摘要共 5 句话。第一句指出了研究内容：中国学者撰写技术论文中最易出现的中式英语习惯。第二、三句强调本文的研究方法与手段：这些习惯性错误来源于 200 多篇中国学者书写的真实的技术论文，并给出了改进的方法，具有相当的真实性与实用性。第四句进一步强调本文的特色，即作者探讨了发生这些习惯性错误的原因。最后，作者指出了本文的意义。

（2）翻译文摘：本文提出了在叶片更换过程中利用力矩平衡技术，并运用计算机进行叶片优化排序用以指导动叶片的安装。采用该方法可以在不需要进行动平衡的情况下，确保更换叶片后机组原有的振动水平变化不大，从而大大缩短了机组启动时间，同时减小了动平衡所需要的花费。该方法通过现场实践证明准确可靠，效果令人满意。

分析：本摘要共 3 句话。第一句提出论题，主语是"本文"，谓语是"提出了"，后面的内容是宾语；作为文摘的起始句，可以采用如下两种常用的方法。

采用主动语态：This paper presents that the movable blades can be erected under the guidance of computer-based optimal blade sequencing and a new torque balancing technology in the process of replacing blades on steam turbine.

采用被动语态：The erection of movable blades under the guidance of computer-based optimal blade sequencing and a new torque balancing technology in the process of replacing blades on steam turbine is presented in this paper.

显然，这里采用主动语态更合适，因为被动句中主语修饰成分过多过长，使得整个句子头重脚轻；此外，"更换"利用词汇 replace 而不是 change 较为准确。

第二句介绍了该方法所起的作用和达到的效果，应采用被动语态；这句话的前半部分谈该方法起到的作用，后半部分谈起到的效果，后半部分是前半部分的承接与结果，故可以翻译成 This method ensures small variation of original vibration level of the unit after replacing blades without need for conducting dynamic balance, therefore, periods of all units start-up is greatly shortened, and expense for dynamic balance is saved at the same time.

第三句是该方法的实践结果，应用被动语态。可翻译为：This method has been proved to be accurate, reliable and satisfied through field practice。注意，为了简洁，把句子 The effect is satisfied through field practice 换成一个形容词形式 satisfied through field practice，显得简洁对称。

（3）This paper discusses CDMA system performance with multimedia services and analyzes interference-based admission control strategy with multi-dimensional Markov model. Moreover, considering priority of handover users and different QoS requirements, multi-level admission thresholds are set in system for different types of users, which can guarantee the quality of existed links and maximize the system capacity. Simulations are also given to confirm the usefulness of proposed strategies.

分析：第一句运用主动语态与并列结构指出了研究内容，即本文讨论了 CDMA 系统多媒体业务性特点，采用多维马尔可夫过程模型分析了基于干扰水平的接入控制策略。第二句指出研究方法：考虑到切换用户的优先级，以及不同类型用户的不同 QoS 要求，通过在系统中设置多级接入门限，保证了系统已有的链路质量，扩大了系统容量。第三句进一步表明：仿真实验进一步说明了推荐策略的实用性。

（4）下面看看某一英文文摘：A technology based on PSPICE for fault modeling of simulation of analog circuit is discussed in this paper. A fault modeling method of physical fault of basic element and functional fault of integrated circuit is proposed. Different methods are utilized under DC and AC test. An example is given to prove the feasibility of this kind of technology.

分析：首句指出研究内容，即基于 PSPICE 的模拟电路故障仿真中的故障建模问题。第二句指出研究方法，即通过对基本元件的物理故障和集成电路的功能故障建立故障模型的方法。第三句对研究方法进行补充，即在直流诊断和交流诊断中，故障建模的方法有所不同。最后一句用例子说明了这种方法的可行性。整段结构紧凑、结构合理，统一采用被动语态，语态一致。

在英文摘要的撰写中，还应注意以下几点：

（1）力求简捷。如 at a temperature of 250℃ to 300℃ → at 250℃ to 300℃；at a high pressure of 2 kPa → at 2 kPa；has been found to increase → increased；from the experimental results, it can be concluded that → the results show。

（2）能用名词作定语的尽量不用动名词作定语，能用形容词作定语的尽量不用名词作定语。如 measuring accuracy → measurement accuracy；experiment results → experimental results。

（3）可直接用名词或名词短语作定语的情况下，要少用 of 句型。如 accuracy of measurement → measurement accuracy；structure of crystal → crystal structure。

（4）可用动词的情况下尽量避免用动词的名词形式。如 Measurement of thickness of plastic sheet was made → Thickness of plastic sheet was measured。

（5）一个名词不宜用多个前置形容词来修饰，可改用复合词，兼用后置定语。如 thermal oxidation apparent activation energy → Apparent active energy of thermo-oxidation。

（6）描述作者的工作一般用过去时态（因为工作是在过去做的），但陈述这些工作所得出的结论时，应该用现在时态。

（7）一般都应使用动词的主动语态，如 B is exceeded by A → A exceeds B。

（8）尽量用短句。

C. Body

科技论文是集假说、数据和结论为一体的概括性描述，而论文主体则是研究工作的具体描述。论文主体的撰写一般始于论文提纲。论文提纲是一篇论文的行文计划，是论文目的、假说、内容与结论最清楚的表述形式。

如何起草论文提纲？主要解决 3 个问题。

① 为什么我要做这个工作，主要的目的和假设是什么？

② 我的研究方法与结果是什么？

③ 这一结果意味着什么？意义何在？提纲本身应该文字简练、思路完整，如果提纲准备充分，那么正文组织起来就更容易。

一般论文提纲与相对应的主体部分包括相关研究简介（Introduction）、研究方法或者系统制作（Methods）、实验与讨论（Experiment & Discussion）及结论（Conclusion）几个部分。

1. 基本结构及其要求

（1）Introduction。Introduction 是本项研究的导读，主要包括谁做了什么？做得怎么样？我们做了哪些工作？做得怎么样？体现出一篇论文的研究起初和创新要素。应该说外刊论文对于 Introduction 的要求是非常高的，可以毫不夸张地说，一个好的 Introduction 就相当于文章成功了一半。

要写好一个 Introduction，最重要的是要保持层次感和逻辑性。

首先，要阐述自己的研究领域，尽量简洁；

其次，相关工作的总结回顾，要把该领域内的过去和现在的状况全面地概括总结出来，不能有丝毫的遗漏，特别是最新的进展和过去经典文献的引用，否则，很可能意味着你做得不够深入或者全面；

再次，分析过去研究的局限性，并且阐明自己研究的创新点。阐述局限性时要客观公正，实事求是。在阐述自己的创新点时，要仅仅围绕过去研究的缺陷来描述，完整而清晰地描述自己的解决思路。中文文章的特点是创新性要多要大，而英文文章的特点恰恰相反：深入系统的解决一到两个问题就算相当不错。

最后，总结性描述论文的研究内容，作为 Introduction 的结尾。

（2）Methods。Methods 部分是描述论文的实践过程，应该按照逻辑思维规律来组织结构，包含材料、内容，应有概念、判断、推理、最终形成观点。通常按照研究对象可分为：以系统为主的研究论文与以方法研究为主的论文。以系统为主的研究论文主要介绍系统的设计或制作；以方法研究为主的论文主要介绍某种研究方法，一般包括实验方法与理论推理两种。由于研究对象的千差万别，难以形成统一的模式，但是主要构件一般包括如下。

- 研究目的：研究目的是正文的开篇，要写得简明扼要，重点突出。先介绍为什么要进行这个研究，通过研究要达到的目的是什么。如果课题涉及面较广，论文只写其某一方面，则要写清本文着重探索哪一方面的问题。并交代探索原因，效果或方法。
- 研究方法：科研课题从开始到成果的全过程，都要运用实验材料、设备，以及观察方法。因此，应将选用的材料、设备和实验的方法加以说明，以便他人据此重复验证。
- 研究过程：研究过程主要说明研究的技术路线，以及具体操作步骤。对于实验型研究，主要说明实验条件、实验设备和操作过程；对于理论性研究，主要说明问题的假设、推理工具与推理过程，达到严谨的科学性、逻辑性。
- 实验结果或仿真结果分析与讨论：该部分是整篇论文的心脏部分。一切实验成败由此判断，一切推理由此导出，一切议论由此引出。因此，应该充分表达，并且采用表格、图解、照片等附件。要尽量压缩众所周知的评论，突出本研究的新发现，及经过证实的新观点、新见解。这一部分一般应包括：主要原理或概念、实验条件；本研究的结果与他人研究结果的相同或差异讲明；解释因果关系，论证其必然性；提出本研究存在的问题或尚需探索的问题。

此外，Methods 撰写中特别要注意表述的完整性和科学性。

（3）Conclusion。该部分是整个研究工作的总结，是全篇论文的归宿，起着画龙点睛的作用。一般说来，读者选读某篇论文时，先看标题、摘要、前言，再看结论，才能决定阅读与否。因此，结论写作也是很重要的。撰写结论时，不仅要对研究的全过程、实验的结果、数据等进一步认真地加以综合分析，准确反映客观事物的本质及其规律，而且，对论证的材料，选用的实例，语言表达的概括性，科学性和逻辑性等方方面面，也都要一一进行总判断、总推理、总评价。同时，撰写时，不是对前面论述结果的简单复述，而要与引言相呼应，与正文其他部分相联系。总之。结论要有说服力，恰如其分。语言要准确、鲜明。结论中，凡归结为一个认识、肯定一种观点、否定一种意见，都要有事实、有根据，不能想当然，不能含糊其辞，不能用"大概"、"可能"、"或许"等词语。如果论文得不出结论，也不要硬写。凡不写结论的论文，可对实验结果进行一番深入讨论。

此外，论文结构上，要思路清晰，层次分明，逻辑性强；文字表述上，要语句通顺，通俗易懂，文字简练准确；特别要强调的是，表格与图像图形信息能够达到文字描述所不易达到的效果。表格的优点是能够清晰地展示文章的第一手结果，便于后人在研究时进行引用和对比；图的优点在于能够将数据的变化趋势灵活地表现出来，表达上更为直接和富于感染力。总体上来说，图表应该结合使用，取长补短，使结果的展现更加丰富。

D. Others

1. Order of Authors and Affiliation

科技论文的作者在享受科技成果和荣誉的同时，也要承担同样的责任。严谨的科学工作者并不会无原则地分享成果和荣誉，要成为一篇论文的作者，必须对论文的思想和写作有实质性的贡献。只要你的名字出现在论文作者中，你就要对整篇文章负全部责任。实际上，很多著名学者很后悔成为某些论文的作者；当导师和研究生合作的论文出现问题时，导师无论怎样辩白都是十分无力的，国内学生与导师尤其需要注意。

科技论文作者的署名顺序也需特别注意，许多著名学者也会因为科技论文的署名问题导致合作关系的破灭。一般应注意以下几点。

（1）通常，署名顺序取决于学科领域与学会的惯例，如在医学界，署名顺序一般根据作者的资历来决定，第一作者一般是实验室主任或者是课题负责人；又如某些领域，作者的署名往往根据作者姓氏顺序来决定。

（2）一般认为文章的成果是属于通讯作者的，说明思路是通讯作者的；而第一作者是最主要的参与者，应该说，通讯作者多数情况和第一作者是同一个人，通讯作者的另一个好处是能和外界建立更广泛的联系，这会大大地提高你在科学界的地位。

（3）现在，大多数作者建议按照作者的贡献来确定作者的署名顺序，因为这样比较公平，也符合 IEEE 与 IEE 的惯例。如果出现争议，建议慷慨分享成果和荣誉，从长期合作的角度出发，某一篇论文的署名顺序并不重要。

（4）大家知道，中国人人名与外国人人名顺序也有差异，中国人姓在前，名在后；而外国人名在前，姓在后。如中文名字曹晓红，则英文应写成 Xiaohong Cao；有些外国学者了解中国人的姓氏习惯，又有可能把本已经正确的英文名字 Xiaohong Cao 理解成为 Xiaohong 为姓氏、Cao 为名字，因此，更多学者建议采用 Xiao-hong Cao。

（5）通常，如果有多个作者，则应在作者姓名的右上角用阿拉伯数字注明作者所在的单位。由于各国各单位对成果的归属都有较严格的控制，因此，不要使用几个大写字母所组成的完全缩写或简称，单位内部级别按照从小到大的顺序。如：

Xiao-hua Xia[1], Alan S.I. Zinober[2]

[1]Department of Electrical, Electronic and Computer Engineering, University of Pretoria, South Africa

[2]Department of Applied Mathematics, University of Sheffield, Sheffield S10 2TN, UK

2. Keywords

关键词（Keywords）是论文的文献检索标识，是表达文献主体概念的自然语言词汇。列出关键词有助于读者对全文的理解，同时便于查阅和检索。

按照 GB 7713—87 规定：关键词一般使用名词形式，词数为 3～6 个，以显著的字符另起一行，排在摘要的下方。关键词的选用要语意准确，能概括出论文所要论述的主要内容或中心，要尽可能避免词汇的语意过宽或过窄。

3. Acknowledgement

通常，Acknowledge 包含两个主要的内容：第一是表明研究的基金来源，如中国的国家自然科学基金 Nature Science Foundation of China（NSFC）等。标注基金的时候一般都要明确基金号（Grant Number），只有这样才算是该项基金的研究成果；第二是对参与人员（没有列在作者中的研究人员）和单位表示感谢；此外，如果研究论文得到了编辑与匿名审稿人的大力帮助，还需要添加上对编辑（editor）和匿名审稿人（Anonymous Reviewers）的感谢，这是一种基本的礼貌。

下面给出几个例子：

- This work is supported by Bogazici University Research Fund (Project No: 99A202).
- This project is supported by Perkins Engines, TRW and EPSRC Grant Reference GR/L42018. The invaluable assistance of our colleague Mr. John Twiddle during the data capture phase of this work is gratefully acknowledged.
- Financial support for the present work was granted by the Iranian Telecommunication Research Center under grant number T500/10177. The authors, hereby, gratefully acknowledge this support.
- We would like to thank an anonymous reviewer for assistance with the proof of Theorem 1. This research was partially supported by the Engineering and Physical Sciences Research Council (EPSRC), United Kingdom, by Grant GR/S41050/01, and partially supported by the RSA-China Scientific Agreement.

下面给出几个中国基金项目的翻译。

- 国家自然科学基金：Chinese National Natural Science Foundation.
- 国家"863 计划"（国家高技术研究发展计划项目）：Chinese National Programs for High Technology Research and Development.
- 国家"973 项目"（国家基础研究发展规划项目）：Key Project of Chinese National Programs for Fundamental Research.
- 国家"十五"重点科技攻关项目：The 10th Five Years Key Programs for Science and Technology Development.
- 国家杰出青年科学基金：National Science Foundation for Distinguished Young Scholars.

4. Reference

References 重要之点在于格式。不同的杂志对于参考文献的格式要求不一样。作者一般要注意以下几个问题。

作者：有的是简写在前，有的简写在后，有的简写附加上一点表示，有的简写没有。

文章：有的要加上引号，有的没有引号。

文章的期刊：有的要简写，有的要全称，有的要斜体，有的则不需要。

文章年和期卷号的顺序：有的是年在前，有的是年在后。

文献的排列顺序：有的是按照字母的顺序，有的则是按照在论文中出现的顺序用阿拉伯数字排序。

下面给出实例如下。

- Tao, C. W., Chan, M.-L., & Lee, T.-T. (2003). Adaptive fuzzy sliding mode controller for linear systems with mismatched time-varying uncertainties. *IEEE Transactions on Systems, Man, and Cybernetics—Part B: Cybernetics,* 33(2), 283-293.
- Harb A. Nonlinear chaos control in a permanent magnet reluctance machine. Chaos, Solitons & Fractals 2004;19(5):1217-24.
- B.K. Yoo, W.C. Ham, Adaptive control of robot manipulator using fuzzy compensator, IEEE Trans. Fuzzy Systems 8 (2000) 186.

以上是一般科技论文参考文献的格式。注意到有些年代写在前面，有些在后面；有些作者写完后用"，"，有些则用"."；有些把页码写全，如 283-293，有些只写初始页码，如 283。

- A.J. Koivo, Fundamentals for Control of Robotic Manipulators, *Wiley, New York,* 1989.

参考书籍的格式一般写明出版社、地点、年代，以及版本号。

- Silpa-Anan C, Brinsmead T, Abdallah S, Zelinsky A. Preliminary experiments in visual servo control for autonomous underwater vehicle. IEEE/RSJ international conference on intelligent robotics and systems (IROS); 2001. Available from: http://www.syseng.anu.edu.au/rsl/.

有些参考文献是通过网络获取的，一般作者也应该著名。

此外，有些杂志在标注所应用论文时，还特别要注明文献的类别，如专著 monograph（M）、论文集 conference(C)、期刊 journal（J）、学位论文 doctrinal（D）、报告 report（R）、标准 standard（S）与专利 patent（P），具体可以参考中华人民共和国国家标准 UDC 025.32 与 GB 7714—87。

5. Supplement

前面已经谈到，适当的表格与图像图形信息能够达到文字描述所不易达到的效果，使得表达上更为直接和富于感染力。一般来说，表格与图像图形应该出现在正文引用部分适当的地方。有时，为了文章的简洁清晰，常常把复杂表述放在文章结尾处 Supplement 中，如某定理的公式证明、某方法的详细描述等。

PART 2

投 稿 指 南

A. 如何选题

科技论文是科学工作者对创造性成果进行理论分析和科学总结，并进行发表或答辩的文字表达形式。科技论文的关键要素是创新性，如何寻找创新性则需要在选题上下工夫。

随着科技的进步与发展，像牛顿、爱因斯坦、爱迪生时代依靠灵感与天才寻找原始火花已经非常困难了。许多人选题喜欢标新立异，然后再从杂志上找题目，似乎这才是创新。显然这样做出的文章难有创新性，几年，甚至十几年的工作一下子就看透了，并且发现了问题所在。如果这时匆匆忙忙写文章，退稿率会很高。

一般而言，研究者应多与导师、指导老师讨论，听取导师的看法，不要只追求标新立异，在大方向上不要偏离导师的研究方向，这样才能取得导师的指导和帮助。一般的建议是：

- 按导师指导的方向大量阅读，增加自己的知识储备量，了解本学科本方向的研究历史与现状，明确过去已经进行了哪些研究，有什么成果，哪些问题尚未得到解决。要泛读和精读相结合，合理搭配，节约宝贵时间。
- 研究领域不要涉及太广，要选几个自己感兴趣的领域深挖，逐步从广泛性中找出特殊性，即先广再博。
- 善于总结。注意平常思考的记录，尤其是对突然来临、转瞬即逝的灵感的记录。
- 勤于思考。一旦发现问题，要抛开对权威刊物的迷信，抛开原定的结论，穷追下去，应该充分运用自己的思考力，通过分析、综合、演绎、归纳、分类、组合、加减、反逆、类推等，对文献资料进行积极的加工，这是一种创造性的想象，缺少它就得不到新的题目。
- 在确定选题之前，要了解选题的创新性和价值性。一般要通过检索来证实这个想法是否具有创新性。此外，还要注意这个选题的现实意义或者长远意义。
- 可行性论证，这包括方法、材料、资金、设备等。

一旦创新性与可行性得到初步保证，则得到了一个不错的选题，从而有可能得到一份很有分量的研究结论。

B. 投稿过程与投稿信（COVER LETTER）

1. 投稿过程

写论文的真正意义在于把你的知识与别人分享而获得肯定的那种成就感，尽管大多数人写科技论文的直接目的是为了获得某种荣誉，如晋职、晋级、获得学位等。目的不同，但目标一致，将论文刊出。正确的投稿将有助于科技论文的发表，一般应该注意以下问题。

（1）正确选择期刊。首先要掂量一下自己论文的分量，想想在哪个杂志上发表最合适。因为期刊种类繁多，即使在同一学科也有许多期刊，且各个期刊的办刊宗旨、专业范围、主题分配、栏目设置及各种类型文章发表的比例均不相同。因此，选择一本恰当的期刊并非易事，然而这是论文得以发表的一个极其重要的环节。选择期刊应考虑的因素：

- 论文主题是否在刊物的征稿范围内。投稿论文可能极为优秀，但如果不适合于该刊物，则不可能在该刊物被发表。
- 期刊的声望，期刊的学术水平高，其声望就高。当然期刊声望越高，被引用的可能性就越大，影响力就越大。
- 期刊的审稿周期。一般而言，期刊声望越大审稿周期越长。当然，期刊又分为一般期刊、快报（Letters）等（如 IEEE Communication Letters，Physics Review Letters 等），通常快报的效率较高。

（2）认真阅读投稿须知。确定期刊后，要阅读投稿须知，认真浏览目录，以确定该刊物是否发表你研究领域的文章及发表的比例有多大。一般应该注意：

- 注意栏目设置，确定拟投稿件的栏目。
- 了解稿件的撰写要求。
- 根据刊登文章的投稿日期、接收日期，以及见刊日期，估算发表周期，以便出现问题即时与编辑沟通。

（3）正式投稿：一般来说，投稿程序分以下 3 步进行。

- 准备投稿信（cover letter or submission letter）。
- 投稿及其包装：目前投稿更多地提倡网络在线投稿，无论是网络投稿还是邮寄投稿，一般要把稿件及其拟投期刊所需的伴随资料一并寄出，一般包括：投稿信、刊物要求的稿件（包括文题页、文摘页、正文、致谢、参考文献、图注、表及图）、版权转让声明、作者地址等。有些还需要提供程序、图片等。
- 稿件追踪：如果投稿两周仍无任何有关稿件收到的信息，也可打电话、发 E-mail 或写信给编辑部核实稿件是否收到。

2. 投稿信（COVER LETTER）

对国外期刊投稿时，除了正文文章外，还需要写一封 cover letter，一封好的 cover letter 可以起到很好的作用，就好比求职时的自荐信一样，如果能吸引编辑的注意，你就成功了一半了。

Cover letter 的内容主要目的是希望编辑详细了解文章的主要内容，因而要突出文章的创新性价值，还有你为什么要发表这篇文章，还可以简要指出目前该领域的发展方向。此外，特别要注意用语恰当与格式规范等。

实例 1：

Dear Dr：

Enclosed are three copies of a manuscript by XXXXX, XXXXX, and XXXXX titled "XXXXXXXXXXXXXXXXXXXXX". It is submitted to be considered for publications a "Original Article" in your journal. This paper is neither the entire paper nor any part of its content has been published or has been accepted elsewhere. It is not being submitted to any other journal. We believe the paper may be of particular interest to the readers of your journal because XXXXXXXXXXXXXXXXXXXXXXX.

Correspondence and phone calls about the paper should be directed to XXXXXXX at the following address, phone and fax number, and E-mail address：

Department of XXXXXXXXX,

Tsinghua University,

Beijing, 100084,

P.R.China

Tel: XXXXXX

Fax: XXXXX

E-mail: XXXXX

实例 2：

Dear Prof. XXX:

I want to submit our manuscript with title "XXXXXXXXX" for publication in "XXXXXX XXX". It is not being submitted to any other journal or is under consideration for publication elsewhere.

The authors claim that none of the material in the paper has been published or is under consideration for publication elsewhere.

I am the corresponding author and further information is as follows:

Address: Department of XXXXX,

Huazhong Normal University,

Wuhan, HuBei, 430079,

P.R.China.

Tel: XXXXXXX

Fax: XXXXXXX

E-mail: qushaocheng@mail.ccnu.edu.cn

Thanks very much for your attention to our paper.

Sincerely yours,

Shao-cheng Qu

C. 审稿过程以及与编辑的沟通

1. 审稿过程

一般不同领域，审稿的过程可能不太一样，大致过程是初选、送审、修改和终审。一般要了解以下基本步骤与内容。

（1）编辑内部审查：一般包括论文文字、格式的审查与论文题材方面的检查，这种审查通常是编辑部内部的专家进行的。由于一些重要期刊投稿众多，许多好的中文期刊内部审查拒稿率达到 60%；投稿英文期刊时，因英文表达不好拒稿率也相当高。如果论文形式不合格，无论你论文内容多么好，都有可能直接被拒绝，因为你的稿件根本没有到真正专家的手中。此外，如果编辑觉得论文题材不适合所投刊物，也会回信退稿。

（2）正式审稿：编辑会挑选 2~5 名同行对论文的创新性和正确性进行审查。有些期刊采取匿名审稿，有些公开审稿。国内审稿一般有少量审稿费，国外评审是自愿花时间评阅论文，由于评阅人一般是已经在本领域建立了地位，比较忙，因此评审时间较长，投稿者应对此予以理解。审稿期间，作者一般应耐心等待。除按收稿通知建议时间与编辑联系外，一般应给评审 4~6 个月时间。若仍无消息，可以与编辑联系催促一下。

（3）评审内容：主要包括论文内容的创新性；采用理论、方法、和数据的正确性；论文表述方法、写作缺陷等提出批评。

（4）评审结果一般有以下情况。

- 接收（accepted or without minor revision）：作者会收到最终稿的指南，有时需要补充提供数字文件等。
- 修改后可接收（conditional acceptance upon satisfactory revision）：应按照评审意见修改论文，将修改部分单独写成报告提供给编辑。一般来说编辑比评审者更具同情心，一般可以最终接受。
- 可以修改后再投：这种情况要分析评审意见，如果编辑希望继续修改提高，不要轻易放弃，修改后被接收的机会还是很大。对于高质量的杂志，多数论文第一次投稿时都会被按这种情况退回来。作者应根据评审意见认真修改。当然也可以提出对某些部分不修改的理由。
- 拒绝：这种情况应根据评审意见修改文稿，然后投往其他刊物。千万不要较劲与编辑过不去，甚至指着谩骂编辑，这样会对你所在学校甚至国家类似的投稿带来永久的障碍。

（5）论文发表：收到印刷编辑寄回的校样后，应尽快订正，尽快寄还给印刷编辑。寄校样时，出版商会要求填写版权转让书（transfer of copy right），并告知支付版面费的办法和订购单行本的方法。许多刊物不收版面费，但对特殊印刷（如彩版印刷）收费。有的超过定额免费页数的页面还可能按页面收费。不少收版面费的刊物费用都挺高，不过作者可以写信告知自己的情况，申请免费。

总之，作者对审查意见首先应高度重视，考虑审稿人为什么要提出这些建议。审稿人毕竟是来自一个旁观者的意见，总有一定道理。有的作者觉得审稿人没有读懂自己的文章，拒绝修改，这当然不好。当然，尽管审稿人是同领域的专家，但隔行如隔山，审稿人可能提出一些并不十分中肯的意见也不奇怪。好在评审人一般在3个人以上，这至少最小化了由个人偏见而产生的不公正现象。

2．与编辑的沟通

在投稿期间，为及时了解稿件信息，难免要与编辑进行沟通；对评阅人的审稿意见，作者要认真对待，因而与评阅人进行沟通也是必要的。

与编辑进行沟通，主要是询问稿件状况。下面给出几个例子。

例1：Dear Editor:

I want to know if you have received our manuscript with the title "XXXXXXXX" for submission in "XXXXXXXX". We submit our manuscript from E-mail: XXXXXXXX on Friday, 27, Feb, but we cannot receive the reply. Thank you for your kindly consideration of this request.

Sincerely yours:
XXXXXXXXX

例2：Dear Editor:

I'm not sure if it is the right time to contact you again to inquire about the status of my submitted manuscript (Paper ID: XXXXXXXXXX; Title of Paper: XXXXXXXXXXXXX) although nearly one month have passed since I contacted you last time. I would be greatly appreciated if you could spend some of your time check the status for me.

Best regards
XXXX

例3：Dear Editor:

Thanks for your reply for time and patient. We have sent many dates and figures to you according to reviews. We want to know if you have received it.

Please contact us, if you have any question.

We are looking forward to hearing from your letters.

由于同行评审是匿名的，评审人的批评通常是直率、无情的，甚至是错误的，有些学者认为论文被要求修改或者被拒绝很丢面子，甚至认为这些批评是人身攻击。事实上，事情可能没有那么复杂。作者主要目的是发表论文，因而按照审稿人的意见修改论文显得尤为必要；如果对自己论文很有信心，认为评审人的意见是错误的，这时候一定要讲究策略。一般而言，要对每一个审稿人的意见都要逐个回答，如果可能的话，应该在回复中附上审稿人提出的意见，这样可以简化审稿人的二审工作，也能显示作者的真诚，以及对审稿人工作的尊重。

根据审稿人意见完成论文修改之后，作者还应该写一封信对责任编辑表示感谢，同时表明你已经考虑了每一位审稿人的意见。绝对不能对审稿人写了很长的解释，但对论文本身却没有多少修改。一般而言，评阅人对按照他们的建议所付出的努力及其有条有理的修改工作会留下深刻的印象，这样你的工作得到评阅人承认的可能性就越大。

Dear Editor:

We have revised the manuscript according to reviews and your comments. Our point-to-point response attached below. At the same time, we would like to thank you and anonymous reviewers for your kindly patience and constructive suggestions, which are very important information to revise this paper.

With my kind regards,

Faithfully yours, XXXX

D．如何修改论文

不管在哪里，稿件的评审都不可能是百分之百的公平的。丘吉尔曾经有一句名言：同行评审（Peer Review）是最坏的体系。一般说来，作者拿出的初稿都不是尽善尽美的，有必要进行认真的修改和润色，正如唐朝李沂所说："能改则瑕可为瑜，瓦砾可为珠玉。"下面介绍几种常用的改稿方法。

其一，诵读法。初稿写成后要诵读几遍，一边读，一边思考，并把文气不接、语意不顺的地方随手改过来。叶圣陶先生十分推崇这种"诵读法"；鲁迅先生写完文章后，总要先读读，"自己觉得拗口的，就增删几个字，一定要它读得顺口"。可见，诵读法实在是一种简便易行、效果显著的方法。

其二，比较法。比较是认识事物的有效方法。把自己的初稿和同类文章中的优秀范文对照、比较，反复揣摩，分析得失，然后加以修改。这是初学者最需要掌握的。

其三，旁正法。"三人行，必有我师焉"，在修改稿件上，多听取各方面的意见，扬长避短，去粗取精，是大有益处的，作者必须高度重视修改这一环，通过反复推敲、加工，使文稿从内容到形式都达到精粹、完美的高度。

E. How to Give a Technical Talk

进行学术报告对一个学者是至关重要的，它不仅展示了你的研究成果，同时也锻炼了你把握事情的能力。通常中国出国留学生遇到的最苦闷的事情就是做报告（presentation），这当然是中西教育上的差异造成的。目前，许多高校教学中正在积极鼓励做报告。

好的论文并不等于好的报告。要做好报告，准备充分是关键。一般应考虑以下因素。

- 好的报告工具，如 PPT。
- 清晰的报告结构。
- 适当的字体。
- 得体的姿势与肢体语言，包括手势、语调等。
- 适中的语速。
- 掌握好时间。

必须要记住，报告人感兴趣的内容听众不一定感兴趣，报告人的任务是所讲的内容让听众感兴趣，因而必须提倡以听众为中心的报告风格。

下面是一段注意力与时间关系图的论述。

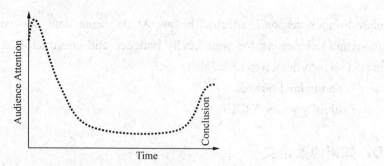

Fig. Typical attention the audience pays to an average presentation.

The average attendee of a conference is by all means willing to listen to you, but he is also easily distracted. You should realize that only minor part of the people have come specifically to listen to your talk. The rest is there for a variety of reasons, to wait for the next speaker, or to get a general impression of the field, or whatever. Figure 1 illustrates how the average audience pays attention during a typical presentation of, let's say, 30 minutes. Almost everyone listens in the beginning, but halfway the attention may well have dropped to around 10-20% of what it was at the start. At the end, many people start to listen again, particularly if you announce your conclusions, because they hope to take something away from the presentation.

下面是一位著名专家总结出的文章与报告结构安排上的区别。

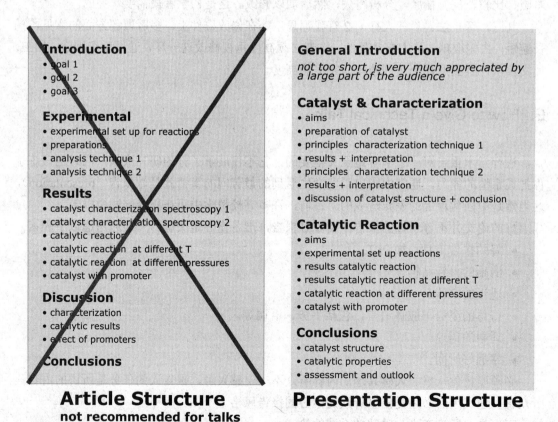

F. 科技论文中常见的错误

科技论文是一种专门的文体，由于许多科技论文都由英文写成，加之众多国内学者没有海外求学经历，因而想写出一篇准确规范的英文科技论文还是有相当的难度，正如 Felicia Brittman 所言，即使以英语为母语的学生要写出一篇规范的科技论文也需要半年到一年的训练时间。

下面是 Felicia Brittman 总结出的中国学生撰写科技论文时的常见错误。

- The single most common habit is the omission of articles a, an, and the.
- Very long sentences are especially common in Chinese-English writing because the writers often translate directly from Chinese to English.

  An example as follows.

  Too long: The clear height of the case is 6.15 meters; the thickness of the roof is 0.85 meters; the thickness of the bottom is 0.90 meters, the overall width is 26.6 meters, the overall length of the axial cord is 304.5 meters, the length of the jacking section is about 148.8 meters; the weight of the case is about 24 127 tons.

  Modification:

  Case clearance height 6.15 meters

  Roof thickness 0.85 meters

  Bottom thickness 0.90 meters

  Overall width 26.6 meters

  Overall length of the axial cord 304.5 meters

  Length of the jacking section 148.8 meters (approx.)

  Weight of the case 24 127 tons (approx.)

- Prefacing the main idea of a sentence by stating the purpose, location or reason first.

  Incorrect: For the application in automobile interiors, this paper studies the nesting optimization problem in leather manufacturing.

  Correct: This paper studies the nesting optimization problem in leather manufacturing for application in automobile interiors.

- Tendency of placing phrases which indicate time at the beginning of a sentence.

  Incorrect: When U is taken as the control parameter, the BDs for Δ = 0.0, 0.001, 0.005 are shown in Fig. 8.

  Correct: Figure 8 shows the BDs for Δ = 0.0, 0.001, and 0.005 when U is taken as the control parameter.

- Place the most important subject at the beginning of the sentence for emphasis.

  Incorrect: Based on the triangulation structure built from unorganized points or a CAD model, the extended STL format is described in this section.

  Correct: The extended STL format is described in this section based on the triangulation structure built from unorganized points or a CAD model.

- Avoid redundancy in the following types of phrases frequently used by Chinese English writers.

Instead of	Say
Research work	Research or work
Limit condition	Limit or condition
Layout scheme	Layout or scheme
Arrangement plan	Arrangement or plan
Output performance	Output or performance
Simulation results	Simulation or results
Application results	Application or results
Knowledge information	Knowledge or information

- Certain words demand that the noun they modify is plural. These include different, various, and number words.

Don't write	Instead write
Different node	Different nodes
Various method	Various methods
Two advantage	Two advantages
Fifteen thermocouple	Fifteen thermocouples

PART 3
应用文写作

A. 信函

1. 信函的基本原则和种类

一直以来，信函都是人们交际的一种重要的手段，即使在通信技术高度发达的今天，信函在社会交际和商业事务中仍然扮演着非常重要的作用，这是其他交际形式所无法取代的。信函具有独特的结构、格式和一些惯用的表达方式，掌握这些特点是十分重要的。信函的侧重点在于传递信息，表达情感，它要求内容简明扼要，条理清楚，表意准确，礼貌适度。随着时代的发展，写信的原则（writing principles）已从最原始的 3 个 C——简洁（conciseness）、清晰（clearness）、礼貌（courtesy）发展到 5 个 C：清晰（clearness）、简洁（conciseness）、正确（correctness）、礼貌（courtesy）、周到（consideration），继而到现在的 7 个 C，它在 5C 的基础上又增加了完整（completeness）、具体（concreteness）。

具体来说，信函可以分为商业信函或公函（business letter or official correspondence）和个人信函（private letter）两种。商业信函一般谈论或处理重要事物，可能是推荐信、邀请信、或者询问，答复某事。商业信函通常还需要加上"完整"和"具体"两个要求，即 7C 原则。个人信函一般比较随意，只需要满足以上的 5C 原则即可，在后面也将会以实例进行讲解。

而对于商业信函，在此基础上还需要加上"完整"和"具体"的两个要求，因为商业信函精确的特点决定了它必须"完整"和"具体"，完整而具体的书信更能达到预期的目的；更有助于建立友善的关系；还可以避免不必要的麻烦。

2. 信封的写法

（1）邮票应该贴在信封右上角。
（2）寄信人的姓名、地址应该写在信封的左上角。
（3）收信人的姓名、地址应该写在信封的正中或右下角的 1/4 处。

（4）也有人喜欢把收件人的名字、地址写在信封正面中央，把寄件人的姓名、地址写在信封的反面。

（5）如果信是由第三者转交给收信人，则要在收信人姓名下面写明转交人的姓名，其前加（C/O=Care Of）。

（6）住址的写法与中文相反；英文住址原则上是由小至大，如必须先写门牌号码、街路名称，再写城市、省（州）和邮政区号，最后一行则写上国家的名称。

3. 信函的组成部分和格式

英语书信通常包括下面几个组成部分：信内地址、称呼、开头语、正文、结束语、签名、附件等。下面逐一介绍。

（1）信内地址（inside address, introductory address）。信内地址收信人的姓名和地址，写在信纸的左上角，从信纸的左边顶格开始写，低于写信人地址和发信日期一、二行，也分并列式和斜列式两种，但应与信端（即信头）的书写格式保持一致。其次序是，先写收信人姓名、头衔和单位名称，占一、二行，然后写地址，可占2～4行，例如：

① 并列式。

Ms. Zhang
Wuhan University
Hongshan District, 430022
Wuhan
China

② 斜列式。

Ms. Zhang
　Wuhan University
　　Hongshan District, 430022
　　　Wuhan
　　　　China

（2）称呼（salutation）。称呼是收信人展开信后最先看到的文字，所以称呼也很有讲究。对收信人的称呼一般自成一行，写在低于信内地址一两行的地方，从信纸的左边顶格开始写，每个词的开头字母要大写，末尾处的符号，英国人用逗号，但美国和加拿大英语则多用冒号。称呼用语可视写信人与收信人的关系而定。

常用的收信人称呼有：先生（男人）Mr.；夫人（已婚）Mrs.；小姐（未婚）Miss；夫人、小姐统称 Ms.；夫妇俩人 Mr. and Mrs.。

（3）开头语（initial sentences）。开头语一般是一些寒暄语，用来引出正文。可以表示对对方的真挚的问候，也可以是表示对对方来信的感谢，还可以是对对方的想念之情。一些常用的开头语有：

- Many thanks for your last kind letter.
- I hope everything goes well.

- I miss you so much that…
- I beg to inform you that…
- I have the pleasure to tell you that…
- I regret to inform you that…
- I feel indebted for the kind note which you sent me on Saturday.
- I am going to answer your letter immediately and with pleasure.
- I am sorry that I have delayed answering your letter of recent date.

（4）信的正文（body of the letter）。信的正文每段第一行应往右缩进约 4～5 个字母。在写事务性信件时，正文一般开门见山，内容简单明了，条理清楚、易读、语气要自然诚恳。在写私人信件时，信写好之后若有什么遗漏，可用 P. S. 表示补叙。

（5）结束语（complimentary close）。结束语是指写信人的结尾套语。结束语一般低于正文一、二行，可写在左边，也可以从信纸的中间或偏右的地方开始写。第一个词的开头字母要大写，末尾用逗号。结束语视写信人与收信人的关系而定。例如写给机关、团体或不相识的人的信，一般用：Yours (very) truly，Yours (very) sincerely，Yours (very) respectfully，Yours appreciatively，Comradely yours 等。

在欧洲一些国家里，多把 Yours 放在 sincerely 等词的前面。在美国和加拿大等国，则多把 yours 放在 Sincerely 等词之后。Yours 一词有时也可省略。

（6）签名（signature）。信末的签名一般低于结束语一、二行，从信纸中间偏右的地方开始写。若写信人是女性，与收信人又不相识，则一般在署名前用括号注上 Miss, Mrs. 或 Ms., 以便对方回信时知道如何称呼。

（7）附件（enclosure）。信件若有附件，应在左下角注明 Encls. 或 Enc.。若附件不止一个，则应写出 2（或 3，4，5 等）Encls., 例如：

Enc: Resume

Encls: Grade Certificate

4．范例

（1）祝贺信。在国际交往中，祝贺信使用场合很多。国家之间，团体之间，以及个人之间常对一些值得庆祝的大事互致祝贺，这也是增进国家之间的关系，加强个人的友谊的一种方式。这类书信也有正式的和普通的两种。正式的祝贺主要用于政府间、官员间，普通的祝贺则多用于个人交往。前者用词拘谨，经常使用一些套语，后者用词亲切，不拘格式，但也有些常用的词句。

① 祝贺新年。

Your Excellency Mr. Ambassador,

On the occasion of New Year, may my wife and I extend to you and your wife our sincere greetings, wishing you a happy New Year, your career success and your family happiness.

Minister of Foreign Affairs

② 祝贺信常用套语。

- On the occasion of…, I wish to extend to you our warm congratulation on behalf of…

and in my own name.
值此……之际，我代表……，并以我个人的名义，向你致以热烈祝贺。

- As…, may I, on behalf of the Chinese people and Government, express to you and through you to the people and Government of your country the heartiest congratulations.
当……之时，我代表中国人民和政府，向你并通过你向你们的人民和政府表示衷心的祝贺。

- May the friendly relations and co-operation between China and Japan develop daily.
祝愿中日两国友好合作关系日益发展。

- May your session be a complete success.
祝大会圆满成功。

（2）感谢信。感谢信在国际交往中是一种很常见的书信形式。按照西方的惯例，当收到邀请、接待，收到祝贺、慰问，接受礼品、帮助等，都应该写信致谢，以示礼貌。感谢信没有固定格式。语言要求诚恳、适当，不宜过长。

① 感谢招待。

Dear Minister,

  I am writing this letter to thank you for you warm hospitality accorded to me and my delegation during our recent visit to your beautiful country. I would also like to thank you for your interesting discussion with me which I have found very informative and useful.

  During the entire visit, my delegation and I were overwhelmed by the enthusiasm expressed by your business representatives on cooperation with China. I sincerely hope we could have more exchanges like this one when we would be able to continue our interesting discussion on possible ways to expand our bilateral economic and trade relations and bring our business people together.

  I am looking forward to your early visit to China when I will be able to pay back some of the hospitality I received during my memorable stay in your beautiful country. With kind personal regards.

Faithfully yours,
Chao Cai
Minister of Economic Cooperation

② 感谢讲学。

Dear Mr Brown,

  I am writing on behalf of all members of our department to say how much we all enjoyed your excellent lecture on Tuesday. We have learned a lot about the changes in present-day Information Technology and are very grateful to you for coming to our university and giving us such an interesting and informative talk.

  Thank you very much and we look forward to hearing you again.

Yours sincerely,

③ 用于各种场合的感谢语。

- I can't sufficiently express my thanks for your thoughtful kindness.
  对你给予我们的无微不至的关怀，我难以充分表达我的谢意。
- This is to thank you again for your wonderful hospitality.
  再次感谢你的盛情款待。
- We acknowledge with gratitude your message of good wishes.
  感谢你的良好的祝愿。
- Many thanks for the fine desk lamp that you send me, and I feel deeply moved by this token of your affection.
  非常感谢你送给我的精致的台灯。这一友情的象征，使我深受感动。

（3）投诉信。投诉信一般是用来向被投诉单位的领导或者负责人提出交易过程中出现的失误，可能是服务的质量问题，态度问题，还有可能是所需商品没有及时达到，或者数量上或者质量上存在问题。这个时候，我们可以写一封投诉信，向对方的负责人说明情况。

Dear Sir/Madam:

  I am writing to you to complain about your hotel. I had a terrible stay in room 3008 of your hotel from the 4th to the 16th of August 2006, when I came to Guangzhou on business.

  Firstly, the air-conditioning in my room could not be turned down or switched off. When I asked the reception staff to do something about it, they laughed and told me it was better than being hot. I asked your front of house manager and she told me she would send someone to my room immediately. No one came. As a result, I was very cold every time I was in the room.

  Secondly, I found the bathroom dirty and the hot water was always warm.

  Thirdly, the noise at night was extremely loud and I found it difficult to sleep. I asked to change rooms, but was told it was impossible because the hotel was full.

  I paid a lot for my stay in your hotel and expect much better service from such a well-known hotel. In future, I will not be staying at your hotel again and will inform my business associates of the terrible service. Wish your service can be improved.

（4）道歉信。在日常生活中难免会出现一些差错，因为失约，损坏了别人的东西等。在这种情况下，应及时写信表示道歉，以消除不必要的误会。写道歉信时应注意态度要诚恳，原委要解释清楚，措辞要委婉。

来看一个因未能及时还书致歉的例子。

Dear Miss Liu:

  Excuse me for my long delaying in return to you your *Robinson Crusoe* which I read through with great interest. I had finished reading the book and was about to return it when my cousin came to see me. Never having seen the book, she was so interested in it that I had to retain it longer. However, I hope that in view of the additional delight thus afforded by your book, you will overlook my negligence in not returning it sooner.

  Thank you again for the loan.

Sincerely yours,
****

（5）申请信。申请信的篇幅一般不超过一页，其语气必须诚恳。申请信的正文一般由3~4个段落组成，内容大致如下。

① 说明向某单位申请工作的理由；例如见广告应征，熟人介绍，本人专业与该单位业务对口等。

② 概括本人经历和特长，表明自己能够胜任此项工作。

③ 希望聘方积极考虑和尽早答复；按西方惯例，录用前，聘方对申请人进行面试（interview），因此，申请信经常以要求安排面试结尾。

来看一个申请任汉语教师的例子。

Dear Dr Smith:

Mr. Liu Yang who has just returned to China from your university informed me that you are considering the possibility of offering a Chinese language course to your students in the next academic year and may have an opening for a teacher of the Chinese language. I'm very much interested in such a position.

I have been teaching Chinese literature and composition at college level since 2000. In the past six years, I have worked in summer programs, teaching the Chinese language and culture to students from English speaking countries. As a result, I have got to know well the common problems of these students and how to adapt teaching to achieve the best results.

With years of intensive English training, I have no difficulty conducting classed in English and feel quite comfortable working with American students.

I will be available after July 2006. Please feel free to contact me if you wish more information. Thank you very much for your consideration and I look forward to hearing from you.

Sincerely yours,
LiuWei

B. 简历

简历是我们打开人生之门的钥匙，现在社会的竞争日益激烈，在求职的过程中，简历的重要性不言而喻。

1. 英文简历的组成及常见的类型

（1）简历的组成部分和内容。简历是针对自己想应聘的工作把求职意向、经验、个人情况等简要地列举出来，以达到向雇主推销自己的目的，所以在简历中，应该突出自己的强项。一般来说，简历可以由以下几部分组成：

- 姓名、地址、电话（name, address, telephone number）。
- 个人资料（personal data）。
- 求职目标和资格（objective and qualifications）。
- 经历（work experience）。
- 学历（education）。

- 著作/专利（publications or patents）。
- 外语技能（foreign languages skills）。
- 特别技能（special skills）。
- 课外活动/社会活动（extracurricular activities or social activities）。
- 业余爱好/兴趣（hobbies or interests）。
- 证明材料（references）。

以上各项不需要全部列举。一般而言，各项内容要根据个人的具体情况或应聘的职位而定。

（2）常见的英文简历类型。个人简历没有固定的格式，应聘者可以根据个人情况，对简历的某些方面有所侧重。例如，对于即将毕业的学生或工作经验很短的人而言，简历可以以学历为主；对于工作经历丰富的人来说，工作经历和工作成绩是简历的亮点。按照简历的不同侧重点，可以把简历分为4类。

① 以学历为主的简历。以学历为主的简历的重点是学习经历，适合于即将毕业的学生或有很短工作经历的人。它一般包括以下几项内容。

- 个人资料。
- 学历（education）：一般从最高学历写起，写出就读学校的名称、所获学位、所学专业、各阶段学习的起止时间、与应聘职位相关的课程，以及成绩、所获得的奖励如奖学金、优秀学生称号等。
- 兼职。
- 特别技能。
- 兴趣爱好。

② 以经历为主的简历。有工作经验的应聘人写简历时可以侧重自己的工作经历，把和应聘工作有关的经历和业绩写出来。此类简历主要包括以下几项内容。

- 个人资料。
- 求职目标。
- 工作经历（work experience）：按照时间顺序列出所工作单位的名称、负责的工作、工作业绩等，最好是工作的创新点和收获是可以重点写的内容。
- 特别技能。

③ 以技能、业绩或工作性质为中心的简历。此类简历主要是强调应聘人的技能和工作业绩，即以所取得的成绩或具备的技能等来概括工作经历，即把成绩和技能先行列出，不再是将工作经历按照时间顺序一一列出，工作经历在最后可简单地提及。

④ 综合性简历。这是以上第3种和第4种简历的综合，既要突出技能与业绩，也要把工作经历列出。所以简历的书写不能一概而论，可以根据自身的情况做出选择。

2. 英文简历常用词汇与句型

（1）常用词汇。

① 个人情况。

Name 姓名	Sex 性别
Male 男	Female 女

Height 身高　　　　　　　　　　　Birth 出生
Birth date 出生日期　　　　　　　Born 生于
Province 省　　　　　　　　　　　City 市
Street 街　　　　　　　　　　　　Road 路
District 区　　　　　　　　　　　Citizenship 国籍
Address 地址　　　　　　　　　　postal code 邮政编码
home phone 住宅电话
② 学历。
Education 学历　　　　　　　　　Curriculum 课程
Major 主修、主课、专业　　　　　Minor 选修、辅修
Courses Taken 所学课程　　　　　Part-Time Job 业余工作、兼职
Professor 教授　　　　　　　　　Summer Jobs 暑期工作
Vacation 假期工作　　　　　　　 Social Activities 社会活动
Rewards 奖励　　　　　　　　　　Scholarship 奖学金
Semester 学期（美）　　　　　　 Term 学期（英）
President 校长　　　　　　　　　Vice-president 副校长
Abroad Student 留学生　　　　　 Master 硕士
Department Chairman 系主任　　　Guest Professor 客座教授
Teaching Assistant 助教　　　　　Doctor 博士
Bachelor 学士
③ 经历。
Achievements 业绩　　　　　　　 Earn 获得、赚取
Cost 成本、费用　　　　　　　　 Effect 效果、作用
Direct 指导　　　　　　　　　　 Assist 辅助
Guide 指导、操纵　　　　　　　　Accomplish 完成（任务等）
Create 创造　　　　　　　　　　 Launch 开办（新企业）
Lead 领导　　　　　　　　　　　 Manage 管理、经营
Analyze 分析　　　　　　　　　　Profit 利润
Manufacture 制造　　　　　　　　Reinforce 加强
Spread 传播、扩大　　　　　　　 Motivate 促动
Mastered 精通的激发　　　　　　 Negotiate 谈判
④ 其他。
Hobbies 业余爱好　　　　　　　　Fishing 钓鱼
Boating 划船　　　　　　　　　　Golf 高尔夫球
Oil painting 油画　　　　　　　　Skiing 滑雪
Interests 兴趣、爱好　　　　　　 Skating 滑冰
Boxing 拳击　　　　　　　　　　 Writing 写作
Jogging 慢跑　　　　　　　　　　Traveling 旅游
Dancing 跳舞　　　　　　　　　　Cooking 烹饪

Collecting Stamps 集邮   Swimming 游泳

（2）实用句型举例。

① 求职目标。

- A responsible administrative position that will provide challenge where I can use my creativity and initiative.
  负责行政事务的、具有挑战性的职位，能发挥创造力与开拓精神。
- A position as an editor that will enable me to use my knowledge of editing.
  能发挥所学编辑知识的编辑之职。
- A position as a Chinese language instructor at college or university level.
  大学汉语讲师之职。
- Editor of a publishing company.
  出版公司的编辑。
- To apply my accounting experience in a position offering variety of assignments and challenges with opportunity of advance.
  申请能提供各种机遇、挑战、提升机会以及能发挥本人在财会方面经验的职位。
- Seeking a teaching position where my expertise in American literature will be employed.
  能运用我在美国文学方面专业知识的教师职位。
- To offer my training in business administration in a job leading to a position of senior executive.
  能运用我在商业管理方面知识的职位，最终目标是高级主管。
- To devote my talent in computer science as a computer engineer to a position with growth potential to a computer systems manager.
  发挥我在计算机方面才能的计算机工程师之职，并有晋升为计算机系统部经理的机会。
- To employ my professional training in the area of electronics engineering.
  能运用我在电子方面专业知识的职位。
- To begin as a system analyst and eventually become a technical controller.
  从系统分析员开始，最终成为技术管理。
- An administrative secretarial position where communication skills and a pleasant attitude toward people will be assets.
  寻求行政秘书之职位，且用得上交际技巧和与人为善的态度为好。

② 学历及所学课程。

- Major courses contributing to management qualifications:
  对管理资格有帮助的主要课程：
- Among the pertinent courses I have taken are…
  所学的有关课程是……
- Courses taken that will be useful for secretarial work:
  所学的对秘书工作有用的课程：
- Academic preparation for electronics engineering:
  电子工程方面的专业课程：

- Completed four years of technical training courses at college:
  完成大学 4 年的技术培训课程：
- Specialized courses pertaining to foreign trade:
  与外贸有关的专业课程：
- To fulfill the plan for continued study in the field of computer science, I have completed the following courses:
  为完成在计算机方面的继续深造的计划，已完成以下课程。
- Following college graduation, I have taken courses in English at Beijing University as part of self-improvement program.
  大学毕业后，作为进修计划的一部分，已完成北京大学的以下英语课程。

③ 经历。

- Engineering sales specialist, responsible for petroleum sales and technical support to the industrial and commercial industries of the Boston metropolitan area.
  工程销售专家，负责推销石油并向波士顿市区内工业及商业性工业提供技术援助。
- Sales manager. In addition to ordinary sales activities and management of department, responsible for recruiting and training of sales staff members.
  销售部经理，除正常销售活动和部门管理之外，还负责招聘与训练销售人员。
- As a mechanical engineer, responsible for developing mechanical specifications, engineering analysis and design for selecting rotating equipment.
- Computer Programmer. Operate flow-charts, collect business information for management, update methods of operation.
  计算机程序员，管理流程表，收集管理商务信息，掌握最新的操作方法。
- As a senior market researcher, responsible for collection and analysis of business information of interest to foreign business offices stationed in the Building.
  高级市场研究员，负责收集和分析住在大厦内的外国商务办事处的商业信息。

3. 英文简历范例

对于已经有工作经验的人来说，可以参考以下的范例。
（1）电子工程师。
BACKGROUND:
Over Eight years of extensive electronics experience. Versed in both digital and analog electronics with specific emphasis on computer hardware/software. Special expertise in designing embedded system. Proficient in VHDL and C# programming languages. Excellent in PCB.
WORK EXPERIENCE:
51-singlechip Systems, Shanghai, China, 1997—1999
Sales Engineer, 1999—2000
Responsible for the characterization and evaluation of, and approved vendors list for: Power supplies, oscillators, crystals, and programmable logic used in desktop and laptop computers.

Evaluated and recommended quality components that increased product profitability. Interacted with vendors to resolve problems associated with components qualification. Technical advisor for Purchasing.

Design Evaluation Engineer, 2000—2003

Evaluated new computer product designs, solving environmental problems on prototype computers. Conducted systems analysis on new computer products to ensure hardware, software and mechanical design integrity.

Assistant Engineer, 2003—2005

Performed extensive hardware evaluation ion prototype computers, tested prototype units for timing violation using the latest state-of-the-art test equipment, digital oscilloscopes and logic analyzers. Performed environmental, ESD and acoustic testing. Designed and built a power-up test used to test prototype computers during cold boot.

EDUCATION:

Bachelor of Science in Electrical Engineering
—Beijing University, 1997

Job descriptions:

Work that is related to the analyzing, designing and evaluation of the embedded system.

下面再来看一个应届毕业生的简历。

（2）市场营销员。

Chinese Name: Wei Zhang

English Name: Andy

Sex: Male

Born: 7/18/82

University: Tsinghua University

Major: Marketing

Address: 110#, Tsinghua University

Telephone: 1356****321

E-mail: ****@yahoo.com.cn

Job Objective:

A Position offering challenge and responsibility in the realm of consumer affairs or marketing.

Education:

2002—2006   Tsinghua University, College Of Commerce

Graduating in July with a B.S. degree in Marketing.

Fields of study include: psychology, economics, marketing, business law, statistics, calculus, sociology, product policy, social and managerial concepts in marketing, marketing strategies, consumer behavior, sales force management, marketing research and forecast.

1999—2002   The No. 2 Middle School of Beijing.

Social Activities:

2000—2002   Class monitor.

2003—2005　Chairman of the Student Union.

Summer Jobs:

2004 Administrative Assistant in Sales Department of Beijing Samsung Company. Responsible for selling, correspondence, expense reports, record keeping, inventory catalog.

Hobbies:

Swimming, Internet-surfing, music, travel.

English Proficiency:

College English Test-Band Six.

Computer Skills:

Dream weaver, Flash, Adobe Photoshop, AutoCAD, Microsoft office, etc.

References will be furnished upon request.

C．求职信

1．求职信的特点和技术要求

（1）求职信的特点。

求职信（application letter）属于商业信件，因此文体及格式要正式；语言要简洁、客观、明了；表达要准确；语气要客气。

（2）技术要求。

① 正式的文体及格式。求职信的文体及格式要正式，这表明求职者的尊重和礼貌，也反映求职人的性格和办事作风。如果求职信写得很随便，会让读信人认为求职者不重视此事或给人马马虎虎的感觉。

② 简洁、客观、明了的语言。求职人要以客观、事实求是的态度、运用简练的语言把事情表达清楚；要做到主题突出、层次分明、言简意赅。表达要直接，不可绕圈子。此外，不要提与主题不相关的事；在说明个人经历或能力时，要说出具体的业绩，不可笼统概括。

③ 准确的表达。表达不要模棱两可，不可过多使用形容词和副词。要避免生僻的词。对有疑问的词语，要多请教他人或词典。

④ 客气的语气。话语要礼貌，充满自信。既要表现出对对方的尊重，又不要表现的过分热情或恭维。

2．求职信的内容

一般来说，求职信包括以下4个方面的内容：①你得知这份工作的管道。②学历及经历的概要。③你的个性，以及能力。④联络地点、联络方式，以及最后的感谢语等，可以发挥创意的空间非常的大。求职信在于延续履历表的内容，更清楚地表现工作企图心、个性、性质等。

3．写英文求职信要点

（1）篇幅不宜过长，简短为好；态度诚恳，不需华丽词汇；让对方感觉亲切、自信、实在即可；不要误看其他错误的写作方法，以免耽误了你的求职机会。

（2）纸张的选用：建议你用灰色，黄褐色或米色纸作最终打印信纸，象牙色也是可以接受的；灰色或任何其他颜色的信纸因缺乏对比度不易看清最好不用。当然还应该注意要配合信封的颜色。

（3）书写：字体要写得整洁可辨，使用打印机把信打出来具有专业感。98%的求职信和简历都是用黑墨打印在白纸上的。

（4）附邮票：英语求职信内需附加邮票或回址信封。这会给别人的回信带来方便，而且也会让别人感受到你的真心。

（5）语法：准确无误的语法和拼写使读信人感到舒畅。错误的语法或拼写则十分明显，一目了然。且不可把收信人的姓名或公司地址拼错了。

（6）标点：正确地使用标点符号可以更好地表达自己的意愿。

- 标题中除冠词（a，an，the）外每一个字都要大写，4 个字母以下的介词（of，in）等不大写，第一个字始终要大写。

    I have read Gone With the Wind.

- 书籍和杂志用斜体或下划线表示。

    The business Women

- 所有商标一律大写。

    Coca Cola   Wahaha

- 家庭成员的称呼在不用名字时大写。

    When I have problems with my homework, I always turn to Brother.

    I cried, "Father, help me!"

- 带名字称呼其他亲属时要大写。

    My Aunt Kate had promised, but she didn't make it.

    My aunt and cousin had promised, but they didn't make it.

（7）数字：数字的使用也有一定的规则，正确地使用它们也是非常重要的。

- 从 1~10 的数字须拼出；11 以上都是多音节词，需要使用阿拉伯数字。如果把 120 写成 one hundred and twenty，读起来就不方便。

- 数字出现在句子开头时必须拼出：Twenty years is the term contained in the contract.

- 数字组合、数字和词组合在一起使用时需要使用连字符。

    150-ton goods / 56-miles from the harbor / thirty-two years ago.

- 如果一句中有一个数字在 10 以下，另一个大于 10，按规则都用数字。

    I asked for 6 Yuan, but Father gave me 16.

（8）引号：引号成对使用，一半在引语之前，一半在引号之后。至于在使用引语时逗号和句号位置的确定，要掌握好规则，即所有的逗号和句号都在引号内（注意逗号和其他标点符号在引语前的用法）；而冒号和分号始终在引号之外。

He said in a low voice, "How much time left to us?" and was told, "Don't worry! We still have plenty of time."

"We will call you back"; this phrase is popular with interviewers.

（9）问号根据句子的结构可以放在引号之内或引号之外。

Where can we find the "real romance"?

My teacher asked me, "Have you finished your homework?"

（10）缩写词：省略语是一个词的缩写，为了节约篇幅和便于使用，它被用来代替一个完整的词。省略的规则是在被省略的词后面加下圆点。例如：Dr.，A.M.，P.M.等。有些是我们熟知的省略语已经很少使用它的全称，而更多的是要使用缩略语，例如：B.A.而不说 Bachelor of Arts，M.B.A.而不说 Master of Business Administration。

4．求职信常用句型

（1）开头句型。

- My interest in the position of Sales Manager has prompted me to forward my resume for your review and consideration.
- The sales Manager position advertised in *China Daily* on July 12 intrigues me. I believe you will find me well-qualified.
- With my thorough educational training in accounting, I wish to apply for an entry-level accounting position.
- Your advertisement for a network support engineer in *China Daily* has interested me very much. I think I can fill the vacancy.
- Attention of Human Resource Manager: Like many other young men, I am looking for a position. I want to get started. At the bottom, perhaps, but started.
- I am very glad that you are recruiting a programmer! I hope to offer my services.
- I am very delighted to know that you have an opening for an English teacher in Beijing Evening News.
- I am forwarding my resume in regard to the opening we discussed in your Marketing Department.
- I want a job. Not any job with any company, but a particular job with your company. Here are my reasons: Your organization is more than just a company. It is an institution in the minds of the Chinese public.

（2）说明经历的句型。

- Since my graduation from Beijing Foreign Studies University 6 years ago, I have been employed as an interpreter in a foreign trade company.
- My three years of continuous experience in electrical engineering has taught me how to deal with all the phases of the business I am in right now.
- As the executive manager assistant of LingDa(China) Investment Co., Ltd, I have had a very extensive training in my field.

（3）说明教育程度的句型。

- I have a PhD from Beijing University of Aeronautics and Astronautics in electronics engineering and was employed by Samsung Computer for 4 years.
- I received my Mater's degree in Chinese literature from Huazhong Normal University in 2000.

- I am a graduate student in the Chemistry Department of Beijing Normal University and will receive my Mater's degree in March this year.
- My studies have given me the foundation of knowledge from which to learn the practical side international trade.
- My outstanding record at school and some experience in business have prepared me for the tasks in the work you are calling for.
- I have a good command of two foreign languages: English and Japanese.
- I am quite proficient in three computer languages:BASIC,C#,.Net.
- I can speak and write English very well and have worked as an interpreter for two years.

（4）说明薪金待遇的句型。

- I should require that your factory provide me with an apartment.
- With regard to salary, I leave it to you to decide after experience of performance in the job.
- I should require a commencing salary of 5000 Yuan per month.
- My hope for welfare is to enjoy free medical care.
- The yearly salary I should ask for would be 100 000 Yuan, with a bed in the school's dormitory.
- The monthly salary of 3800 Yuan will be acceptable if your company houses me.

（5）推荐自己的句型。

- I am presently looking for a position where my experience will make a positive contribution to the start-up or continuing profitable operation of a business in which I am so well experienced.
- I am an innovative achiever. I feel that in nowadays society where competition is fierce, there is a need for a representative who can meet and beat the competition. I feel that I have all the necessary ingredients to contribute to the success of Any Corporation. All I need is a starting point.
- Your advertisement in the June 20th issue of *Lawyers Monthly* appeals to me. I feel that I have the qualifications necessary to effectively handle the responsibilities of Administrative Judge.
- My ten years employment at the LIDOO Company provides a wide range of administrative, financial and research support to the Chief Executive Officer. I have a strong aptitude for working with numbers and extensive experience with computer software applications.
- As you will note, I have twelve years of educational and media experience. I am proficient in the operation of a wide variety of photographic, video, and audio equipment. I am regularly responsible for processing, duplicating, and setting up slide presentations, as well as synchronized slide and audio presentations.

（6）结束语句型。

- I should appreciate the privilege of an interview. I may be reached by letter at the address

given above, or by telephone at 98675213.
- I feel that a personal meeting would give us the opportunity to discuss your shout-and long-term objectives and my ability to direct your organization towards successfully achieving those goals.
- I should be glad to have a personal interview, and can present references if desired.
- Thank you for your consideration.
- I have enclosed a resume as well as a brief sample of my writing for your review. I look forward to meeting with you to discuss further how I could contribute to your organization.
- Thank you for your attention to this matter. I look forward to speaking with you.
- The enclosed resume describes my qualifications for the position advertised. I would welcome the opportunity to personally discuss my qualifications with you at your convenience.
- I would welcome the opportunity for a personal interview with you at your convenience.

5. 求职信范例

（1）软件工程师。

Reading *Beijing Youth Daily* on the web yesterday, I was very impressed by an article on your company's contribution to the development of China's IT industry. I would like to offer my experience in computer science and am writing to inquire whether your company has any position available.

I will graduate in June from Tsinghua University of Science and Technology with a Bachelor's degree in computer's science. Courses taken include Programming, System Design and Analysis, Operating System, .NET, etc. In addition, I have experience with programming as I have worked as a part-time programmer for almost two years in a software company. I have passed College English Test Band 6 and got a score of 650 in TOFEL.

Working with in a company like yours would be a great way to expand my skills and contribute something to the development of computer science. If there is a position available in your company, I do hope that you will consider me. Enclosed is a copy of my resume. I will appreciate if you could give me an opportunity of a personal interview at your convenience. In any event, thank you very much for your time.

Yours sincerely,
Wang Lei

（2）电脑工程师。

Dear Sir or Madam,

In reply to your advertisement in today's Job51, I am respectfully offering my service as an engineer for your company. My college educational background and work experience in the field of IT industry have prepared me for the task in the work you are calling for.

I have worked as a computer programmer in HuaWei Company for three years, during which I become more and more expert in programming. I developed a sales and management software and won a prize for The Administration of Hotel system software. I am diligent worker and a fast learner and really interested in coping with difficulties in computer science.

However, in order to get a more challenging opportunity, I'd like to fill the opening offered in your company, which I am sure will fully utilize my capability, with regard to salary, I leave it to you to decide after experience of my performance in the job.

I would appreciate it if we could set an appointment so you can get to know me better. Thank you for your kind attention. I hope to hear from you.

Yours sincerely,
Zhang Wei

D. 合同书

1. 合同书的构成和分类

合同是缔约双方通过协商就某一项具体事务划定双方各自的权利和义务，达成的文字契约。随着我国对外开放的不断扩大，各类涉外合同协议日益增多。能够正确理解与撰写涉外合同协议已成为当今国际交往中的一个重要而必不可少的环节。由于合同协议是具有法律效力的契约性文件，条款是否周全，措辞是否严谨，是否能体现平等互利原则，都事关重大。

国际贸易中使用的英文合同书通常由以下内容构成：标题、前言、正文部分和结尾部分。

合同分为贸易合同（Contract of Trade）和聘约合同（Contract of Employment）。

2. 贸易合同写法与格式

贸易合同是进出口业务中经过交易磋商，把双方同意的具体条件固定下来。贸易合同不论采用文字条款或表格形式，都必须规定得具体和明确，不得有差错。

一份完整的贸易合同通常包含有以下内容。

- 合同（CONTRACT）:
- 日期（Date）:
- 合同号码（Contract No.）:
- 买方（The Buyers）:   卖方（The Sellers）:
- 兹经买卖双方同意按照以下条款由买方购进，卖方售出以下商品:

This contract is made by and between the Buyers and the Sellers; whereby the Buyers agree to buy and the Sellers agree to sell the under-mentioned goods subject to the terms and conditions as stipulated hereinafter:

（1）货号：Article No.:

（2）品名及规格：Description & Specification:

（3）数量：Quantity:

（4）单价：Unit price:

（5）总值：Total Value:

（6）包装：Packing:

（7）生产国别和制造厂家：Country of Origin and manufacture:

（8）支付条款：Terms of Payment:

（9）装运期限：Time of Shipment:

（10）装运口岸：Port of Lading:

（11）目的口岸：Port of Destination:

（12）保险：由卖方按发票全额110%投保至_____为止的_____险。

Insurance: To be effected by buyers for 110% of full invoice value covering _____ up to _____ only.

（13）付款条件：买方须于_____年_____月_____日将保兑的，不可撤销的，可转让可分割的即期信用证开到卖方。

Payment: By confirmed, irrevocable, transferable and divisible L/C to be available by sight draft to reach the sellers before ___/___/_____.

（14）单据：Documents:

（15）索赔：在货到目的口岸45天内如发现货物品质、规格和数量与合同不符，除属保险公司或船方责任外，买方有权凭中国商检出示的检验证书或有关文件向卖方索赔换货或赔款。

Claims: Within 45 days after the arrival of the goods at the destination, should the quality, specifications or quantity be found not in conformity with the stipulations of the contract except those claims for which the insurance company or the owners of the vessel are liable, the Buyers shall, have the right on the strength of the inspection certificate issued by the C.C.I.C and the relative documents to claim for compensation to the Sellers.

（16）仲裁：凡有关执行合同所发生的一切争议应通过友好协商解决，如协商不能解决，则将分歧提交中国国际贸易促进委员会按有关仲裁程序进行仲裁，仲裁将是终局的，双方均受其约束，仲裁费用由败诉方承担。

Arbitration: All disputes in connection with the execution of this Contract shall be settled friendly through negotiation. In case no settlement can be reached, the case then may be submitted for arbitration to the Arbitration Commission of the China Council for the Promotion of International Trade in accordance with the Provisional Rules of Procedure promulgated by the said Arbitration Commission. The Arbitration committee shall be final and binding upon both parties, and the Arbitration fee shall be borne by the losing parties.

3. 聘约合同

（1）聘约合同的内容。聘约合同多为我国一些高等院校和企事业单位与外国专家本人签订的服务合同，一般规定有聘期、受聘方的工作任务、聘方的要求、受聘方的工资和生活待遇、受聘方应遵守的法律和制度、聘约的生效、终止、解除和延长等。

一般来说，聘约合同里有很多常用的句型，而有一些常用的句型基本上也已经程序化了，成为常用术语，譬如在开头通常这样说："This contract is made on the ___ day of ___ to ___ between ___ as Seller and ___ as Buyer. Both Parties agree to the sale and purchase of ___ under the following terms and conditions".

一般说来，聘约合同的主要内容如下：

- 合同双方在自愿的基础上签订合同。

The two Parties, in a spirit of friendly cooperation, agree to sign this contract and pledge to fulfill conscientiously all the obligations stipulated in it.

- 合同的起始和终止时间。

The period of service will be from the ___ day of ___ to the ___ day of ___.

- 受聘方的责任。

The duties of Party B.

- 聘用期间报酬的计算。

Party B's monthly salary will be Yuan RMB (About USD), the pay day is every month _____. If not a full month, the salary will be will be prorated (days times salary/30).

- 甲方的义务和职责。

Party A's Obligations:

- 乙方的义务和职责。

Party B's obligations:

- 关于修订、取消和终止合同的一些说明。

Revision, Cancellation and Termination of the Contract.

- 违反的处罚。

Breach Penalty.

（2）聘约合同实例。下面来看一个聘用合同的实例：

Contact of Employment

The Foreign Language Department of Huazhong Normal University (the engaging party) has engaged Mr. Smith (the engaged party) as a teacher of English. The two parties in the spirit of friendship and cooperation have entered into an agreement to sign and to comply with the present contract.

1. The term of service is two years, that is, from Sept 1, 2006, the first day of the term of office, to Sept 1, 2008, the last day of the term of office.

2. By mutual consultation the work of the engaged party is decided as follows:

(1) Training teachers of English, research students and students taking refresher courses.

(2) Conducting senior English classes and advising students on extra-curricular activities of the language.

(3) Compiling English textbooks and supplementary teaching materials, undertaking tape recording and other work connected with the language.

(4) Having 18 up to 22 teaching periods in a week.

3. The engaged party works five days a week and eight hours a day. The engaged party will have legal holidays as prescribed by the Chinese Government. The vacation is fixed days by the

school calendar.

4. The engaging party pays the engaged party a monthly salary of Three Thousand *Yuan*(Chinese Currency) and provides him with various benefits.

5. The engaged party must observe the regulations of the Chinese Government concerning residence, wages and benefits, and travel for foreigners when entering, leaving and passing through the territory of the country, and must follow the working system of the engaging party.

The engaged party welcomes any suggestion put forward by the engaged party and will take them into favorable consideration in so far as circumstances permit. The engaged party will observe the decisions of the engaging party and is to do his work in the spirit of active cooperation to accomplish the tasks assigned.

6. Neither party shall without sufficient cause or reason cancel the contract.

If the engaging party finds it imperative to terminate the contract, then, in addition to bearing the corresponding expenses for wages and benefits, it must pay the engaged party one month's extra salary as compensation allowance, and arrange for him and his family to go back to their own country within a month.

If the engaged party submits his resignation in the course of his service, the engaging party will stop paying him his salary from the day when his resignation is approved by the engaging party, and the engaged party will no longer enjoy the wages and benefits provided. When leaving China, the engaged party and his family will have to pay for everything themselves.

7. The present contract comes into effect on the first day of the term of service herein stipulated and ceases to be effective at its expiration. If either party wished to renew the contract, the other party shall be notified before it expires. Upon agreement by both parties through consultation a new contract may be signed.

8. The engaged party agrees to all the articles in this contract.

9. The present contract is done in Chinese and English, both versions being equally valid.

··· (The engaging party)

··· (The engaged party)

August 20, 2006

Wuhan, Hubei

E．产品说明书

随着科学和经济的发展，各种现代化的机械、化工、电子产品层出不穷。说明书的主要目的是用来说明产品的性能、特点、用途和使用方法，其语言应当简洁、通俗易懂、确切，注意科学性和逻辑性，使消费者一看便知道所购商品的用途、安装、使用方法和保养方法，以免由于对产品的不了解，造成不必要的差错或损失。

1．产品说明书的结构

英语产品说明书，根据产品的性能、特点、用途和使用方法的不同，其语言形式也有所不同。一般来讲，产品说明书由标题（包括副标题）和正文两部分组成。有的说明书在最后还附注厂商的名称。

（1）说明书标题。说明书标题并不如广告的标题那么重要，所以有些英文产品说明书中并没有标题。但从宣传效果上讲，其标题也很重要，在说明中会起到很好的引导作用，如同广告标题，说明书标题同样分为直接性标题和间接性标题，有时也附有副标题。

（2）说明书正文。说明文的主要目的是用来说明产品的性能、特点、用途和使用方法。其语言应当简洁、通俗易懂、准确，注意科学性和逻辑性，使消费者一看便知道所购买商品的用途、安装、使用方法和保养方法。

各类产品的性质和用途不同，产品说明书的方法及内容也各不相同，以及正文究竟包括哪几个部分，应根据不同产品的具体情况来确定。

一般来说，各类产品的说明书应包括的内容不尽相同，分类如下。

① 饮料类的产品说明书应包括以下几点：
- 食品的主要成分，即组成成分和配料；
- 冲调方法，水的比例，水的温度，即服用方法；
- 要表明生产厂家；
- 保质期；
- 存放方法。

② 医药用品的说明书包括：
- 药品的主要成分；
- 药品的主要功效，以及适用哪些症状；
- 药品的用法及用量；
- 存放方法；
- 注意事项（包括禁忌，以及药品的副作用）；
- 有效期。

③ 电子产品的说明书一般包括：
- 技术参数或产品规格；
- 各部件名称、或称为功能指示；
- 使用方法、控制及操作程序；
- 使用时的注意事项；
- 接地线、天线说明；
- 确保安全要点；
- 接电注意事项；
- 操作方法；
- 机器的维护和保养；
- 常见故障及排除方法；
- 生产厂家、联系地址、电话、邮箱及网站等。

④ 化学产品说明书的内容包括：
- 产品成分；
- 用途；

- 产品的性能特点；
- 产品的适用范围；
- 使用方法；
- 注意事项；
- 保存期。

2. 产品说明书的语言特征

产品说明书的语言不同于广告语言，它的目的不像广告那样在于宣传，而是朴实详细地说明产品的功能和用途等，所以其鼓动性不及广告语言强。一般来说，产品说明书的语言要求简练朴实，切忌夸大其词，以免造成不良的影响和后果。总的来说，产品说明书的语言有以下一些特征。

（1）多用简单句。由于说明书的语言具有简洁、清晰的特点，而且其层次结构明了，所以说明书中常采用简单的句子结构。

- The battery life should be about one year under normal use.
- It is an ideal instrument.
- Purified water for drinking.

（2）多用名词短语。名词性短语使用频繁也是英语产品说明书的一大特色，这些句型大多是祈使句型的动词省略。

- Three times daily. = Take it three times everyday.
- Two tablets each time.
- Cooking time 15 minutes. = The cooking time is 15 minutes.
- Adults and children over 12 years old.

（3）常用祈使句。因为产品说明书通常用来告诉消费者如何正确地使用某种产品，所以祈使句是一种很好的表达方法，它能给人亲切的感觉。

- Do keep out of the reach of children.
- Press the record button when you start to record.
- Adjust the sound Volume with the – /+ buttons.
- Set the Washer Timer to the time you want.
- Store in upright position.

（4）常用复合名词。在英文产品说明书中，复合名词的使用能够简洁而准确地表达产品说明书中所要说明的内容。

- Purified water 纯净水
- Needle-head 针头
- Multi-vitamins 多种维生素
- Push-pull button 推拔式按钮

（5）非谓语结构多。英语中的非谓语动词有动词的不定式、现在分词和过去分词。在产品的英文说明书中，使用非谓语动词，不仅可以提高语言的表达层次，还可以精炼句子的结构。

- Insert batteries with the poles in the right direction as marked.

- Shake well before taken.
- Adjust the echo effect to your taste with the Echo Control while singing.

3. 产品说明书范例

现代家庭生活已经离不开电子产品，大中小型企业更是如此。电子产品的问世，给生活带来了方便，也给生产带来了活力和效益。但是电子器械如果不按说明书安装或使用，会造成经济的损失甚至是人员的伤亡，因此这类产品说明书写具体，详细，哪怕是一个小螺钉、小线头，都要标明。总体来说，最起码应该写出产品性能、特点、适用范围，即产品简介。下面来看一个说明书的例子。

Precautions in the Use of Microwave Ovens for Heating Food

(1) Inspection for Damage. A microwave oven should only be used if an inspection confirms all the following items.

① The grill is not damaged or broken.
② The door fits squarely and securely and opens and closes smoothly.
③ The door hinges are in good condition.
④ The door does not open more than a few millimeters without an audible operation of the safety switches.
⑤ The metal plates of the metal seal on the door are neither buckled nor deformed.
⑥ The door seal are neither covered with food nor have large burn marks.

(2) PRECAUTIONS Microwave radiation ovens can cause harmful effects if the following precautions are not taken:

① Never tamper with or inactivate the interlocking devices on the door.
② Never poke an object, particularly a metal object, through the grille or between the door and the oven while the oven is operating.
③ Never place saucepans, unopened cans or other heavy metal objects in the oven.
④ Clean the oven cavity, the door and the seals with water and a mild detergent at regular intervals. Never use any form of abrasive cleaner that may scratch or scour surfaces around the door.
⑤ Never use the oven without the trays provided by the manufacture.
⑥ Never operate the oven without a load(an absorbing material such as food or water) in the oven cavity unless specifically allowed in the manufacturer's literature.
⑦ Never rest heavy objects such as food containers on the door while it is open.
⑧ Do not place sealed containers in the microwave oven.

微波炉使用说明书

使用微波炉烹调应注意的事项：
（1）检查是否有损坏。使用微波炉前应先按下列各项检查。
① 烤架是否损坏。
② 炉门是否妥当，开关是否良好。
③ 门栓是否妥当。

④ 除非听到安全开关的操作信号，炉门不能开启。
⑤ 炉门上镶着金属绝缘孔网的金属板不可弯曲或变形。
⑥ 炉门上的绝缘孔网不可沾上食物或积聚油污。
（2）预防事项。
① 切勿损坏炉门的安全锁。
② 当微波炉操作时，请勿置入任何物品，特别是金属物体。
③ 切勿放置任何金属物体于炉内，包括金属容器、碟或任何金属装饰品等。
④ 经常清洁炉内，使用温和洗洁液清理炉门及绝缘孔网，不可使用具有腐蚀性的清洁剂，以免损坏炉门。
⑤ 使用微波炉时必须应用附设的转盘。
⑥ 使用微波炉时，炉内应放有可吸收能量的物质（例如：食物，水），除本说明书特别许可的情况外。
⑦ 炉门开启时，请勿在炉门上放置重物。
⑧ 切勿使用密封的容器于微波炉内。

General Use

1. In order to maintain high quality, do not operate the oven when empty. The microwave energy will reflect continuously throughout the oven if no food or water is present to absorb energy.

2. If a fire occurs in the oven, touch the STOP/RESET Pad and Leave Door Closed, or turn TIMER to zero and Leave Door Closed.

3. Do not dry clothes, newspapers or other materials in oven. They may catch fire.

4. Do not use recycled paper products or other materials, as they may contain impurities which may cause sparks and /or fires when used.

5. Do not use newspapers or paper bags for cooking.

6. Do not hit or strike control panel. Damage to control may occur.

7. POT HOLDERS may be needed as heat from food is transferred to the cooking container and from the container to the glass tray. The glass tray can be very hot after removing the cooking container from the oven.

8. Do not store flammable materials next to, on top of, or in the oven. It could be a fire hazard.

9. Do not cook food directly on glass tray unless indicated in recipes.

10. Do not use this oven to heat chemicals or other non-food products. Do not clean this oven with any product that is labeled as containing corrosive chemicals. The heating of corrosive chemicals in this oven may cause microwave radiation leaks.

一般使用

1. 为保持烘炉的质量，切勿让烘箱空操作，因为当没有食物或水分在炉内吸收能量的情况下，微波能量会不停地在炉内反射。

2. 如果炉内着火，请紧闭炉门，并按停止或重置或关掉（timer）时计，然后拔下电源导线，或关闭电路闸刀板或保险丝的开关。

3. 不要在烘箱内烘干布类，报纸或其他东西。
4. 不可使用再生纸制品类，因其含有容易引起电弧和着火的杂质。
5. 不可将报纸或纸盒用于烘烤。
6. 不可敲击控制板以免导致控制器损坏。
7. 取出烘完的食物时，必须使用锅夹，因为热力会从高温的食物传至烘烤容器，然后再由烘烤容器传至玻璃盛盒，当烘烤容器从炉内取出，玻璃盒会非常热。
8. 不可将易燃物放在烘箱内或烘箱上，以免导致起火。没有放入玻璃盒和轴环时则不可使用烘箱。
9. 如非食谱所指定，不可直接在玻璃盘上烘烤食物。
10. 请勿使用烘炉加热化学剂或其他非食制品。不可用含有腐蚀性化学剂的制品洗涤烘炉。在炉内加热腐蚀性化学剂可能会引起微波外泄。

FOOD

1. Do not use your oven for home canning or the heating of any closed jar. Pressure will build up and the jar may explode. In addition, the microwave oven can't maintain the food at he correct canning temperature. Improperly canned food may spoil and be dangerous to consume.
2. Do not attempt to deep fat fry in your microwave oven.
3. Do not boil eggs in their shell.
4. Potatoes, apples, egg yolks, whole squash and sausages are examples of foods with nonporous skins. This type of food must be pierced before cooking, to prevent bursting.
5. Stir liquids several times during heating to avoid eruption of the liquid from the container, e.g. water, milk or milk based fluids.
6. To check the degree of cooking of roasts and poultry use a Microwave Thermometer. Alternatively, a conventional meat thermometer may be used after the food is removed from the oven. If undercooked, return meat or poultry to the oven and cook for a few minutes at the recommended power level. It is important to ensure that meat and poultry are thoroughly cooked.
7. Cooking Times given in the cookbook are APPROXIMATE. Factors that may affect cooking time are preferred degree of moisture content, starting temperature, altitude, volume, size, shape, of food and utensils used. As you become familiar with the oven, you will be able to adjust for these factors.
8. It is better to Undertake Rather than Overcook foods. If food is undercooked, it can always be returned to the oven for future cooking. If food is overcooked, nothing can be done. Always start with minimum cooking times recommended.

食　物

1. 不可用密封罐将食物或瓶子放入烘箱，当气压增加，瓶子可能会爆炸，而且微波烘箱不可能使食物维持在适当温度，可能会引起罐装食物变质。
2. 不可用烘箱煎炸食物。
3. 不可带壳煮蛋，因压力会使鸡蛋爆裂。
4. 土豆、苹果、蛋黄、板栗、红肠等带皮的食物在烘烤之前必须用叉或刀穿孔以防止烘焦。

5. 在加热含有气体的液体时，请搅动数次以避免液体溢出容器。

6. 使用微波炉测肉温计检查牛肉或鸡肉的烘烤结果。如果烘烤不足，则再放入烘箱用适当温度强度多烘几分钟。不可用一般的测肉温计测微波烘箱。

7. 烘烤手册提供了烘烤的大约时间，影响烘烤时间的因素有：所喜欢的烘烤程度、开始温度、海拔高度、分量、大小、食物形状和盛载器皿。如果你熟悉烘箱操作，则可以适当参照以上这些因素加以修正烘烤时间。

8. 烘烤食物时最好是宁可烘烤不足，也不要烘烤过度。如果食物烘烤不足则可以重新再加以烘烤，但如果烘烤过度时无法补救。启动时请用最短时段烘烤。

Important Instructions

Warning—to reduce the risk of burns, electric shock, fire, injury to persons or excessive microwave energy:

1. Read all instructions before using microwave oven.
2. Some products such as whole eggs and sealed containers may explode and should not be heated in microwave oven.
3. Use this microwave oven only for its intended use as described in this manual.
4. As with any appliance, close supervision is necessary when used by children.
5. Do not operate this microwave oven, if it is not working properly, or if it has been damaged or dropped.
6. To reduce the risk of fire in the oven cavity:

   a. Do not overlook food. Carefully attend microwave oven if paper plastic, or other combustible materials are placed inside the oven to facilitate cooking.

   b. Remove wire twist-ties from bags before placing bag in oven.

   c. If materials inside the oven should ignite, keep oven door closed, turn oven off at the wall switch, or shut off power at the fuse or circuit breaker panel.

使用指南

注意：为避免产生烧伤、触电、火灾、人员伤亡或过多的能量外泄。

1. 在使用本设备前，请参阅使用要点。
2. 生鸡蛋及密封盒之类的东西，例如：密封玻璃瓶盒奶瓶容易引起爆裂，故不能放入烘箱加热烘烤，细节请参照烹调书。
3. 本设备只适用于本册所指示之用途。
4. 小孩使用本设备时必须注意看管。
5. 当烘箱操作不正常时，或受损坏及跌撞时，应停止继续使用。
6. 为避免烘箱起火：

   a. 不可过度烘烤食物，若放入炉内包装纸、佐料或其他易燃物品等材料要特别注意。

   b. 放盒子入箱时，请撤去金属包装袋。

   c. 万一烘箱内的东西着火，请保持烘箱内紧闭，然后拔去电源插头，或关掉屋内电源总联。

Earthing Instructions

This microwave oven must be earthed. In the event of an electrical short circuit, earthing reduces the risk of electric shock by providing an escape wire for the electric current.

This microwave oven is equipped with a cord having an earthing with an earthing plug. The plut must be plugged into an outlet that is properly installed and earthed.

Warning—Improper use of the earthing plug can result in a risk of electric shock.

接地线说明

本设备必须接地线，万一漏电，则接地线可以提供电流回路，以避免触电。本设备配有接地线以及一个接地线插头，此插头必须接插在确实接地的插座上。

Warning

1. The appliance should be inspected for damage to the door seal and door seal areas. If these areas are damaged the appliance should not be operated but be delivered to the manufacturer to service.

2. It is dangerous for anyone other than a service technician trained by the manufacture to service appliance.

3. If the supply cord of this appliance is damaged, it must be replaced by the special cord available only from the manufacture.

注意事项

1. 需检查这套设备的用具的门边线缝，若有损坏，必须停止使用，并送去制造商让服务修理员修理。

2. 必须由指定制造商所训练的修理员做调整或修理服务，让他人修理，会有危险。

3. 产品的电源若有损坏，必须更换由制造商提供的特别电源线。

Care of Your Microwave Oven

1. Turn the oven off and remove the power plug from the wall socket before cleaning.

2. Keep the inside of the oven clean. When food splatters or spilled liquids adhere to oven walls, wipe with a damp cloth. Mild detergent may be used if the oven gets very dirty. The use of harsh detergent or abrasives is not recommended.

3. The outside oven surfaces should be cleaned with a damp cloth. To prevent damage to the operating parts inside the oven, water should not be allowed to seep into the ventilation openings.

4. Do not allow the Control Panel to become wet. Clean with a soft, damp cloth. Do not use detergents, abrasives or spray on cleaners on the Control Panel. When cleaning the Control Panel, leave the oven door open to prevent the oven from accidentally turning on. After cleaning touch STOP/RESET Pad to clear display window, make sure oven timer is set to off position.

5. If steam accumulates inside or around the outside of the oven door, wipe with a soft cloth. This may occur when the microwave oven is operated under high humidity conditions and in no way indicates malfunction of the unit.

6. It is occasionally necessary to remove the glass tray for cleaning. Wash the tray in warm sudsy water or in a dishwasher.

7. The roller ring and oven cavity floor should be cleaned regularly to avoid excessive noise. Simply wipe the bottom surface of the oven with mild detergent, water or window cleaner and

dry. The roller ring may be washed in mild sudsy water or dish washer. Cooking vapours collected during repeated use will in no way affect the bottom surface or roller ring wheels. When removing the roller ring from cavity floor for cleaning, be sure to replace in the proper position.

8. When it becomes necessary to replace the oven light, please consult a dealer to have it replaced.

微波烘箱的保养

1. 清洗微波烘箱前,须关闭烘箱,并从插座上拔下插头。
2. 保持烘箱内部清洁。如溅出的食物或漏出的液体积在烘箱壁上,则请用湿布擦去。如烘箱十分肮脏,则可以使用软性洗剂。最好不要使用粗糙、磨损性洗剂。
3. 请用微湿布来清洗微波炉表面部分,为防止损伤烘箱内的操作部分,不要让水分由通口渗入。
4. 如控制扳手湿了,则请用软的干布抹擦,不能用粗糙、磨损性的物体擦控制板。擦控制板时请将炉门打开,以防止不小心启动烘箱。擦完之后按停止/重置以消除显示窗上的显示或确保定时计回到零时的位置。
5. 如有水蒸气积在烘箱内或炉门周围,可用软布擦净。这种情形在烘箱正常运转和温度高的情况下都可能产生。
6. 必须经常清洗玻璃盘,可用温肥皂水清洗或置于洗碗机内清洗。
7. 必须经常擦洗轴环和烘箱壁以避免产生噪声,请用软性洗剂或擦窗剂清洗烘箱底面。而轴环则可用热肥皂水清洗。从箱底下取下轴环清洗后必须妥善放回原位。
8. 如需要更换炉灯,请向有关厂商查询后更换。

部分参考译文与习题参考答案

UNIT 1

A. Text 电和电子

我们都有一个很好的帮手,在任何时候,它都准备好帮助我们。当你打开房间开关的时候,它让我们的房间变得明亮;当你拧开电视开关的时候,它会给我们展示清晰的画面。当你在电话里与别人通话时,它将你的声音带到对方。它是什么呢?对,这个帮手的名字就叫做电。我们对电灯、无线电广播、电视和电话非常熟悉,很难想象如果离开了电,我们的生活将会是什么样子。在没有电的时候,人们只能摸索在微弱的烛光下,因为没有交通灯的引导,汽车只能在街上缓慢行走,食物在冰箱中慢慢腐烂,人们长距离交流只能通过已经抛弃的烽火信号和信件进行。

很多年前,科学家们对电的概念还是很模糊的。大约 2000 年以前,中国哲学家王充发现,将一块琥珀在一块兽皮或者木头上摩擦时,随时都能产生电。现在科学家就认为这块琥珀已经带电了。19 世纪以前,除了上述电现象以外,没有人知道更多关于电的情况了。随着时代的进展,很多科学家们认为它不过是一种"流体",就像水流过管道一样流过导线,但是他们并不知道是什么让它流动。很多人认为电是由某种微小的颗粒构成的,但是如果要将电分解为单个的微小颗粒就很难了。

此后,1909 年,一位伟大的科学家密利坎让整个科学界震惊不已,因为他真正的称出了单个电粒子的质量并算出了它的电荷。这可能是人类做过的最细致的计量工作之一,因为单个的电粒子的质量仅为一磅的百万分之一的百万分之一的百万分之一的百万分之一的百万分之一的一半左右的质量。它比我们所能想象的还要小得多。要得到一磅质量的粒子数比整个太平洋的水滴数还要多。

这些电粒子对我们来说并不陌生,因为我们知道它就是电子。我们所看到的每一样东西都是由成千上万的原子组成的。这些原子都含有电量。电来源于电子,每一个原子都包含有一个或者更多的电子。当大量的电子脱离原子的"束缚"并通过导线运动时,这时我们就说电通过导线在"流动"。所以,早期科学家所说的电的"流体"只不过是通过导线流动的电子!

单个的电子如何摆脱原子的束缚而跑出来的呢？答案就在原子本身的结构上。在很多物体中，电子被紧紧地束缚在原子的周围。木头、玻璃、塑料、陶瓷、空气、棉花……这些物体中的电子很忠于它们的原子；因为电子并不移动，所以这些物体不能很好的导电。如果不导电，我们就称之为绝缘体。

但是很多金属的电子能够与它们的原子分离，到处漂移，于是它们就成为自由电子。金、银、铜、铝、铁等都含有自由电子。它们丢失电子，让电流很轻易地通过，所以把它们称为导体。它们导电。移动的电子从一端到另一端传送电能。

譬如，一个铝原子，总是在不停地丢失一个电子，重新收回它（或另外一个电子），然后又失去它。一个铝原子一般有 13 个电子，它们排列在原子核周围 3 个不同的轨道上，最里层的轨道上有 2 个电子，外面较大的轨道上有 8 个电子，第三层轨道上有 3 个电子。铝原子不断丢失的就是这些最外层的电子，因为它们受原子的约束最小。它游离而去，然后被另外游离的电子取代，然后再丢失第二个电子。

因此，在铝导线中自由电子在铝原子周围四处飘荡。所以，尽管对我们普通肉眼来说，铜导线看起来是完全不动的，但在它的内部却不断进行着大量的活动。

如果导线把电输送到一盏电灯或者另外某个电气设备那里，这些电子就不会杂乱无章地到处跑来跑去，而是它们中的许多电子将会向一个方向奔去——从导线的一端到另一端。

所以，电流必须通过导体传送。人们已经找到方法让电从导体的一端移动到另一端。一种方法就是利用发电机。发电机使用磁场让电子流动。法拉第和亨利发明了怎样利用磁场让电在导线中流动的定律。另外一种方法就是化学的方法，伏特电堆，或者电池就是一种能够使电流在导线中流动的化学装置。

Exercises

I.
1. C 2. D 3. B 4. A 5. C 6. D

II.
Electricity	电，电学
Electron	电子
Atoms	原子
Orbit	轨道
Electrical energy	电能
Magnetic	磁的

UNIT 2

A. Text 电阻和电抗

电阻是限制电流在电路中流动的电子器件。它是最简单的电子器件。它主要用来保护电路或者限制电流。电阻有两端，并且电流都必须通过。当电流从一端流到另一端时，电阻上就有电压降。

电阻可以分为两类：固定电阻和可变电阻。固定电阻有预先固定的阻值，可变电阻的阻值则可以根据不同的阻值进行调整。可变电阻也叫做分压计，在音频设备中也经常用来控制音量。可变电阻是专门为了在高电流的场合使用的。还有金属氧化物变阻器，它们能根据电压的改变而改变阻值；电热调节器，也能根据温度的上升或者下降而增加或者降低阻值；还有光敏电阻。

电阻都有阻抗。电阻抗就是物体阻碍电荷流动的特性。电阻的单位是欧姆。在直流电路中，通过电阻的电流与它的阻抗成反比，与加在其上的电压成正比。这就是著名的欧姆定律。它可以用等式 $V=IR$ 表示，其中，V 代表电压，I 代表电流，R 代表电阻。欧姆值很大的话就代表对电流的阻抗越大。在交流电路中，只要电路中不含有电感电抗的话，这个规律同样适用。根据欧姆单位的不同，可以用不同的方法来表示阻抗的大小。譬如，$81R$ 表示 81Ω，而 $81k\Omega$ 则表示 $81\ 000\Omega$。

不同物体的阻抗不同。譬如，金、银和铜的阻抗都很低，这意味着电流能顺利地通过它们。玻璃、塑料和木头的阻抗都很高，这意味着电流不能轻易地通过它们。

电阻可以用不同的方法制作。最常见的类型是用于电子设备和系统中的碳合电阻，将精细的颗粒状的碳（石墨）与泥土混合并使其变硬。它的阻抗取决于碳与泥土的比例，这个比例越大，阻抗就越低。

另外一种电阻是用缠绕的镍铬铁合金或者相似的导线以绝缘的方式制成的。这种部件叫做线绕电阻，与相同体积的碳合电阻相比，它更能够承受高电流。然而，因为导线绕成了圈，这个元件在显示电阻特性的同时，也具有电感的一些特性。在直流电路中这并没有影响，但是对交流电路却有反作用，因为电感效应使得该器件对频率的变化很敏感。

电阻的阻抗是由它的物理结构决定的。碳合电阻是在陶瓷柱体中注入了具有阻抗性的碳，而碳薄膜电阻器则是由相似的陶瓷管组成，在外面包有导电薄膜。金属薄膜或者金属氧化物电阻器也是以同样的方式做成的，但是在里面放的是金属而不是碳。而线绕电阻则是将金属线包裹于泥土、塑料或者玻璃纤维管的外面，在高功率的时候提供更大的阻抗。在温度很高的场合中，金属陶瓷，或者含有金属陶瓷成分的物体，就可以用来做成电阻，因为它们可以经受高温，如钽，一种稀有金属。

电阻会被瓷漆油漆，或者在外面浇一个塑料模型来保护它。因为电阻体积很小所以不好在上面写字，所以人们就用一个标准的色标系统来标示它们。开始的 3 个色标是欧姆挡，第四个表示容差，或者说电阻与它的真实的欧姆值相接近的百分比。这种重要性体现在两个方面，一是电阻在制作的过程中本身就是不精确的，二是如果它工作在最大电流之上，它的值会发生改变或者它会被烧坏。

Exercises

I.
1. B 2. B 3. A 4. A 5. B 6. D

II.

1. Resistor: A resistor is an electrical component that limits or regulates the flow of electrical current in an electronic circuit.

2. Resistance: Resistance is a feature of a material that determines the flow of electric charge.

3. Tolerance: Tolerance is an acceptable range how close by percentage the resistor is to its

standard value.

UNIT 3

A. Text 电容器和电容

电能能储存在电场内,具有这种能力的器件称之为电容器。

一个简单的电容器是由被介质隔开的两块金属板组成的。如果电容器连接到电池上,电子将从电池的负极流出堆积在与负极相连的极板上。同时与电池正极相接的极板上的电子将离开极板流入电池正极,这样两极板上就产生了与电池上相等的电位差。我们就说电容充上了电。

电容器储存电能的能力叫电容。电容的标准单位用法拉,F。然而这个单位太大了,通常使用微法,μF ($1\mu F = 10^{-6}$ F)和皮法 pF ($1pF = 10^{-12}$ F)。

电容是并联在电路当中,根据它存储电荷的多少来定义的。

$$C = \frac{Q}{V}$$

其中,Q是每个极板存储电荷的大小,V是极板间电压。

集成电路中就应用了电容器。通常在动态随机存储器中,将电容器与晶体管连接在一起。电容器帮助保存存储内容。

所有型号的电子设备,包括计算机及其外围设备的电源的补给,就使用了大电容器。在这些系统中,电容器能进一步平滑经整流过的公用交流电,使其提供如电池产生的纯直流电一样。

Exercises

Ⅰ.
1. Alternating Current
2. Direct Current
3. Integrated Circuit
4. Dynamic Random Access Memory

Ⅱ.
1. D　　2. C　　3. D　　4. D　　5. B

UNIT 4

A. Text 晶体管

晶体管是一种由半导体材料组成的器件。它能够放大信号或打开闭合电路。它是1947年由贝尔实验室发明的。

晶体管有两种标准类型:NPN 和 PNP,它们分别具有不同的电路特征。晶体管上的字母与用于制造该晶体管的半导体材料相关。今天所使用的晶体管大部分是 NPN 型，因为 NPN 型比较容易用硅制成。如果你是电子学的初学者，最好现在就开始学习如何使用 NPN 型晶体管。

晶体管在电路中有三种正确的连接方式：共基极、共发射极、共集电极法。由于错误的连接会在接通电路时导致电路的毁坏，所以需要特别注意。

晶体管可以放大电流。例如，它们可以放大一个逻辑芯片上的小输出电流，使得它可以操作一个电灯，或其他高电流设备。在许多电路中，晶体管可以转换电压，所以晶体管也可用于放大电压。

今天，晶体管已经成为了所有数字电路的关键元件，包括计算机。一个微处理器包含数千万个微型晶体管。

在晶体管发明之前，数字电路是由真空管组成的，这样存在很多劣势，例如电路规模更大，需要的能量更多，散热性也差，而且大多电路寿命更短。可以这么说，没有晶体管这项发明，今天我们所知的计算是完全不可能的。

Exercises

I.

1. Because this is the easiest type to make from silicon.
2. Transistors.
3. Its computing as we know it today would not be possible.

II.

TRANSLATION	VOCABULARY
Movement of electrically charged particles	Current
Electromotive force expressed in volts	Voltage
Disposed, liable	Prone to
Coming before in time	Prior to

III.

电动势、电流和电阻之间的关系，是 19 世纪初由德国科学家乔治·西蒙·欧姆发现的。处于对他的尊敬，用欧姆来命名电阻的单位。被称为欧姆定律的这种关系，在数学上用下式表示：

$$电流 = \frac{电动势}{电阻} \quad 即 \; I = \frac{E}{R}$$

其中，I 的单位为安[培]，E 的单位为伏[特]，而 R 的单位则为欧[姆]。这意味着电动势越大，电流就变得越大。但电阻越大，电流却变得越小。

UNIT 5

A. Text 计算机系统的基本组成

计算机系统的基本部件包括中央处理器、存储器、输入输出设备以及连接这些组件的数据总线。

冯·诺依曼是计算机设计的先驱，他提出的计算机结构沿用至今。一个典型的冯·诺依曼计算机系统主要包括3个部分：中央处理器、存储器和输入输出设备，如何设计这三个部分会影响到系统的性能。在冯·诺依曼计算机系统体系中，如80x86系列，所有事务都在中央处理器执行，所有的运算都在中央处理器进行。数据和CPU指令存储在存储器里，直到中央处理器需要时才被读取出来。对CPU而言，大部分输入输出设备可看作存储器，因为CPU可以把数据存储在输出设备中，也可以从输入设备中读取数据。存储器和输入输出设备的主要区别在于：输入输出设备一般与计算机外的设备相连。

冯·诺依曼计算机系统中系统总线连接着各个组件。80x86系列有三大总线：地址总线、数据总线和控制总线。电信号通过总线传输到系统的各个组成部分。例如，80386和8086的数据总线虽然执行方式不同，但它们都在处理器、输入输出和存储器间传输数据。80x86处理器通过数据总线在计算机各部件间传递数据。80x86系列中总线的大小差别很大，事实上，总线大小决定了处理器的容量。

80x86系列中，数据总线在某一特定的存储单元或输入输出设备及CPU之间传递信息。问题是："究竟哪个是特定的存储单元或输入输出设备？"地址总线回答了这个问题。

为了辨别存储单元和输入输出设备，每个存储单元和输入输出设备被分配了一个唯一的内存地址。当软件需要访问存储单元或输入输出设备时，它把相应的地址传送到地址总线上，与存储器或输入输出相连的电路能够识别地址，并命令存储器或输入输出设备从数据总线读取数据或把数据写到数据总线。

控制总线是控制处理器与系统其他部件如何通信的信号枢纽。考虑数据总线，CPU通过数据总线向存储器发送数据或从存储器接收数据，这就产生了一个疑问："它是在发送还是在接收呢？"在控制总线上有两条线，即读线和写线，它们指明了数据流的方向。其他信号包括系统时钟、中断信号、状态信号等。80x86系列控制总线的具体结构因处理器的不同而不同，但一些控制线对所有的处理器是共同的，简单介绍一下。

读写线控制数据总线上的数据流方向。当读写信号都是逻辑1时，CPU和内存-I/O间不能相互通信，如果读信号是逻辑0，那么CPU从内存读取数据（也就是说系统从内存传输数据到CPU）。如果写信号是逻辑0，那么系统从CPU传输数据到内存。

主存储器是计算机系统的主要存储单元，它是一个容量相对较大的快速存储器，存放计算机运行期间的程序和数据。主存的基本原理是基于半导体集成电路的。集成电路RAM（只读随机存储器）有两种可能的运行方式：静态和动态。静态RAM实质是由存储二进制信息的内部触发器构成，只要系统通电，存储信息都是有效的。动态RAM则是以电容器的电荷形式存储二进制信息的，电容器由金属氧化物半导体晶体管组成。电容器内储存的电荷随着时间慢慢放电，因此，必须定期给电容器充电来刷新动态内存。在单个存储芯片中，动态RAM能提供更低功耗和巨大的存储能力，静态RAM则更易使用，而且读写周期较短。

Exercises

I.

1. A VNA computer has three basic parts: the central processing unit (or CPU), memory,

and input/output (or I/O).

2. The major difference between memory and I/O device is that I/O device is generally associated with external device in the outside world.

3. When the read line and the write line contain logic 1, the CPU and memory – I/O do not communicate with one another. If the former is low (logic 0), the CPU reads data from memory. If the latter is low, the system transfers data from the CPU to memory.

4. The 80x86 family has three major buses: the address bus, the data bus, and the control bus.

5. A typical Von Neumann System has three major parts: the central processing unit (or CPU), memory, and input/output (or I/O).

II.

CPU: central processing unit.

I/O: input/output.

RAM: Read random memory.

MOS: Metal-oxide semiconductor.

UNIT 6

A. Text ARM-数字世界的架构

ARM 公司[（伦敦证交所：ARM）；（纳斯达克：ARMHY）]，在半导体革命中显示出了一种卓越的力量，并被 Dataquest 排列为全世界第一的半导体 IP 提供商。在 20 世纪 90 年代初，为发展基于 SoCs 的 32 位 RISC 微处理器，该公司永久地改变了动态半导体产业的 ARM 首创的概念——公开许可知识产权：通过许可而不是制造和出售它的芯片技术。该公司重新定义了微处理器设计、生产和销售的方式，从而建立了一种新的商业模型。

更重要的是 ARM 塑造了下一代电子产品的新时代：强大的 ARM 微处理器在我们使用的电子产品中无孔不入，在不同的市场应用中，包括汽车、消费娱乐、影像、工业控制、网络、存储、安全和无线技术中都起着关键作用。ARM 向其网络合作伙伴许可知识产权，这里面有一些世界领先的半导体和系统公司，其中包括世界上 20 个顶尖的半导体厂商中的 19 家。这些合作伙伴利用 ARM 的低成本、省电的内核设计来创造和制造微处理器、外设和系统芯片解决方案。作为公司全球技术网络的基础，这些合作伙伴在广泛采用 ARM 架构方面起到了举足轻重的作用，迄今为止，ARM 合作伙伴已经使用了超过 10 亿的 ARM 微处理器内核。

为了支持和补充公司的 RISC 微处理器内核和系统芯片知识产权，ARM 开发了强大的软件能力。合作伙伴已经获得了无可匹敌的一系列基于软件的知识产权、操作系统和软件设计服务。通过这种方式，ARM 提供给合作伙伴一整套旨在降低风险并能快速获取市场利益的投资产品。为了支持这个全球技术网络，ARM 最近又引进了两项先进技术，并在一些重要的半导体公司投入使用。

公司现在为合作伙伴提供 ARM PrimeXsys™平台，封装好的 IP 以平台形式解决特殊应用的需要。初始的 PrimeXsys 平台开发于 2001 年 9 月，是 PrimeXsys 无线平台，这是一个高集成的、可扩展的平台，它具有所有的硬件、软件和所需集成工具，使其合作伙伴能更容易地、更快、更低风险地开发出各种各样的以 ARM 供电装置为重点的设备。为了满足市场上更多的综合解决方案的需求，ARM 在 2002 年上市进一步改善的 PrimeXsys 平台。ARM 为加速 Java™技术提出了 Janelle™ 技术，这样就可以将 Java 的优越性能引入到世界领先的 32 位嵌入式 RISC 结构中，这项技术使平台开发商能自由运行操作系统、中间件和应用程序代码建立在单一处理器上的 java 应用程序。与协处理器和双处理器解决方案相比，单处理器解决方案提供了更高的性能、更低的系统成本和能耗。

Exercises

I.

1. By licensing IP, rather than manufacturing and selling its chip technology.
2. The ARM Powered® microprocessors' advantages include: low-cost and power-efficient core designs.
3. ARM provides Partners with solutions to expand their business while Intel provides customers with products to apply in the computer operation.

II.

1. Firstly, an eminent semiconductor IP supplier. Secondly, ARM provides Partners with a full portfolio of offerings that deliver significant risk reduction and faster time-to-market benefits. Thirdly, its Partners utilize ARM's low-cost, power-efficient core designs to create and manufacture microprocessors.
2. By yourself.

UNIT 7

A. Text 数字信号处理器基础

数字信号处理器有多种定义，严格来说，DSP 是处理用数字表示信号的微处理器。例如，DSP 滤波器输入一个或多个离散数据 $x_i[n]$，产生一个与之对应的输出 $y[n]$，其中 $n=\cdots$, $-1, 0, 1, 2, \cdots, i=1, \cdots, N$，这里 n 表示第 n 次输入或输出，i 是第 i 次的系数，N 是滤波器的长度。实际上，DSP 处理的是离散时间系统。顾名思义，连续时域信号必须要经过某种形式的预处理才能被处理，当然这很容易由模数转换器来完成。

一般来说，DSP 是对实时信号的重复、累积的数学运算。实时信号的样本数以百万计，因此需要大容量的存储器带宽。正是由于这一特性，在发明 DSP 处理器时采用了一种与传统的微处理器不同的结构体系。大部分 DSP 算法并不复杂，只需要多次的累积运算。DSP 处理器大多通过组建的电路和有线硬件来尽可能快地执行这些运算。

信号处理算法和函数决定了合适的运行结构。我们以一个简单 FIR 滤波器为例子来看看 DSP 的结构。

一种算法是构造一个 FIR 滤波器，其 $M+1$ 次的延迟线结构采用直接的抽头形式。最近

的第 $M+1$ 次输入样本被存储为"过滤器状态",根据方程(2-1)

$$y(n) = \sum_{i=0}^{M} c_i x(n-i) \qquad (2-1)$$

每个滤波器的输出状态变量 $x(n-i)$ 和其相应的系数 c_i 的乘积累加得到当前输出样本 $y(n)$。我们也可以用图 2-1 中的信号流程表示这个运算规则。不过,看起来好像所有的操作同时进行,所以运算的次序不是很清楚,因此图 2-2 通过使用寄存器传输级的微操作,更加准确地描述了运算从左至右的顺序。

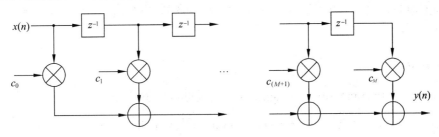

图 2-1　FIR 滤波器的抽头延迟线结构

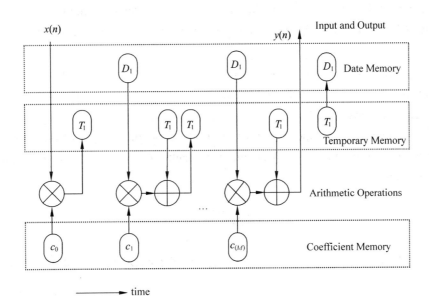

图 2-2　滤波器的寄存器传递描述

　　延迟输入存储在数据存储器 D_1、系数存储器系数 c_0,c_1,$c_{(M)}$ 的数据,把这两个存储器获取的数据相乘,将其结果放到临时存储器 T_1 中,T_1 中存放着上一次抽头的结果。用不同的系数重复这个循环直到结束——生成最后的结果 $y(n)$。

　　为了解通用 DSP 的基本架构,可以做一些假设。从我们已经了解的 DSP 算法来看,大部分的运算都是相乘和累加。从前一节的例子中可以看到,我们需要多种内存单元来储存不同的数据和算术运算序列。寄存器可作为临时存储单元,它们通过系统总线连接在一起。

　　在这一点上,读者可能会忍不住问,这样的设计与通用微处理器有什么不同?如果我们将问题集中在 DSP 的功能,即大部分 DSP 的运算是重复的,它需要很大的内存带宽和数字精度，以及处理的实时性，也许有人认为现代的通用处理器比 DSP 有更高的处理速度和指令周期，但是通用处理器有许多对于 DSP 不必要的运算和灵活多变的编程。尤其是在移动运算时代，DSP 必须以较低的成本、较少的能耗、较低的内存使用以及较短的程序调试时间来有效地执行任务。

由于许多信号处理应用过程中每秒处理的样本数据数以百万计，因此，最低采样周期通常比处理器的计算时延更为重要。采样周期即为输入每个连续样本的时间间隔，数据输入和其计算所产生结果之间的时间差称为计算时延。经过一定的时延计算出最初采样，通过采样周期率就可以计算出随后的结果。随着运算次数的增加，对采样率来说相对较大的处理器时延可以忽略不计。

Exercises

Ⅰ. Please answer the following questions according to the text.

1. To each filter of the products, state and its corresponding coefficient c_i are accumulated or added to produce the current output sample $y(n)$.
2. The signal flow graph as shown in Fig. 2-1 represents the DSP algorithm.
3. Fig. 2-2 described the algorithm sequence from left to right more accurately.

Ⅱ.

1. The signal flow graph as shown in Fig.2-1 represents the DSP algorithm, but the sequence of the computations hasn't been described. Fig. 2-2 described the algorithm sequence from left to right more accurately.

2. The sample period is the time between each sequential sample of the input data. The time difference between the input data and the result of its computation is known as the computational latency.

UNIT 8

A. Text 数字串行方式和可重构超大规模集成电路的体系结构

1. 数字串行方式

1.1 数字串行执行

传统结构主要有两种执行方式：位串行和位并行。位串行系统一次处理输入字（或样本）的一个比特。这些系统的优势在于它们之间互联少、引脚少、内部硬件少、时钟速度更快、耗电量更少，其主要缺点是速度慢，因为对于一个 W 位字长，位串行结构需要 W 个时钟周期来计算一个字或采样，因此，它们主要适合低或中等速度的应用。位并行系统一个时钟周期处理字的所有输入比特，它是应用最普遍的执行方式，其主要优点是它可以在一个时钟周期计算出一个字，因此，具有高性能，适合高速应用，缺点是芯片面积较大、互联多、引脚多、能耗大。

为了避免位串行和位并行计算的缺点，提出了字串行执行的概念。字串行系统在一个时钟周期里根据位长来处理输入字的多个比特。位长从 1 到该字长变化以实现速度、面积和输入输出引脚限制的平衡。在字串行算法中，一个字的位长为 N 比特，W 位的数据字需要 W/N 时钟周期来处理，首先处理最低位，一次处理一个字，连续进行。例如，如果一个字长 16 位，位长是 4 位，那么一个时钟周期处理 4 位，一个字就需要 4 个时钟周期，如图 2-3 所示。这使得字串行算术运算比相应的位并行的算术设计占用更小的范围，而比相应的位串行的算术设计有着更大的吞吐量。假设位长是个整体，其结构可简化成位串行系统，位长等于字长，则其结构变成位串行系统。基于字串行方式的结构能够提供速度、有效面积利用率、吞吐量、输入输出引脚的限制和电力消耗的均衡。考虑到字串行方式的一系列优点，可以为某一特定应用寻找合适的设计以实现最佳的执行方式。

Time									
Bit0	a0	a4	a8	a12	b0	b4	b8	b12	c0	c4
Bit1	a1	a5	a9	a13	b1	b5	b9	b13	c1	c5
Bit2	a2	a6	a10	a14	b2	b6	b10	b14	c2	c6
Bit3	a3	a7	a11	a15	b3	b7	b11	b15	c3	c7
Reset	1	0	0	0	1	0	0	0	1	0

图 2.3　字串行数据格式（字长为 W=16 比特和位长 N=4 比特）

字串行方式在位串行和位并行方式，以及数据吞吐量和运算大小之间提供了灵活的均衡性（见图 2-4）。基于这种方式的系统能把高吞吐量的并行运算和小规模的串行运算的优势结合起来。字串行格式为字宽大的系统存在的互连问题提供了一种解决方法，尤其是布线区域非常大的分布式数据流系统。我们之所以选择字串行方式，是因为它可以通过改变位长而实现速度和面积的最佳均衡。

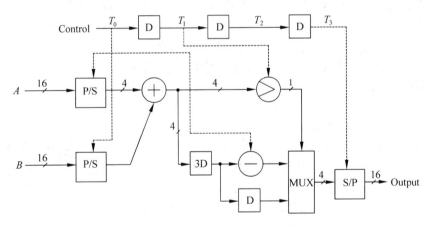

图 2-4　字串行结构的控制原理

文献[A]中报道的字串行结构，第一种实现的方式是从位并行结构开始，然后通过折叠得到字串行结构，第二种方式是从位串行结构开始，然后通过展开得到字串行结构。基于这些方法的结构主要缺点是，它们不能以位传输，这严重地限制了吞吐量，也是高速应用的主要障碍之一。这种结构不能以位传输的主要原因是进位反馈环路的存在，而这种环路是不可能传输的。近来，以位级别传递字串行的结构已在文献[B]-[C]报道。进位前馈的应用解决了传统字串行设计进位反馈环路的主要瓶颈问题，高速传输的可能性增加了字串行结构的吞吐率。

1.2 定时的控制信号

每一字串行操作中，为操作者增加一些控制信号来标识字的边界是必要的。由于数据字之间没有间隔，需要一些机制来标识一个字在哪里结束，下一个字从哪里开始，这是由一个被称为控制信号的周期信号来提供的，并且这个信号被传递给各个操作者。在每个采样周期的严密的时钟周期里，也就是说在每一个 W/N 循环周期里，控制信号表现很活跃。一般情况下，各个不同延迟版本的控制信号可在字串行电路中获得，操作者可以连接一个或者更多的控制信号进而实现同步。对一个周期来说只需要 W/N 个不同的控制信号，可以通过移位寄存器环产生并在整个芯片传播，或通过移位寄存器链分发。图 2-5 是实现位长 $N=4$ 位和字长为 $W=16$ 位的字串行电路的一个典型完整的控制设计图。这个典型的电路接受两个 16 位的并行输入：A 和 B，并计算他们求和后的绝对值。由延迟的输入控制信号产生四个延迟控制信号：T_0, T_1, T_2, T_3，在 i 时刻，控制信号 T_i 产生一个脉冲，接着每一次做 4 个循环。

2. 可重构超大规模集成电路的体系结构

由于 VLSI 技术增值快、成本低，事实上，现在每种新的数字设计几乎完全是由高密度器件组成。专用结构的使用对大容量应用而言几乎是妄想。在市场要求高，而且经常不断变化的今天，为原型化和低容量应用设计专用体系结构所花的费用（以设计时间和财务费用的形式表示）正受到限制。基于这个原因，许多原型甚至是生产设计，都在用可重构的 VLSI 结构或可编程逻辑器件构建（PLDs）。

其主要优势在于瞬时周转时间快、创建成本低，而且设计合并易于更改。现在可利用多种可重构的超大规模集成电路结构，如 FPGAs 和 CPLDs（复杂可编程逻辑器件），它们是构建可重构系统的关键。产品上市时间的压力和低财务风险使得 FPGAs 和 CPLDs 成为原型化以及许多情况下实际制作过程中日益流行的工具。几乎所有的可重构系统使用的都是在商业上可用的 FPGAs/CPLDs，但也有些利用的是定制的可重构芯片。

现场可编程门阵列

现场可编程门阵列（FPGAs）是可编程逻辑器件的一种形式，它允许设计许多不同的复杂数字电路。1986 年，Xilinx 首次把基于内存的编程技术引入了 FPGAs。此后还有许多新的商业结构出现，有人也提出了少数的非商业 FPGAs 结构，其设计细节更易获得。可编程逻辑区别于传统硬件的关键特性在于它的可重构性。从执行的强度和速度来看，这种装置不能与传统硬件相比，但它们的可重构性能的开发和硬件设计改变的迅速性，缩短了产品上市时间，降低了成本。通常情况，可编程逻辑是由主机系统外部的特殊程序员设定的。但目前许多 FPGAs 有 SRAM 配置存储器，它可以在系统内进行编程。

因此，将配置器装入 FPGA，它就可以像软件程序一样运行，但其性能和专用硬件差不多。FPGAs 可用个人计算机和简单的硬件界面编程，其灵活性和上市时间优于传统的专用集成电路 ASICs，专用集成电路必须在装配工厂完成所有的布线。根据通用结构、逻辑块类型和编程技术的不同，FPGAs 可以分成许多不同的类型。因此，有很多种不同类型的 FPGAs。商用的 FPGAs 主要由 Xilinx、Altera、Latice、Actel 和 Lucent Technologies 等设计。

虽然 FPGAs 为实现数字信号处理器运算电路提供了一定的支持，但它们仍然是优越的通用设备。由于 DSP 的广泛应用、精深计算，为 DSP 设计专用的现场可编程门阵列 FPGA 是必要的。因此，提出了针对特定应用的 FPGA 结构。

Exercises

Ⅰ.

1. The advantages of bit-serial systems include fewer interconnections, fewer pin-outs, less internal hardware, faster clock speed, and less power consumption and their disadvantage is that they are slow. The main advantage of bit parallel systems is that they can provide high-performance and are ideal for high-speed applications. Their disadvantages include larger chip area, interconnection, pin-out, and they consume more power.

2. In a digit-serial arithmetic implementation, the W-bit of a data word are processed in units of the digit-size N-bits in W/N clock cycles, and are processed serially one digit at a time with the least significant digit first.

3. To indicate the word boundary for each digit-serial operator because there is no gap between successive words of data, the control signal is necessary to indicate where one word ends and the next one begins.

4. FPGAs are a form of programmable logic devices which permits the design of many different complex digital circuits.

Ⅱ.

One bit of a word (or sample) at a time is input in the Bit-serial systems. Bit-parallel systems process all input bits of a word in one clock cycle. Digit-serial systems process multiple bits of the input word, referred to as the digit-size, in one clock cycle.

The advantages of FPGA are as follows: firstly, FPGAs' reconfigurability permits the design of many different complex digital circuits and allows hardware designs to be created and changed rapidly so as to reduce time-to-market and costs. Secondly, FPGAs can be programmed using just a personal computer and simple hardware interface, giving them flexibility and time-to-market advantages over traditional ASICs. The application of FPGA is FPGAs provide some support for the implementation of DSP arithmetic circuit.

Ⅲ.

半导体的电气性质介于导体和绝缘体之间，像锗和硅这样的元素以及氧化铜和硫化镉这样一些化合物，都属于这种类型，其名称正式来源于此。例如，在普通的室温情况下，$1cm^3$ 的纯铜（导体）对电流形成的电阻约为 $0.000\,001\,7\Omega$。$1cm^3$ 的岩石（绝缘物）具有的电阻约为 $100\,000\,000\Omega$。$1cm^3$ 的锗（半导体）具有的电阻约为 60Ω。

正如所学过的那样，我们讨论的原子是包含着质子和中子的原子核。原子是被位于 1 个或多个在同心壳体轨道上电子旋转的一种结构。质子的正电荷被电子的负电荷中和。在中性原子中，轨道上的电子与原子核中的质子数量是相同的。

UNIT 9

A. Text 信号的数学表示

承载信息的任何事物可以看做是一个信号。信号可以描述变化万千的物理现象。例如，语音、音乐、利率、汽车的行驶速度等都是信号。虽然信号可以用许多方式来表示，但是在所有情况下，信号所载有的信息总是包含在以某种形式变化的波形中。例如，考察人类的发声机制，即是通过声压的起伏波动产生的语音信息。图 3-1 是一个语音信号的录音波形，它是通过拾音器来感知声压的变化，然后将这种变化再转化为电信号。如图所示，不同的声音对应不同的声压变化波形，人的声道系统通过产生特别的波形系列来产生可理解的语音。另一个例子是一幅黑白照片，这时照片上各点的亮度变化波形才是重要的。

信号是描述口语单词 should we chase 声压随时间变化的函数，第一个波形对应单词 should，第二个是 we，最后两个是 chase。

信号在数学上表示为一个或多个自变量的函数。例如，一个语音信号在数学上可以用声压随时间变化的函数来表示，而一张照片可以表示为亮度随二维空间变量变化的函数。为了方便起见，通常用时间来表示自变量，尽管在某些具体应用中自变量不一定是时间。例如，在地球物理学研究中用于研究地球结构的一些物理量如密度、气隙度和电阻率就是随地球深度变化的信号。

信号分为两种基本类型：连续时间信号和离散时间信号。连续时间信号的自变量是连续的，因此，这些信号定义为自变量的值是连续的一类信号。另一方面，离散时间信号只定义自变量是离散时刻的信号，这些信号的自变量只取一系列离散的值。作为时间函数的语音信号和随海拔高度变化的大气压信号都是连续时间信号的例子。每周的道琼斯指数是离散时间信号的例子。在人口统计学的研究中可以找到其他离散时间信号的例子，例如像平均预算、犯罪率或捕鱼的重量等各种属性都可以分别对家庭大小、总人口数或捕鱼船的类型等离散变量列成表格。

为了区别连续时间信号和离散时间信号，我们用符号 t 来表示连续时间自变量，用 n 来表示离散时间自变量。另外，给连续时间信号的自变量加上圆括弧(·)，给离散时间信号的自变量加上方括弧[·]。 我们常常用图解的方法来表示信号。图 3-2 表示的是一个连续时间信号 $x(t)$ 和一个离散时间信号 $x[n]$ 的波形。值得强调的是，离散时间信号 $x[n]$ 仅仅在自变量的整数值上有定义。为了更进一步强调，有时我们把 $x[n]$ 看做是离散时间序列。

一个离散时间信号 $x[n]$ 可以描述一个自变量固有离散的现象，比如人口数据就是这类信号的例子。另一方面，一类非常重要的离散时间信号来源于连续时间信号的取样。既然这样，离散时间信号 $x[n]$ 描述了自变量是连续的基本现象的连续采样。

不管数据是什么来源，信号 $x[n]$ 只在 n 为整数时有定义。所谓的一个数字语音信号的第 $3\frac{1}{2}$ 个样本和所谓的具有 $2\frac{1}{2}$ 个家庭成员的家庭平均预算一样都是毫无意义的。

Exercises

Ⅰ.

1. Anything that bears information can be considered a signal. For example, speech, music, interest rates, the speed of an automobile are signals.

2. Continuous-time signals are defined for a continuum of values of the independent variable, for these signals, the independent variable is continuous. For example, a speech signal as a function of time and atmospheric pressure as a function of altitude are continuous-time

signals.

Discrete-time signals are defined only at discrete times, for these signals, the independent variable takes on only a discrete set of values. For example, the weekly Dow-Jones stock market index, average budget and crime rate are examples of discrete-time signals.

3. Signals are presented mathematically as functions of one or more independent variables, we will generally refer to the independent variable as time.

4. We will use the symbol t to denote the continuous-time independent variable and n to denote the discrete-time independent variable. In addition, for continuous-time signals we will enclose the independent variable in parentheses (•), whereas for discrete-time signals we will use brackets [·] to enclose the independent variable.

II.
1. signal
2. sequence
3. continuous
4. discrete
5. integer
6. independent
7. tabulate
8. acoustic
9. illustration
10. monochromatic

UNIT 10

A. Text 系统的数学表示

广义的物理系统是各组成部分、设备、或子系统的互联。从信号处理、通讯到电机马达、机动车和化学处理设备，一个系统可看作输入信号的变换器或对输入信号作出某种响应而产生出另外的输出信号。例如，一个高保真度的系统对输入音频信号进行录制，并重现原输入信号。如果高保真系统有音调控制，我们可以改变重现信号的音质。同样的，电路可看作是输入电压为 $x(t)$，输出电压为 $v(t)$ 的系统，而汽车可以看做是输入为动力 $f(t)$，输出为汽车速度 $v(t)$ 的系统。某个图像增强系统可把一副输入图像转化成为具有某些所需性质的输出图像，如增强图像对比度。

一个连续时间系统是施加连续时间输入信号，而产生连续时间输出信号的系统。这个系统的框图表示如图 3-4（a）所示，其中 $x(t)$ 为输入，$y(t)$ 为输出。另一方面，我们常用符号来表示连续时间系统的输入输出关系：

$$x(t) \rightarrow y(t)$$

同样的，一个离散时间系统，将离散时间输入转化为离散时间输出的描述如图 3-4（b）所示，有时用符号描述为：

$$x[n] \rightarrow y[n]$$

许多实际的系统由多个子系统互联而成。把这样一个系统看做是它的各组成部分的互联，可以用对各部分系统以及它们之间的互联方式的理解来分析整个系统的作用和性能。另外，根据简单系统的互联来描述一个系统，事实上可以通过定义有用的方法来从简单基本的模块中合成复杂的系统。

当我们构造多种系统互连的时候，经常碰到几种基本的互连方式。两个系统的串联或级联如图3-5（a）所示，这种图称为框图。这里系统1的输出是系统2的输入，整个系统首先按系统1，然后按系统2来变换输入。一个级联系统的例子是收音机接一个扩音器。类似的，级联可以是三个或更多系统的连接。

两个系统的并联如图3-5（b）所示，在这里相同的输入信号施加于系统1和系统2。图中符号"⊕"表示相加，因此并联系统的输出是系统1和系统2的输出之和。简单的音频系统是一个系统并联的例子，几个麦克风输入到一个单一放大器和扬声器系统。除了图3-5（b）所示的简单的并联结构外，系统的并联可以是两个以上的系统的连接，我们还可以将级联与并联结合在一起得到一种更为复杂的系统。图3-5（c）所示就是这种结构的例子。

另一种重要的系统互连是反馈系统，如图3-6所示。这里系统1的输出是系统2的输入，而系统2的输出反馈回来与外加的输入信号相加，一起组成系统1的实际输入。反馈系统有很广泛的应用。例如，汽车感应系统的巡航控制系统感应汽车的速度并调整燃油流量来保持所希望的速度。

Exercises

Ⅰ.

1. Physical systems in the broadest sense are an interconnection of components, devices, or subsystems. A system can be viewed as a process in which input signals are transformed by the system or cause the system to respond in some way, resulting in other signals as outputs.

2. A continuous-time system will often be represented symbolically as $x(t) \rightarrow y(t)$, and a discrete-time system will be represented symbolically as $x[n] \rightarrow y[n]$.

3. There are several basic system interconnections: series (cascade) interconnection; parallel interconnection; series-parallel interconnection; feedback interconnection.

Ⅱ.

1. system
2. fidelity
3. signal
4. series (cascade) interconnections
5. receiver
6. amplifier
7. feedback
8. reproduction
9. tone

10. depict

UNIT 11

A. Text 傅里叶变换和频域描述

实际遇到的信号大多是连续时间信号，这类信号可以用 $x(t)$ 表示，其中 t 是连续变量。虽然有些信号，例如股票市场、储蓄账户和库存本来就是离散时间信号，但大多数离散时间信号，是从连续时间信号采样而来，可以表示为：$x[n] := x(nT)$，其中 T 为采样周期，n 为只能取整数的时间量。$x(t)$ 和 $x[n]$ 都是时间的函数，称为时域描述。在信号分析中，我们研究信号的频谱。为了能做到这点，必须开发不同但等效的描述方法，称为频域描述法。从这种描述中能很容易确定各个频率的能量分布。

连续时间信号的数字处理，第一步是选择一个采样周期 T，然后采样 $x(t)$ 产生 $x(nT)$。很明显，周期 T 越小，$x(nT)$ 约接近 $x(t)$。然而，T 越小计算量越大。因此，数字信号处理的一项重要任务，是要找出最大可能 T，使 $x(t)$ 的所有的信息（如果不能，那么信号的所有基本信息）仍然保留在 $x(nT)$ 中。没有频域描述，就不可能找到采样周期。因此，数字信号处理的第一步是计算信号的频谱。

频域描述来自于傅里叶变换。信号的傅里叶变换称为信号的频谱

$$\text{傅里叶变换} \leftrightarrow \text{频谱}$$

连续时间傅里叶变换定义为下面两个等式：连续时间傅里叶正变换：

$$X(j\omega) = \int_{-\infty}^{\infty} x(t) e^{-j\omega t} dt$$

连续时间傅里叶反变换：

$$x(t) = \frac{1}{2\pi} \int_{-\infty}^{\infty} X(j\omega) e^{j\omega t} d\omega$$

式（3-1）和式（3-2）称为傅里叶变换对，函数 $X(j\omega)$ 称为 $x(t)$ 的傅里叶变换或傅里叶积分，而式（3-2）称为傅里叶反变换。$X(j\omega)$ 通常称为信号的频域表示或信号的频谱，因为 $X(j\omega)$ 告诉我们这样一个信息，就是 $x(t)$ 可以描述成不同频率正弦信号的线性组合。同样，$x(t)$ 是信号的时域描述，我们表述这两种域之间的关系如下：

$$\text{时域} \qquad \text{频域}$$
$$x(t) \xrightleftharpoons{F} X(j\omega)$$

其中，符号 F 表示时域与频域变换是一一对应的。

已知数学函数 $x(t)$，可以通过式（3-1）的积分运算得到相应的频谱函数 $X(j\omega)$。换句话说，式（3-1）定义了一个数学运算，将 $x(t)$ 变换为新的等效表示 $X(j\omega)$。通常说得到了 $x(t)$ 的傅里叶变换，就意味着确定了 $X(j\omega)$，这样我们就可以运用信号的频域表示方法。

同样，已知函数 $X(j\omega)$，就可以利用式（3-2）通过计算积分确定相应的时间函数 $x(t)$。因此，式（3-2）得到了由频域到时域的傅里叶反变换。

运用傅里叶变换这个强大的工具，我们可以：①定义一个信号的精确带宽概念；②解释通过共享可用带宽来同时发送多个信号的现代通信系统的内部工作机理；③确定在这样的频率共享系统中分离信号的滤波方式。傅里叶变换有很多其他应用，也就是说，傅里叶分析为确定和设计现代工程系统提供了精确的方法。

Exercises

Ⅰ.

1. The continuous-time Fourier transform is defined by the following pair of equations:
Forward Continuous-Time Fourier Transform

$$X(j\omega) = \int_{-\infty}^{\infty} x(t)e^{-j\omega t} dt \tag{3-1}$$

and Inverse Continuous-Time Fourier Transform

$$x(t) = \frac{1}{2\pi}\int_{-\infty}^{\infty} X(j\omega)e^{j\omega t} d\omega$$

2. $x(t)$ is referred to as the time-domain representation of the signal and $X(j\omega)$ is referred to as the frequency-domain representation.

We indicate this relationship between the two domains as

Time-Domain　　　　Frequency-Domain

$$x(t) \xleftrightarrow{F} X(j\omega)$$

3. We are given $x(t)$ as a mathematical function, we can determine the corresponding spectrum function $X(j\omega)$ by evaluating the integral in $X(j\omega) = \int_{-\infty}^{\infty} x(t)e^{-j\omega t} dt$.

4. There are many applications of the Fourier transform, for example, we will be able to: ①define a precise notion of bandwidth for a signal, ②explain the inner workings of modern communication systems which are able to transmit many signals simultaneously by sharing the available bandwidth, and ③define filtering operations that are needed to separate signals in such frequency-shared systems.

Ⅱ.

1. Frequency
2. Bandwidth
3. Continuum
4. Evaluate
5. Power
6. Transmit
7. Spectrum
8. Combination
9. Filter

UNIT 12

A. Text 抽样理论

在一定的条件下,一个连续时间信号完全可以由该信号在时间等间隔点上的瞬时值或样本值来表示,并且能用这些样本值恢复出原信号来。这个性质来自于基本的结论,即抽样定理。这个定理非常重要并且得到了广泛的应用。例如,抽样定理在电影里得到了利用。电影由一组按时序排列的单个画面所组成,其中每一个画面都代表着连续变化景象中的一个瞬时画面(即时间样本)。当这些画面以足够快的速率按顺序观看时,我们看到的是对原始连续影片的精确重现。

抽样理论的重要性同样在于它在连续时间信号和离散时间信号之间起了桥梁的作用。在一定的条件下,可以用信号的时序样本值完全恢复出原连续时间信号,这就提供了用一个离散时间信号来表示一个连续时间信号的机理。在许多方面,处理离散时间信号要更加灵活些,因此往往比处理连续时间更为可取。这主要归功于在过去几十年里高速发展的数字技术,使我们可以得到廉价,重量轻,可编程且易再生的离散时间系统。我们利用抽样把连续信号转换为离散时间信号,通过离散时间系统来处理离散时间信号,然后再把离散时间信号转换成连续时间信号。

抽样定理叙述如下:

假设 $x(t)$ 是一个带宽受限信号,且 $X(j\omega)=0$,$|\omega|>\omega_m$。如果 $\omega_s>2\omega_m$,其中 $\omega_s=2\pi/T$,那么 $x(t)$ 可以通过它的样本值 $x(nT)$,$n=0$,± 1,± 2,…来唯一确定。

已知这些样本值,我们可以用以下方法重新构造 $x(t)$:产生一个周期的冲激串,其冲激的强度就是依次而来的样本值,然后将冲激串通过一个增益为 T,截止频率大于 ω_m,而小于 $\omega_s-\omega_m$ 的理想低通滤波器,该滤波器的输出就等于 $x(t)$。

在抽样定理中,采样频率必须大于 $2\omega_m$,频率 $2\omega_m$ 通常称作奈奎斯特抽样率。

在前面的讨论中,假设抽样频率足够高,因而满足抽样定理的条件。如图 3-10 所示,由于 $\omega_s>2\omega_m$,取样信号的频谱是 $x(t)$ 频谱的周期性延拓。这构成了抽样定理的基础。当 $\omega_s<2\omega_m$,$X(j\omega)$ 即 $x(t)$ 的频谱不再在 $X_p(j\omega)$ 中被复制,因此通过低通滤波器也不能被恢复。重构的信号不再等于 $x(t)$,这种现象称作频谱混叠。

抽样有许多重要的应用,一组特别重要的应用是利用微计算机,微处理器,或任何一种专门用于离散时间信号处理的器件,通过这些离散时间系统利用抽样来处理连续时间信号。

Exercises

Ⅰ.

1. It is exploited in moving pictures, which consist of a sequence of individual frames, each of which represents an instantaneous view (i.e., a sample in time) of a continuously changing scene. When these samples are viewed in sequence at a sufficiently fast rate, we perceive an accurate representation of the original continuously moving scene.

2. The fact that under certain conditions a continuous-time signal can be completely recovered from a sequence of its samples provides a mechanism for representing a continuous-time signal by a discrete-time signal.

3. Sampling theorem can be stated as follows:

Let $x(t)$ be a band-limited signal with $X(j\omega)=0$ for $|\omega|>\omega_m$. Then $x(t)$ is uniquely determined by its samples $x(nT)$, $n=0, \pm1, \pm2,\cdots$, if

$$\omega_s > 2\omega_m$$

where

$$\omega_s = 2\pi/T$$

The frequency $2\omega_m$ is commonly referred to as the Nyquist rate.

4. When $\omega_s > 2\omega_m$, the spectrum of the sampled signal consists of scaled replications of the spectrum of $x(t)$, and this forms the basis for the sampling theorem. When $\omega_s < 2\omega_m$, $X(j\omega)$, the spectrum of $x(t)$, is no longer replicated in $X_p(j\omega)$ and thus is no longer recoverable by lowpass filtering. The reconstructed signal will no longer be equal to $x(t)$. This effect is referred to as aliasing.

II.
1. Sampling
2. Instantaneous
3. Gain
4. Cutoff
5. Replication
6. Programmable

UNIT 13

A. Text 移动通信

20世纪70年代，当时还属于AT&T公司的贝尔电话实验室，研制出了第一套可以对移动用户提供服务的无线传输系统。该系统包括三个主要组成部分，这些部分进而构成了如今更加现代化的移动系统的基本结构。这些组成部分包括基站，移动电话交换局（MTSO）以及手机等。

自20世纪70年代以来，无线移动通信领域已经取得了重大技术进展，但蜂窝系统基本组成部分的结构关系仍然保持不变。此外，蜂窝系统的基本概念仍是一样的。

移动通信的基本结构

在移动通信环境，地理区域细分为能支持不同频率业务的蜂窝。为防止蜂窝间的干扰，第一类的无线移动通信系统，即模拟移动电话系统采用了七蜂窝模式，如图4-1所示。图4-1中的蜂窝图形确保没有相邻的蜂窝工作在相同的频率。实际上，每一个蜂窝包括一个基站与天线，它们支持在很宽的频率范围工作。

然而，对任意给定的时刻，一个小区中的一个频率上只能存在一个呼叫，蜂窝模式用来确保相邻的蜂窝不会同时使用同一频率。

蜂窝组成部分的关系

每个蜂窝由一个基站和天线构成，基站中有用于支持所用无线传输方法的电子产品。如图 4-2 所示，每个基站连接到一个 MTSO。MTSO 依次连接到公共交换电话网络并提供互联机制。

当一个手机用户开始离开某一特定蜂窝的覆盖区域，该蜂窝的基站记录该用户信号强度的降低。当用户向一新的蜂窝移动时，一个或多个基站记录下功率的增加。无论是正在提供服务的基站，还是和该基站毗邻的基站将该信息传送给 MTSO，MTSO 在功能上如同一个交警，选择信号功率增加最强的那个基站，该基站接收来自于当前蜂窝基站的用户的切换。

在切换操作的实现过程中，MTSO 检查其数据库，以确定用户正在进入的蜂窝中哪些频率是可用的。然后，该 MTSO 将这一信息传送给用户正在进入的被称为"增益"的蜂窝中的基站。该基站接下来调整其发射和接收频率，并以用户先前的接收频率向其发送一个信息，通知手机调整到新的频率对。

先进移动电话系统

由贝尔实验室发明的模拟移动电话系统被认为是代表了第一代的无线移动通信。该系统采用频分多址（FDMA）技术作为网络接入技术的。图 4-3 说明了 FDMA 的使用。

在 FDMA 情况下，由联邦通信委员会（FCC）在 800MHz 频段为 AMPS 工作而分配的 50MHz 的频谱被细分为 30 千赫带宽的不同子信道，每个子信道能支持单一的通话。当 FCC 为 AMPS 分配频率时，许可这两家公司各有 25MHz，这样每个呼叫有 832 个蜂窝信道。然而，每 25MHz 细分为前向（基站至用户）和反向（用户至基站）的业务，称为发送和接收业务。采用这种方式可以为全双工通信提供支持，但它限制了全双工通话的数量，一个蜂窝中减少到 416 个。

作为一种模拟技术，在 AMPS 中传输数据是相对容易的。你只需要将调制解调器和 AMPS 兼容的手机连接。不过，由于可能的干扰，你通常需要一个为无线传输设计的，支持可调包长度和纠错能力的调制解调器。因为 AMPS 采用的 25kHz 信道包括为特定用途预先分配的频率，所以 9.6 Kbps 的数据速率通常是你所期望达到的最高数率。

直至千年之交，AMPS 在所有移动无线系统中拥有最广的覆盖范围。不幸的是，它的成功也导致人们寻求其他的网络接入技术。当一般用户购买了 AMPS 兼容的手机后，他们开始体验到无法拨打电话，尤其是在市区，这种情况被称为阻塞。它发生在一个最大容量支持 416 个同时呼叫的蜂窝中，出现第 417 个试图呼叫时。AMPS 用户遇到的第二个问题，当一个移动用户到达某个蜂窝的覆盖区域时，该蜂窝容量不足，不能为这个用户分配一个信道。这种情况导致了通话过程中的掉话。请注意，固定模拟电话不能支持越来越多的用户，蜂窝技术开发人员推出了两种新的接入方式。这些接入方式被称为时分多址（TDMA）和码分多址（CDMA）。每种接入方式，支持同时通话用户数量，即蜂窝传输容量的增加。

时分多址

时分多址将 AMPS 分配的频率细分为时隙。如图 4-4 所示，每个 AMPS 信道被分为各包含三个时隙的重复的序列，每个用户分配了一个频率和一个时隙。

在北美，基于 TDMA 的蜂窝系统工作在 800MHz 或 1900MHz。当工作在 800MHz 时，时分多址通常可以和模拟信道在同一网络中并存。这就使拥有双模手机的用户在它们四处走动时，也就是漫游的情况，可以利用 AMPS 或 TDMA。TDMA 和 AMPS 的第二个区别在于语音传送的方式。在 AMPS 的情况下，它是一个模拟系统，30~20 000MHz 范围内的人声，首先被过滤，以消除对理解会话不很重要的非常低和高的频率。

接下来，保留下来的频率在信道中使用载波进行调制。相比较而言，在 TDMA 情况下，语音首先是以一个低比特率进行数字化编码，通常采用一种混合编码器以 64Kbps 的速率对语音进行编码。接着产生的数据流被调制到一个无线信号上。作为语音数字编码的结果，工作在 800MHz 的 TDMA 起先也被称为数字先进移动电话服务（D-AMPS）。

个人通信系统

工作在 1900MHz 的第二代 TDMA 被称为个人通讯系统(PCS)。PCS 工作在比 D-AMPS 更高的频率上，由于波长和频率成反比，结果是 PCS 使用更短的波长。PCS 相关的较短的波长导致了一个较小的蜂窝直径，这意味着 1900MHz 系统每个地理面积需要比 800MHz 系统更多的蜂窝。这也解释了为什么在市区或洲际公路上使用 PCS 电话拨打电话相对容易些。然而，当你到农村地区，你的双模手机更适合采用 AMPS 进行通信。

世界上，有几种 PCS 系统正在运作。PCS 系统的实例包括 D-AMPS1900（当其工作在 1900MHz），全球移动系统（GSM）以及 CDMA。GSM 是基于 TDMA 的，这一点和 D-AMPS 是相似的，然而 CDMA 使用完全不同的接入技术。

PCS 的关键优势在于一个 TDMA 帧可以被修改以支持两个呼叫，而不是针对某一特定时间范围内的三个呼叫。在这种情况下，时隙可以用来支持数字控制信道（DCC）。通过使用 DCC，向 PCS 电话发送和接收字母数字信息成为可能，这称为短信服务（短信）。这使得 PCS 兼容的手机具有传呼机的功能。

和 AMPS 电话相比较，D-AMPS 和 GSM 中 TDMA 的使用使得电话的电池寿命延长。电池寿命延长的关键原因是采用 TDMA 通常导致只需使用 AMPS 电话三分之一的传输时间。第二个原因是 PCS 电话能够在空闲模式时，能定期检查控制信道，以查看是否有来电。如果在控制信道上没有发现一个信号，则电话进行另一个瑞普凡温克尔操作并返回睡眠状态。

全球移动通信系统

GSM 可以追溯到 20 世纪 80 年代，当时北欧国家的模拟蜂窝系统经历了快速的发展，由此一种新的数字蜂窝标准得以发展。经过 5 年的努力，13 家网络运营商和管理机构签署了 GSM 标准化的章程。当时，GSM 指的是其法文名称。但是移动特别小组目前在世界范围都是以全球移动通信系统被大家熟知的。

欧洲版的 GSM 工作在 900MHz 频段上，该频段在欧委会成员国中是可用的。遗憾的是，900MHz 频段在美国是不可用的，因此，在美国 GSM 个人通信系统使用的是 1900MHz 频段。

GSM 是 PCS 的 TDMA 的一个实例。作为数字技术，在数据调制前，语音首先是使用混合编码器以约 13Kbps 的速率进行数据压缩。采用这种数字技术，你可以直接将 GSM 手机连接到一个数据源，而不用使用调制解调器。不过，你能获得的最高数据传输率约为 14.4 Kbps。

码分多址

第三种移动无线接入技术是 CDMA。它不像 AMPS 和 TDMA 那样存在于某一频率，CDMA 信号存在于一个扩展的频带，这被称为宽带或扩频通信。根据香农定理，扩展信号最主要的优点在于信道容量可维持在一个较低的功率水平上。因此，CDMA 支持低功率运行。

在 CDMA 情况下，扩展是通过使用一种可以扩展每一比特的伪随机（PN）数字码而发生。PN 信号指的是片码，每片代表 PN 码的一个数据位。每一个在 CDMA 下传输的数据位首先进行模 2 加成为 PN 码，则扩展的位序列调整为高于 1.23MHz 的信道。

图 4-5 举例说明了一个直接序列扩频过程。在这个例子中，5 位 PN 的扩频码用来传播一个 3 位的信息。结果是，每个数据位传送了 5 次，或一次片操作。在接收机端，进行模 2 减法过程，以恢复数据为它的原成分。如果代表 1 个数据位的一个 5 位序列（在这个例子中）因为传输受损而恶化，接收机将选择序列中最常用的位设置。举例来说，如果 4 位被设为 1 和 1 位被设为 0，那么接收器会判断正确的数据位的值是 0。

在 CDMA 情况下，1.23MHz 的频谱容纳一个信道。虽然这明显高于 AMPS 和 TDMA，但 CDMA 情况下的所有可用的频谱可在每个蜂窝中重复使用。此外，通过改变伪随机码，CDMA 系统使可以支持数倍于 TDMA 系统容量成为可能。根据一些研究，CDMA 可以支持 10 倍于 TDMA 系统的容量，这反过来又能够支持 3 倍于一个 AMPS 蜂窝的容量。

Exercises

Ⅰ.
1. 传输损伤
2. 双重方式，双模
3. 基站
4. 码分多址

Ⅱ.
1. of
2. as
3. to
4. with, at

UNIT 14

A. Text 光纤

光纤传输作为电信业一项重大变革的时代已经到来。光纤系统提供了非常高的带宽，它不受外界干扰，不能通过外部手段进行信号截取，它的原材料是廉价的（硅，地球上最丰富的物质)。

光纤系统基础

光纤在纤维材料中引导光射线。之所以能这样是因为当光射线从一个介质传播到另一个介质时会弯曲或改变方向。光纤弯曲是因在不同的介质中，光的传播速度是不同的。这种现象称为折射。一个发生折射的常见例子是当你站在水池边看着池底的一个物体。除非你直接在这个物体之上，否则它看上去比它实际情况要远。这种现象发生的原因是，当来自于物体的光线从水中到空气后，其速度会增加。这会导致光线倾斜，改变你观察物体的角度，使得在该角度上看到该物体的距离与实际不同。研究一下 Snell 定理，你就可以理解光线传播的方式。

Snell 定理

光纤如何工作可以通过 Snell 定理来解释，该定理阐明入射角正弦与反射角正弦的比值和两个不同介质中的光波传播速度的比值相等。这个比值是一个常数，即第二个介质的折射率和第一个介质折射率的比值。用一个等式来表示，Snell 的定理如下所示：

$$\frac{\sin A_1}{\sin A_2} = \frac{v_1}{v_2} = k = \frac{n_2}{n_1} \tag{4-1}$$

在这个等式中，A_1 和 A_2 是入射角和折射角，V_1 和 V_2 分别是光波在两个介质中的传播速度，n_1 和 n_2 的是这两种介质折射率。

这些参数图示于图 4-6 中。每种情况中，A_1 是入射角，A_2 是折射角。材料 1 的折射率是 n_1，大于材料 2 的折射率 n_2。这意味着光线在材料 2 中的传播速度比在材料 1 中要快。

图 4-6（a）说明了从材料 1 到材料 2 的光线，当 A_1 小于临界角时，该光线在材料 2 中被反射的情况。图 4-6（b）说明了当 A_1 是临界角时，A_2 是 90°的情况。光线沿着两种材料的边界直线传播。

如图 4-6（c）所示，任何入射角大于图 4-6（b）中的 A_1 的光线将会返回到材料 1，此时 A_2 角和 A_1 角相等。图 4-6（c）的情况就是光纤特别有趣的情况。

光纤构成

光纤是一种由玻璃或塑料制成的绝缘（非导电体）波导。它由 3 个不同的区域组成：纤芯、包层和护套。护套用于保护光纤但不能控制光纤的传输能力。

构成光纤的各部分的折射率大小会沿着光纤的半径而发生改变，纤芯的折射率 n_c 是常数或均匀变化。包层区域的折射率是另一个常数 n，纤芯具有高的折射率，而包层做成具有较低的折射率。折射率不同的结果是，即使光纤弯曲或打结，也能保持光在进入纤芯后能在纤芯中传播。对于设计为要在相同时间传输几种传播模式的光纤，纤芯的直径必须是传输光波长的数倍。波长是同一波的两个周期距离的度量，单位是 nm，而包层的厚度比纤芯的半径大得多。以下是多模光纤的一些典型值。

该包层光纤的直径为 125μm，光会如图 4-7 所示传播。

光源以相对于光纤中心的许多角度发射光。如图 4-7 所示，光线 A 进入光纤，它垂直于纤芯面而平行于轴线。其入射角 A_1 是 0°，因此，它不会折射，它平行于轴线前行。光线 B 以入射角 A_{1B} 从空气进入纤芯，由于 n_2 大于 n_1，该光线以 A_{2B} 角折射。当光线 B 到达纤芯和包层的边界时，其入射角 A_{1B} 大于临界角，因此，折射角 A_{2B} 和 A_{1B} 相等，而光线反射回纤芯。光线以这种锯齿形在纤芯中传播，直至到达光纤另一端。

如果入射角 A_{1C} 太大、如光线 C，该光线以小于临界角的入射角 A_{1C} 到达纤芯和包层的边。光线进入包层并且传播到或被吸收到包层和护套（对光不透明）。

模式延迟

对于光纤而言，它的纤芯直径是传输光波长的许多倍。光线在纤芯和包层的交界面向前反射从而在光纤中前行。以不同角度进入光纤的光线从光纤的一端到另一端会被反射不同的次数，并且当它们到达较远的一端时，通常不具有和它们出发时同样的相位关系。进入的不同角度称为传播模式（或模式），而承载多个模式的光纤称为多模光纤。

因为大多数的光纤通信系统是以光脉冲构成的数字方式来传输信息的，模式延迟的影响限制了用来传播可识别脉冲的光纤的性能。这是因为模式延迟在时域上将脉冲展宽，如图 4-8 所示，脉冲展宽使得光接收器很难或无法将经历了一段给定传输距离后的一个光脉冲和另一光脉冲区分。因此，在经历了预先设定的传输距离后，多模光纤要么会造成很高的误码率，要么无法识别光脉冲，这样光纤也就无法用于通信当中了。

如果纤芯的直径只有传输光波长的几倍（比如 3 倍），只能传播一条射线或一个模式，这样光线间就不会发生干扰了。这种光纤称为单模光纤，它用于大多数的传输系统中。图 4-9（a）和图 4-9（b）显示了多模光纤以及单模光纤的折射率分布和典型的直径值。单模光纤和多模光纤的一个重要区别在于多模光纤中的大部分能量在纤芯中，而在单模光纤中大部分的能量是在靠近纤芯的包层中传播。在光波长足够长到引起单模传输的地方，大约 20%的能量是在包层中，但是如果光波长加倍，则会有超过 50%的能量在包层中。

折射率

光纤也可以按其折射率进行分类。图 4-10 所示说明了几种类型，它们概述如下：
- 阶跃型光纤——纤芯的折射率一直相同，但在纤芯的覆盖层其折射率突然改变。
- 渐变型光纤——随着离纤芯中心点距离的增加纤芯的折射率逐渐减小。
- 单模光纤——同单一模式一样，它有一致的折射率。这种光纤只允许一种光在电缆中传输。
- 渐变型多模光纤——纤芯的折射率随纤芯直径方向均匀变化，但覆盖层的折射率为常数。因为光在渐变型光纤中传播时延几乎相等，所以光纤的这种处理减小了模内散射。

其他形状折射率的设计主要是为了解决各种具体的问题，如色散的减少等。几种折射率分布如图 4-10 所示，图中再次比较了阶跃型光纤与渐变型光纤。

图 4-11 对阶跃型、渐变型以及单模光纤中的光线传播进行了比较。阶跃型光纤的纤芯直径通常为 $100\mu m$ 和 $500\mu m$。渐变型光纤的纤芯直径通常为 $50\mu m$ 或 $62.5\mu m$，而单模光纤的纤芯直径为 $8\mu m$ 和 $10\mu m$。阶跃型和渐变型光纤都支持多模传输。

Exercises

I.

1. 传播模

2. 折射率分布
3. 光接收器
4. 绝缘材料
5. 破坏性干扰，相消性干扰
6. 阶跃折射率光纤

II.
1. of
2. to, to
3. in
4. from
5. in, to transport

UNIT 15

A. Text 卫星

1. 卫星基础

20 世纪 80 年代末，卫星通信已成为人们日常生活中的一部分。国际通话变得就像和住在街区的一个朋友的本地通话一样。我们还可看到发生的一些国际事件，例如英国的选举，在法国进行的网球比赛，以及当地的一些政治和体育事件。在这种情况下，电视新闻节目每晚将世界的画面和声音带到我们的家。

基于全球范围交流信息的能力，无论是一个电话或一个新闻故事，都能通过强大的通信工具——卫星使之成为可能。对于我们而言，在我们成长时，空间时代并不是人们日常生活中的一部分，基于卫星的通信是我们最高的梦想，回想那个年代，卫星这个词仅仅是少数颇具灵感的人才能思考的东西。这些先驱者包括作家，如 Arthur C. Clarke，他们在 1945 年提出了全球卫星系统的想法。这个想法后来蓬勃发展成为一个先进的卫星网络，这个网络遍布全球。

和当代的航天器相比，第一代卫星是相当原始的。这些早期的卫星体现了有源和无源的设计。

无源卫星，例如 Echo 一号航天器，发射于 1960 年，它没有配备双向传输系统。当卫星放置在地球低轨道上，发送到 Echo 的信号反射回其表面并返回到地球上不同的地方。

基于以上原则，三颗在环绕地球等距位置的卫星就可以构成一个全球通讯系统，在该系统中，卫星能触及地球上几乎所有位置。这个概念是阿瑟克拉克最初设想的全球通信网络的基础。

2. 上行链路和下行链路

根据联邦通信委员会的规定，上行链路是"承载信号的传输功率从地面站源向上传送到卫星"，而下行链路"包括卫星本身，地面接收站，以及两者间向下传送的信号"。不过，为了简化我们的讨论，上行将是指以从地面站到卫星的传输，而下行是由卫星向地面站的传输。

上行和下行双向信息流通过特定装备来管理。中继信号的站点必须具备天线或通常是抛物线形的碟型天线以及能产生高频微波信号的发射机。还应指出的是，有些地面站可以接收和发送信号，而其他的地面站只有接收模式。

通信卫星部分而言在天空是以一个中继站来工作的。在卫星接收到来自于地面站的信号后将该信号转发回地球。这个过程和地面转发站的功能相似，但在这种情况下，中继站位于距离地面 22 000 英里以上的高空。

地面站和卫星之间的传输由以下事项组成：
1. 卫星接收来自于地面站的信号。
2. 由于在 22 300 英里的行程中，信号强度已经衰减了很多，因此要进行信号放大。
3. 卫星改变信号频率，以避免上行和下行间的干扰。
4. 信号转发回到地球上的一个或多个地面站以接收。

为了搭建通信连接，卫星利用卫星转发器，这是一种卫星设备，它可以管理双向传输。一颗通信卫星带有多个转发器，如国际通信卫星家族法的反映，每个卫星的转发器的数量逐年增加。反过来，这种设计导致新一代卫星的发展，新一代卫星借助于它们的转发器及相关电子系统能处理庞大的信息量。

举例来说，原来的国际通信卫星，Early Bird，配备了 2 个转发器，支持一个电视频道或 240 语音（电话）话路。后来国际通信卫星四号在最初的成果上进行改进。这种卫星的推出是在 20 世纪 70 年代初期至中期，每颗卫星携带了 12 个转发器，为卫星提供的总平均传输容量为 4000 个话路和 2 个电视频道。

较新的国际通信卫星 5 号配有 27 个转发器，而最新的国际家族，国际通信卫星 6 号，将配备 48 个转发器。国际通信卫星 6 号将容纳超过 10 万个同时进行的通话以及可能 3 个频道的电视节目。

Exercises

Ⅰ.
1. satellite
2. culmination inspired
3. a series of, earth station
4. geostationary, slots

Ⅱ.
1. T 2. F 3. F 4. T

UNIT 16

A. Text 计算机网络介绍

在 20 世纪 50 年代，大多数计算机在一个方面是相似的。他们有一个主存储器，一个中央处理器（CPU）及周边设备。内存和 CPU 是系统的核心。从那以后，出现了新一代的计算机，其计算和数据存储不必集中。用户可从一个地方获得程序，在任一处理器上运行，并将结果输送到第三方。

连接着不同设备，如计算机、打印机、磁盘驱动器的系统是一种网络。通常情况下，网络中的每个设备为一个或多个用户提供一种特定的服务。举例来说，计算机可能会在你的案头，向你提供你需要的信息或软件。计算机也可以管理一个共享的文件磁盘驱动器。我们称之为文件服务器。一个网络往往覆盖一个小的地理区域，并且在一个单幢建筑或建筑群中连接设备。这样的网络就是局域网（LAN）。一个覆盖更大范围的网络，例如一市、一州、一个国家或世界，被称为广域网（WAN）。

一般来说，大多数网络可能涉及很多人使用许多计算机，每个人都可以访问许多打印机和服务器。对于这些人的访问信息，他们的要求难免会冲突。因此，设备必须按照某种方式连接，该方式使各有关方面有序地传输信息。一个很好的比喻，是一个街头布置在一个大的城市。只有一人驾驶，街道在哪无关紧要，哪些是单行，交通信号在哪里，或如何将它们同步。但随着成千上万的汽车开上大街，在上午交通拥挤时间，一个差劲的布局会造成拥塞，从而造成重大延时。计算机网络也是一样。它们必须以一种能让数据在许多用户间几乎没有延时的传输方式进行连接。我们称这种连接方法为网络拓扑。最好的拓扑结构是根据设备的类型和用户的需求。对某用户组工作很好的网络可能不适用于另外的用户组。

一些常见的网络拓扑如下所示。

图 4-16 显示了一种普通的总线结构，该结构连接了如工作站、大型机和文件服务器等设备。他们通过一条总线（一组并行线）进行通信。通常的方法是给设备提供一个接口，用于监听总线以侦测其数据通信。如果某一接口侦测到数据的目的地址正是它所服务的设备，它就从总线上读取数据并传送给该设备。同样，如果设备要传送数据，接口电路检测到总线何时空闲，然后再传输数据。这就像交通拥堵期间，交通工具等候在高速公路的入口匝道上。

有时，两个设备试图同时进行数据传输。每个设备侦测到交通空闲后，还不清楚其他设备的传输就开始传输数据。其结果是信号冲突。当设备检测到信号冲突它就停止传输，等待一随机时间后又开始尝试发送数据。这一过程称为载波监听，载波监听多路访问多址将在稍后讨论。

一种很流行的总线网络是以太网。其常见的总线通常是以太网电缆，它由铜、光纤或两者结合而组成。其设计允许终端，个人计算机，磁盘储存系统及办公室机器进行通信。以太网的一个主要优点是能非常容易地给网络添加新设备。

另一种较常见的连接形式是星型拓扑结构，如图 4-17 所示。它使用了可以和网络中其他设备进行通信的中央计算机。控制集中化了，如果设备想要通信，它只能通过中央计算机来完成。计算机依次路由数据到它的目的地。集中化起了一个联络点的作用，这正是星型拓扑的优点。而总线结构和星型拓扑相比具有一些优势。由于不需要考虑其他设备，所以不存在中央控制使得添加新的设备很容易。此外，总线网络中某一设备故障或移除并不会引起网络故障。在星型结构中，中央计算机的故障会导致整个网络的瘫痪。

星型拓扑往往可以服务包括很多终端和次级设备的主机。通过适当的终端仿真软件，个人计算机就能够与主机通信。终端间或终端与存储设备间的数据传输只能通过主机完成。

在图4-18所示的环型拓扑中，设备连接成环型。每个设备可以直接和相邻的一方或两方，而不能和其他设备进行通信。如果它想和距离更远的设备通信，它发送一个必须通过两者之间每一个设备的信息。

环型网络可以是单向或双向的。单向意味着所有传输在同一方向。因此，每一设备只能和一个相邻设备通信。双向意味着数据可以在两个方向上传输，也就是设备可以和相邻的两个设备通信。

环型拓扑，如IBM的令牌环网，往往将一个办公室或一个部门的计算机连接在一起。因此计算机上的应用可以访问存储在其他计算机上的数据，而不需要向主机请求以协调通信。相反，通信的协调是通过在环中的所有站点中传递令牌。一个站点只有在它接收到令牌时才能发送数据。

环型拓扑缺点体现在当一个站向另一个站发送数据时，两者之间所有站都参与了。和其他拓扑，例如总线拓扑相比，环型拓扑花费了更多的时间用于传送信息的意思。此外，一个站点的故障就会在环中引起中断，这会影响到所有站点间的通信。

许多计算机网络是不同拓扑的组合。图4-19显示了一种可能的组合形式。

Exercises

Ⅰ.
1. 中央处理单元
2. 局域网
3. 网络拓扑
4. 令牌环网络

Ⅱ.
1. C 2. A 3. D 4. D 5. C

参 考 文 献

[1] Chang Y N, Parhi K K. Efficient FFT implementation using digit-serial arithmetic. Proceedings of IEEE Workshop on Processing Systems, 1999, 645~653

[2] Aggoun A, Ibrahim M K, Ashur A. Bit-level pipelined digit-serial array processors. IEEE Transactions on Circuits and System, 1998, 45(7): 857~868

[3] Chang Y N, Parhi K K. High-performance digit-serial complex number multiplier-accumulator. Proceedings of IEEE Internation conference on computer Design, 1998, 211~213

[4] 常义林，任志纯. 通信工程专业英语. 西安：西安电子科技出版社，2003

[5] 祝晓东，张强华，古绪满. 电气工程专业英语实用教程. 北京：清华大学出版社，2006

[6] 任胜利. 英语科技论文撰写与投稿. 北京：科学出版社，2004

[7] 丁西亚. 英语科技论文写作——理论与实践 西安：西安交通大学出版社，2006

[8] 朱月珍. 英语语科技学术论文——撰写与投稿. 武汉：华中科技大学出版社，2004

[9] 钟似璇. 英语科技论文写作与发表. 天津：天津大学出版社，2004

[10] 张敏瑞，张红. 通信与电子信息科技英语. 北京：北京邮电学院出版社，2004

[11] 曹玲芝. 电子信息工程专业英语. 武汉：华中科技大学出版社，2006

[12] 韩定定，赵菊敏. 信息与通信工程专业英语. 北京：北京大学出版社，2004

[13] 田岚. 电子信息科学专业英语导读教程. 北京：清华大学出版社，2005

读者意见反馈

亲爱的读者：

  感谢您一直以来对清华版计算机教材的支持和爱护。为了今后为您提供更优秀的教材，请您抽出宝贵的时间来填写下面的意见反馈表，以便我们更好地对本教材做进一步改进。同时如果您在使用本教材的过程中遇到了什么问题，或者有什么好的建议，也请您来信告诉我们。

  地址：北京市海淀区双清路学研大厦 A 座 602 室 计算机与信息分社营销室 收
  邮编：100084   电子邮件：jsjjc@tup.tsinghua.edu.cn
  电话：010-62770175-4608/4409   邮购电话：010-62786544

教材名称：电子信息工程专业英语导论
ISBN：978-7-302-17065-5
个人资料
姓名：_____ 年龄：_____ 所在院校/专业：_____
文化程度：_____ 通信地址：_____
联系电话：_____ 电子信箱：_____
您使用本书是作为：□指定教材 □选用教材 □辅导教材 □自学教材
您对本书封面设计的满意度：
□很满意 □满意 □一般 □不满意 改进建议_____
您对本书印刷质量的满意度：
□很满意 □满意 □一般 □不满意 改进建议_____
您对本书的总体满意度：
从语言质量角度看 □很满意 □满意 □一般 □不满意
从科技含量角度看 □很满意 □满意 □一般 □不满意
本书最令您满意的是：
□指导明确 □内容充实 □讲解详尽 □实例丰富
您认为本书在哪些地方应进行修改？（可附页）
_____
_____
您希望本书在哪些方面进行改进？（可附页）
_____
_____

电子教案支持

敬爱的教师：

  为了配合本课程的教学需要，本教材配有配套的电子教案（素材），有需求的教师可以与我们联系，我们将向使用本教材进行教学的教师免费赠送电子教案（素材），希望有助于教学活动的开展。相关信息请拨打电话 010-62776969 或发送电子邮件至 jsjjc@tup.tsinghua.edu.cn 咨询，也可以到清华大学出版社主页（http://www.tup.com.cn 或 http://www.tup.tsinghua.edu.cn）上查询。

高等学校教材系列

已出版教材

ISBN：9787302115816　C语言程序设计教程（王敬华　等编著）
ISBN：9787302124412　C语言程序设计教程习题解答与实验指导（王敬华　等编著）
ISBN：9787302135074　C++语言程序设计教程（杨进才　等编著）
ISBN：9787302140962　C++语言程序设计教程习题解答与实验指导（杨进才　等编著）
ISBN：9787302129066　软件工程（叶俊民　编著）
ISBN：9787302141006　人工智能教程（金聪　等编著）
ISBN：9787302130666　离散数学（李俊锋　等编著）
ISBN：9787302137801　计算机控制——基于MATLAB实现（肖诗松　等编著）
ISBN：9787302132042　数字信号处理——原理与算法实现（刘明　等编著）
ISBN：9787302143338　计算机网络技术及应用教程（杨青　等编著）
ISBN：9787302160694　大学计算机基础教程（杨青　等编著）
ISBN：9787302167327　微机组成与组装技术及应用教程（崔建群　等编著）
ISBN：9787302167334　高级语言程序设计与应用教程（陈静　等编著）
ISBN：9787302168119　数字媒体技术导论（刘清堂　等编著）
ISBN：9787302170655　信息工程科技英语导论（瞿少成　等编著）

即将出版教材

数据结构（C语言版）（魏开平　等编著）
数据结构教学辅导与实验（魏开平　等编著）
操作系统原理（叶俊民　编著）
软件体系结构教程（叶俊民　编著）
非线性编辑原理与技术（左明章　等编著）
多媒体技术原理与应用（刘清堂　等编著）
单片机原理及接口技术（彭文辉　等编著）
计算机组成原理（陈利　等编著）

更详细的教材介绍请登录清华大学出版社网站http://www.tup.com.cn查询。
联系人：魏江江　E-mail：weijj@tup.tsinghua.edu.cn　电话：010-62770175-4604

21 世纪高等学校电子信息工程规划教材

已出版教材

书号	书名	定价
9787302124382	数字信号处理——原理与实践（方勇　编著）	24.00
9787302126126	电磁场基础（钟顺时　编著）	26.00
9787302137771	现代通信原理（上册）——信息传输的基本原理（李颖洁　等编著）	22.00
9787302137788	现代通信原理（下册）——信息传输的相关技术（余小清　等编著）	17.00
9787302134831	光纤通信简明教程（袁国良　等编著）	22.00
9787302167983	自动控制原理（李玉惠　等编著）	24.00
9787302168065	信息科学与电子工程专业英语（王朔中　等编著）	39.00
9787302153542	DSP 原理及应用教程（薛雷　等编著）	26.00
9787302170655	电子信息工程专业英语导论（瞿少成　等编著）	25.00
9787302169437	数字信号处理学习指导与习题详解（方勇　编著）	16.00
9787302171300	电子技术实验教程（汤琳宝　等编著）	24.00
9787302169192	模拟电子技术基础（徐晓夏　等编著）	

即将出版教材

电路分析基础（邹国良　等编著）

电路、信号与系统实验教程（邹国良　等编著）

通信电子线路（侯丽敏　等编著）

信号与系统（彭章友　等编著）

移动通信（赵东东　编著）

概率论与随机过程（石海　等编著）

微波技术基础（杨雪霞　等编著）

自动控制原理学习指导及习题解答（李玉惠　等编著）

信息论与编码基础教程（张丽英　等编著）

更详细的教材介绍请登录清华大学出版社网站 http://www.tup.com.cn 查询。

联系人：魏江江　　E-mail：weijj@tup.tsinghua.edu.cn　　电话：010-62770175-4604